Varieties
of Political Expression
in
Sociology

An American
Journal of Sociology
Publication

Essays by:

Robert K. Merton
Howard S. Becker
Irving Louis Horowitz
Seymour Martin Lipset
Everett Carll Ladd, Jr.
Morris Janowitz
John K. Rhoads
Vernon K. Dibble
Lewis A. Coser
Benjamin Nelson

with an Introduction
by Tom Bottomore
and an Epilogue
by E. Digby Baltzell

The University of Chicago Press
Chicago and London

Varieties
of Political Expression
in
Sociology

This work appeared also as volume 78, number 1
(July 1972), of **American Journal of Sociology**,
edited by C. Arnold Anderson with associate
editors David McFarland and Barry Schwartz,
book review editors Richard Albares and John D.
Kasarda, managing editor Florence Levinsohn, and
published by the University of Chicago Press.

The University of Chicago Press, Chicago 60637
The University of Chicago Press, Ltd., London

International Standard Book Number: 0-226-52087-0
Library of Congress Catalog Card Number: 72-81104

Contents

Preface

We feel privileged to publish this book at this time. The rush of social change in contemporary societies affects the outlook and techniques used by sociologists to study these changes no less than it alters the foci of sociological inquiry or the data used in the research. A discussion of "politics and ideology in sociological inquiry" is timely in every way.

The editors of professional journals are aware that the state of the discipline is measurably affected by the selection of materials for publication. Yet we do not solicit materials, but wait instead for suitable and provocative manuscripts from our colleagues. In its publication as a book this issue of the *Journal* does not depart from these normal procedures; only the Introduction and the Epilogue were solicited. The review of *Science, Technology and Society in Seventeenth-Century England* had been commissioned months before in the normal book-reviewing process. All the articles came to us through regular channels. Some were submitted in the conventional manner; some were invited for publication after we heard them presented to the American Sociological Association at its 1971 meetings.

Diverse in content and source as the materials submitted to us are, the bringing together of these works required the sensitivity to issues and theme and the alert listening of our managing editor, Florence Levinsohn. She was greatly assisted by Patrick Molloy and Moshe Schwartz who were associate editor and book review editor, respectively, in the early stages of this volume.

We hope our colleagues and other readers interested in the role of sociology during a period of social transformation will concur that the following papers embody one of the major debates in our discipline and that the contributors aid substantially in the clarification of some of the conflicting outlooks associated with the work of sociology.

THE EDITORS
American Journal of Sociology

Introduction

Tom Bottomore
University of Sussex

It would be possible to comment on these essays from various points of view. From one aspect, they are explorations in the sociology of knowledge which—mercifully—deal directly with the social influences upon knowledge instead of raising yet again questions about the theoretical possibility of a sociology of knowledge.

More narrowly, however, most of the essays are concerned in some way with the social context of political thought, especially radical thought, and in this respect they mark out, and contribute to, a field of inquiry which has been much neglected. The study of conservative thought which Karl Mannheim published in 1927 has never been adequately complemented by a structural and historical analysis of radical thought, except perhaps in the little known work by C. Bouglé, *Les idées egalitaires* (actually published two years earlier, in 1925), which provides, at the same time, an interesting contrast with Mannheim's approach, inasmuch as it is inspired by Durkeimian rather than Marxist ideas. Marxism itself is an obvious candidate for this kind of investigation, and Lewis Coser's essay in the present symposium is noteworthy for initiating a study along these lines, although I have reservations about his actual procedure which I shall set out later in this paper.

Last, a large part of the symposium is concerned especially with recent radical thought in the United States, not only from the point of view of its social context but also in terms of the relationships—of mutual influence, suspicion, antagonism, or conflict—which may exist between radical political doctrines on one side and sociological theory on the other.

In the following comments I shall limit myself mainly to the second and third set of issues which I have just outlined. For this reason I shall discuss less fully than it deserves the essay by Robert Merton, which approaches the broader questions raised by the sociology of knowledge in a fresh and illuminating way, by examining some of the implications of the contrast between "knowledge from the inside" and "knowledge from the outside." Of course, some of Merton's observations bear directly upon current problems. He notes that in times of acute social conflict and great social change the perspectives offered by the various sociologies of knowledge are closely linked with the problems agitating society. "As the society becomes polarized, so do the contending claims to truth." In short, the sociology of knowledge also has a social context.

Merton illustrates the contrast between "insiders" and "outsiders" particularly by reference to the black movement, and the claims sometimes advanced, in connection with Black Studies, that *only* black historians can truly understand black history, only black sociologists can understand the social life of blacks, etc. Sociologically, this corresponds, he suggests, with a need for group self-affirmation in a situation of conflict and change. Epistemologically, it produces difficulties; for there are multiple group affiliations, and if there are reasons for saying that only blacks can understand blacks, the same reasons would indicate that only women can understand women, only young people can understand young people, and so on. Thus, we should have to admit, for example, that young black women could only be studied properly by other young black women. Any kind of general social science is thereby ruled out. So is all historical writing, since the historian is always an outsider. Merton might have noted that a pure "insider" doctrine would also eliminate a considerable part of Black Studies, for a black historian teaching Afro-American history is no more of an insider (in the sense of a participant in the events) than is a white, yellow, or brown historian.

If it is then argued simply that a black historian would embark on his study from a distinct perspective and would bring a special insight to it, this is to assert a weaker version of the insider doctrine; and the claim would have to be assessed against the claims made for the virtues of the "outsider" approach, namely, the special kind of insight into a situation which the external observer, the "stranger"—who is detached from local prejudices and animosities and able to make comparisons with other situations—can bring to his study.

The problems which Merton explores are posed in somewhat different terms in several of the essays. Obviously Marxism is, in some versions, a form of "insider" doctrine. If Marxism is conceived *only* as the world view of the proletariat, then it is true for this class but not for other classes; it is the self-consciousness of the proletariat in capitalist society, providing an insight into the structure and development of society which the members of other classes cannot acquire. But this idea has usually been qualified in various ways. On one side, Marxism is also presented as an objective science of society—that is, as a body of theory and empirical descriptions formulated from the standpoint of an external observer. On the other side, some Marxists (notably Lukács and Lenin), in discussing the question of "false consciousness," have argued that a *correct* class consciousness is brought to the proletariat by socialist intellectuals, or, in other words, by "outsiders."

Thus, Marxist thought has often embodied a fruitful tension between the "inside" and the "outside" view; and the same is true of other kinds of radical thought, which are partisan from one aspect in that they investigate social life from the viewpoint of the interests and aspirations of particular social groups, but are also objective insofar as they base their interpretations upon the evidence of actual conditions and events. Becker and Horowitz, however, conceive recent radical thought mainly in its partisan character. Unlike Merton, who sees the "insider" and the "outsider" as complementing each other, they are more inclined to emphasize a total disjunction between "radical" sociology, which is an ideological orientation, and "good" sociology, which is an objective science conforming with publicly acknowledged standards of scientific evidence and argument.

Of course, there are grounds for making such a sharp distinction. A good deal of radical thought, in the past decade, has amounted to little more than what Alain Touraine has called the "repetition of ideology." Becker and Horowitz refer to this characteristic by observing that most radical sociology has been "programmatic" and has not taken shape in a body of empirical studies. This is also a characteristic of Marxism, over a much longer period, and there is an interesting contrast between sociology and history in this respect. There have been many good Marxist historians, especially in the fields of economic and social history, who have worked quite comfortably in accordance with the general standards of historical scholarship, however distinctive the conceptual scheme which they have brought to their work. There have been far fewer Marxist sociologists, and their contribution is less impressive, although it is evident that Marxism has inspired, in a diffuse way, much sociological theory and inquiry. The difference seems to arise in the first place from the fact that Marxism and sociology can be conceived as alternative global schemes of interpretation, and this rivalry has produced controversies which are largely methodological and philosophical in character, especially on the Marxist side, where a preoccupation with the inner structure of Marxist thought, and criticism of "bourgeois" thought, tend to assume preeminence over any study of the external world. This tendency is reinforced by the dogmatic element in Marxism; as sociology is very largely concerned with the study of modern (including present-day) societies, and as Marxism already contains some fundamental propositions about the character of modern capitalism, the revolutionary role of the working class, the more or less necessary transition to a socialist society, it may well appear, from an extreme ideological and dogmatic Marxist perspective, that research into such matters is otiose.

Becker and Horowitz point to some other influences which have inhibited the development of radical sociology in a more positive direction: conventional techniques of research, common-sense standards of the credibility of explanations, and agency sponsorship. It would obviously be worthwhile to investigate such influences more fully and, in particular, to look at the consequences of agency financing and sponsorship. The kind of analysis which Vernon Dibble makes of the research reports published by the German Verein für Sozialpolitik could very usefully be extended to other scholarly associations and research bodies, in an attempt to reveal some of the factors which give a particular direction to social research in various countries at different times, and which impart to the evaluation of research findings a more radical or more conservative cast.

There are, however, more general influences which have held back sociological research of a radical kind. One, which I have already noted, is the extremely strong pressure of ideology. Another, perhaps the most important, seems to me to arise from a distinguishing feature of radical thought, namely, its orientation toward the future. In many ways it is much easier to be a conservative sociologist, engaged in the description and analysis of existing social institutions and of the various forces which have given them their present form. A radical sociologist, on the other hand, must try to discern those trends and movements, in the present, which seem likely to bring about a future social transformation, and he has to be concerned, in part, at least, with sketching the characteristics of institutions which do not yet exist. Thus, radical thought has, inevitably, a more speculative character, and it is less easy to embody in programs of research.

But this is not to say that a great deal more empirical research could not be undertaken. There are, after all, many precursors of new social institutions—in the organization of industrial work, in the provision of social services, and so on—which have emerged from the revolutions of this century and yet have been very inadequately studied. There are also other kinds of problems which do not involve, to the same extent, speculation about the future form of society. One set of problems emerges from the failure of socialism in a number of countries in the course of this century. There is now an accumulated historical experience of what can go wrong with the efforts to create a more equal, less coercive type of society; and radical sociologists might well undertake more thorough critical studies of this experience, so that they and others can learn from it. Another problem, which I have always considered extremely important, though few radicals have ever shown much interest in it, is that presented by the sectarian tendencies in radical movements themselves. In some societies, during certain periods, there has been a notable proliferation of radical sects; and the competition, or conflict, among them has generally impeded the development, and the political success, of a broad radical movement. One factor in this situation is probably the degree of social differentiation in modern societies; Merton, in his paper, alludes to the problem of achieving unity in large social movements when their members are differentiated by cross-cutting status sets. But there may well be other influences at work, and it would not be inappropriate, for example, to introduce some hypothetical comparisons between religious and political sects. Once again, research along these lines might prove to be of considerable value to radicals themselves, by revealing such possibilities as there are for overcoming internal divisions.

Whatever the reasons may be, it is apparent that the radical thought of the recent past (and of some earlier periods) confined itself mainly to criticism, rather than establishing an alternative body of knowledge.[1] Even in their critical function, however, radical doctrines are themselves open to criticism. Lewis Coser, in his study of Marxist thought in the first quarter of this century, asserts that "Marxist theorists have contended that Marxism is exempted from the claims of the sociology of knowledge that all thought structures and ideas need to be investigated in relation to . . . existential conditions and social structures." This is not strictly true. Lukács, in *History and Class Consciousness*, recognized explicitly that historical materialism had to be applied to itself and described it, in relativistic terms, as the "self-consciousness of capitalist society," existentially determined by the situation of the proletariat. What *is* true is that Marxists have not generally employed the sociology of knowledge, or the more specifically Marxist theory of ideology, in detailed studies of the diversity of Marxist thought itself and, still more widely, of socialist thought. There have been some attempts along these lines—for example, in the formulation of a connection between "reformism" and the "labor aristocracy"—and there is the outline of a more coherent theory in Gramsci's writings on the intellectuals. Nevertheless, the greater part of Marxist discussion of the divisions within Marxist thought has taken the form of theoretical controversy about the "correctness" or otherwise of a particular interpretation of Marx.

Coser illustrates the possibility of a more detailed interpretation of Marxist thought from the perspective of the sociology of knowledge by examining two forms of Marxist theory—the positivistic and the voluntaristic—in relation to the social milieu in which they originated and developed. However, the approach which Coser adopts, relying upon an analysis of the work of individual thinkers, seems to me inadequate and in some respects misleading. Merton offers some pertinent observations on this point, when he brings against a total "insider" doctrine the objection that it assumes "total coincidence between social position and individual perspectives" and thus "exaggerates into error the conception of structural analysis which maintains that there is a *tendency for, not a full determination of*, socially patterned differences in the perspectives, preferences, and behavior of people variously located in the social structure." Coser, I think, commits this error, and there are many particular objections which can be

---

[1] There are, of course, some notable exceptions. C. Wright Mills, and after him G. William Domhoff and others, carried out serious research on classes and elites, and in this field there is an empirically founded radical theory. Recently, Richard Flacks, in "Towards a Socialist Sociology" (*Insurgent Sociologist* 2 [Spring 1972]: 18–27), outlined an array of research problems for radicals. Although this is still "programmatic," it is so in a very practical way, in the style of an earlier, neglected statement of radical social science, Robert Lynd's *Knowledge for What?*

brought against his analysis. For instance, why emphasize so strongly the formative influence of Gramsci's Sardinian childhood, and not his student years in the industrial city of Turin, or his deep involvement with the factory councils? Again, if Lenin's "voluntarism" was determined by his milieu, how are we to account for the fact that the same milieu produced Bukharin's much more "positivistic" version of Marxism, which both Lukács and Gramsci criticized for its positivism? And if the character of Rosa Luxemburg's Marxism is traceable to her Polish origins, how shall we explain the equally "voluntaristic" version of Marxism expounded by Karl Korsch, whose ideas were developed in the environment of the "industrial heartland"? The most convincing part of Coser's study is that which deals, not with the social determination of the ideas of individual thinkers, but with the influences which affected the acceptance of particular versions of Marxist theory by large social groups. Thus, he draws attention to some differences between the Social Democratic movement in north and south Germany which help to account for the more favorable reception of Bernstein's reformism in the south. Along such lines there are obviously many valuable studies to be made of the social influences upon the historical fluctuations as well as the geographical divergences, in the acceptance of particular formulations of Marxist doctrine (for example, the rise of "humanist Marxism" in the 1960s), and also comparisons with societies in which Marxism never became an important political force at all.

Much of the counter-criticism of radical thought has been concerned with radical accounts of the conservative orientation of postwar sociology. Two essays take up this issue. Rhoads argues, in the latter part of his essay, that Parsons's theory is not fundamentally conservative because it does allow for tensions, conflict, and change. The depiction of a condition of social equilibrium and of conformity to a normative order, he says, is an "ideal-type"; "the continuation of stability is a theoretical assumption, . . . and harmony is only a point of reference for the analysis of empirical events." In practice, however, the "ideal-type" merges into the "ideal"; and the work of Parsons and his followers, as is well known by this time, consistently emphasizes harmony, equilibrium, and the integration of disturbing elements as *empirical* characteristics of modern industrial societies, while persistently neglecting major social conflicts and those social movements which might produce a fundamental change in the social system. In those cases where Parsons has commented on empirical events and problems, as in his essay on the situation of black Americans, he is still primarily concerned with integration into the present social system, and not with any hypothesis so radical as the idea that the system itself might have to be changed in order to solve the problems.

It may well be, as Lipset and Ladd claim, that Parsons's attitude to many social problems is liberal rather than conservative, but this may reflect a disjunction between the theory which he produces as a thinker, and the practical judgments which he makes as a member of society. This supposition is confirmed to some extent by the fact that when Parsons does analyze current social problems, he does not usually begin from any propositions derived from his own general theory but places his discussion within a conceptual framework borrowed from social theorists who differ from him profoundly (in the essay on black Americans, for example, he uses the concepts of T. H. Marshall and Gunnar Myrdal).

There is another, quite startling, example of such disjunction, mentioned by Lipset and Ladd. A survey of Japanese sociologists apparently revealed that those under 30, who were more radical in politics than older age groups, also referred to Parsons more frequently as a non-Japanese sociologist worthy of considerable attention, and did not refer to Marx at all. Findings as surprising as this ought not to be taken simply at face value but should provoke deeper inquiries. However, insofar as they do describe authentically a state of mind, they could be regarded as showing the extent to which academic social scientists have come to accept a separation between the discipline which they teach and any personal conceptions of social life, not in the acceptable sense of making a distinction between facts and values, but in the sense of isolating in separate compartments of the mind two different theories of society—one public and academically acknowledged, the other private.

These examples lead to a wider issue, which is one of the principal themes discussed by Lipset and Ladd. The two questions which they raise in their paper are, first, whether functionalism, and especially the Parsonian version of it, has been the dominant theoretical orientation in American sociology over the past few decades, and, second, if this is so, and if Parsonian theory is as conservative as has been alleged, how it could become so influential in a profession which is markedly "left-wing" or "liberal" compared with other intellectual professions and with the general population. On the first point they conclude, in my view rightly, that neither Parsons's theory nor any other theory was really "dominant." Nevertheless, Parsons was clearly influential, as were the functionalists in general; and the question remains concerning the favorable reception of their theories by sociologists who were liberal or radical in politics. The answer suggested by Lipset and Ladd is that Parsonian and functionalist theories are not fundamentally conservative. But two other answers are possible. One is along the lines that I indicated above, namely, that individual sociologists came to lead a double life and to practice "double think," accepting one theory in their academic role, and another in their private political role. Another answer would be to say that functionalism did have a generally conservative influence, and that sociologists might otherwise have been more radical than they were; a corollary would be that those sociologists who rejected functionalism altogether were in fact more consistently radical (or else that in order to be radical they found it necessary to reject functionalism). Although the data provided by Lipset and Ladd are not sufficient to decide this question, there are some indications that such was the case. The most radical sociologists, notably C. Wright Mills, did find the sociological theory of functionalism incompatible with a radical political theory.

Lipset and Ladd, therefore, do not settle definitively the question they raise but present us, rather, with a series of new questions about the connections between sociological theories and political doctrines. One might say that the symposium as a whole opens up, in a similar way, new fields of inquiry; and I should like to end this comment by indicating some of the main issues which seem to deserve closer attention. In the first place, it would be illuminating to examine in much greater detail the conservative orientation in social and political thought which developed in the Western industrial countries during the 1950s, in an attempt to see how theories in sociology and other social sciences influenced and were influenced by general political doctrines and attitudes, and how these in turn were affected by social conditions. A second issue concerns the rise of a new radicalism during the 1960s, on which much has already been written, but without the kind of structural analysis which would link the appearance of social movements and doctrines with changes in society, in the composition and relationships of groups. From these two questions arises the most difficult problem of all, namely, the succession of radical and conservative orientations in social thought and political action. A comprehensive sociology of political knowledge would have to explore in many different directions the causes of such fluctuations, taking account of the succession of generations, cultural fashions, and longer-term changes in the social structure.

Insiders and Outsiders: A Chapter in the Sociology of Knowledge[1]

Robert K. Merton
Columbia University

The sociology of knowledge has long been regarded as a complex and esoteric subject, remote from the urgent problems of contemporary social life. To some of us, it seems quite the other way.[2] Especially in times of great social change, precipitated by acute social conflict and attended by much cultural disorganization and reorganization, the perspectives provided by the various sociologies of knowledge bear directly upon problems agitating the society It is then that differences in the values, commitments, and intellectual orientations of conflicting groups become deepened into basic cleavages, both social and cultural. As the society becomes polarized, so do the contending claims to truth. At the extreme, an active and reciprocal distrust between groups finds expression in intellectual perspectives that are no longer located within the same universe of discourse. The more deep-seated the mutual distrust, the more does the argument of the other appear so palpably implausible or absurd that one no longer inquires into its substance or logical structure to assess its truth claims. Instead, one confronts the other's argument with an entirely different sort of question: how does it happen to be advanced at all? Thought and its products thus become altogether functionalized, interpreted only in terms of their presumed social or economic or psychological sources and functions. In the political arena, where the rules of the game often condone and sometimes support the practice, this involves reciprocated attacks on the integrity of

[1] A first edition of this paper was read on November 6, 1969 to the seminar celebrating the 50th anniversary of the department of sociology at the University of Bombay, India. A second edition was read at the Centennial Symposium of Loyola University (of Chicago) on January 5, 1970 and at the annual meetings of the Southwestern Sociological Association in Dallas, Texas, on March 25, 1971. This third edition was presented at the annual meeting of the American Sociological Association in Denver, Colorado, September 1, 1971. Any errors I have retained after the critical examinations of the paper by Walter Wallace and Harriet Zuckerman are of course entirely my own. Aid from the National Science Foundation is gratefully acknowledged, as is indispensable help of quite another kind provided by Hollon W. Farr, M.D.

[2] As witness the spate of recent writings in and on the sociology of knowledge, including far too many to be cited here. Some essential discussions and bibliography are provided by Berger and Luckmann (1966), Stark (1958), Wolff (1965), Curtis and Petras (1970). The application of the sociology of knowledge to the special case of sociology itself has also burgeoned since 1959 when the Fourth World Congress of Sociology held by the International Sociological Association focused on the social contexts of sociology. See, for prime examples, Gouldner (1970), Friedrichs (1970), Tiryakian (1971).

the opponent; in the academic forum, where normative expectations are somewhat more restraining, it leads to reciprocated ideological analyses (which often deteriorate into barely concealed *ad hominem* innuendos). In both, the process feeds upon and nourishes collective insecurities.[3]

SOCIAL CHANGE AND SOCIAL THOUGHT

This conception of the social sources of the intensified interest in the sociology of knowledge and some of the theoretical difficulties which they foster plainly has the character, understandably typical in the sociology of scientific knowledge, of a self-exemplifying idea. It posits reciprocal connections between thought and society, in particular the social conditions that make for or disrupt a common universe of intellectual discourse within which the most severe disagreements can take place. Michael Polanyi (1958, 1959, 1964, 1967) has noted, more perceptively than anyone else I know,[4] how the growth of knowledge depends upon complex sets of social relations based on a largely institutionalized reciprocity of trust among scholars and scientists. In one of his many passages on this theme, he observes that

> in an ideal free society each person would have perfect access to the truth: to the truth in science, in art, religion, and justice, both in public and private life. But this is not practicable; each person can know directly very little of truth and must trust others for the rest. Indeed, to assure this process of mutual reliance is one of the main functions of society. It follows that such freedom of the mind as can be possessed by men is due to the services of social institutions, which set narrow limits to man's freedom and tend to threaten it even within those limits. The relation is analogous to that between mind and body: to the way in which the performance of mental acts is restricted by limitations and distortions due to the medium which makes these performances possible. [1959, p. 68]

But as cleavages deepen between groups, social strata or collectivities of whatever kind, the social network of mutual reliance is at best

---

[3] This passage on the conditions making for intensified interest in the sociology of knowledge and for derivative problems of theoretical analysis in the field has not been written for this occasion. It is largely drawn from my paper in Gurvitch and Moore (1945, but now out of print) and reprinted in Merton (1968, pp. 510–14). Since the cognitive orientations of group members and nonmembers has long been a problem of enduring interest to me, I shall have occasion to refer to my writings throughout this paper.

[4] Polanyi's detailed development of this theme over the years represents a basic contribution to the sociology of science by providing a model of the various overlapping cognitive and social structures of intellectual disciplines. Ziman (1968) has useful observations along these lines and Campbell (1969) has contributed some typically Campbellian (i.e., imaginative and evocative) thinking on the subject, in developing his "fish-scale model" of overlapping disciplines.

strained and at worst broken. In place of the vigorous but intellectually disciplined mutual checking and rechecking that operates to a significant extent, though never of course totally, within the social institutions of science and scholarship, there develops a strain toward separatism, in the domain of the intellect as in the domain of society. Partly grounded mutual suspicion increasingly substitutes for partly grounded mutual trust. There emerge claims to group-based truth: Insider truths that counter Outsider untruths and Outsider truths that counter Insider untruths.

In our day, vastly evident social change is being initiated and funneled through a variety of social movements. These are formally alike in their objectives of achieving an intensified collective consciousness, a deepened solidarity and a new or renewed primary or total allegiance of their members to certain social identities, statuses, groups, or collectivities. Inspecting the familiar list of these movements centered on class, race, ethnicity, age, sex, religion, and sexual disposition, we note two other instructive similarities between them. First, the movements are for the most part formed principally on the basis of ascribed rather than acquired statuses and identities, with eligibility for inclusion being in terms of who you are rather than what you are (in the sense of status being contingent on role performance). And second, the movements largely involve the public affirmation of pride in statuses and solidarity with collectivities that have long been socially and culturally downgraded, stigmatized, or otherwise victimized in the social system. As with group affiliations generally, these newly reinforced social identities find expression in various affiliative symbols of distinctive speech, bodily appearance, dress, public behavior patterns and, not least, assumptions and foci of thought.

THE INSIDER DOCTRINE

Within this context of social change, we come upon the contemporary relevance of a long-standing problem in the sociology of knowledge: the problem of patterned differentials among social groups and strata in access to certain types of knowledge. In its strong form, the claim is put forward as a matter of epistemological principle that particular groups in each moment of history have *monopolistic access* to particular kinds of knowledge. In the weaker, more empirical form, the claim holds that some groups have *privileged access*, with other groups also being able to acquire that knowledge for themselves but at greater risk and cost.

Claims of this general sort have been periodically introduced. For one imposing and consequential example, Marx, a progenitor of the sociology of knowledge as of much else in social thought, advanced the claim that after capitalistic society had reached its ultimate phase of development, the strategic location of one social class would enable it to achieve an understanding of the society that was exempt from false consciousness.[5] For another, altogether unimposing but also consequential example involving ascribed rather than achieved status, the Nazi *Gauleiter* of science and learning, Ernest Krieck (1935), expressed an entire ideology in contrasting the access to authentic scientific knowledge by men of unimpeachable Aryan ancestry with the corrupt versions of knowledge accessible to non-Aryans. Krieck could refer without hesitation to "Protestant and Catholic science, German and Jewish science." And, in a special application of the Insider doctrine, the Nazi regime could introduce the new racial category of "white Jews" to refer to those Aryans who had defiled their race by actual or symbolic contact with non-Aryans. Thus, the Nobel Prize physicist, Werner Heisenberg, became the most eminent member of this new race by persisting in his declaration that Einstein's theory of relativity constituted "an obvious basis for further research." While another Nobel laureate in physics, Johannes Stark, could castigate not only Heisenberg but his other great scientific contemporaries—Planck, von Laue, and Schrödinger—for accepting what Stark described as "the Jewish physics of Einstein" (Merton 1968, pp. 538–41).

For our purposes, we need not review the array of elitist doctrines which have maintained that certain groups have, on biological or social grounds, monopolistic or privileged access to new knowledge. Differing in detail, the doctrines are alike in distinguishing between Insider access to knowledge and Outsider exclusion from it.

SOCIAL BASES OF INSIDER DOCTRINE

The ecumenical problem of the interaction between a rapidly changing social structure and the development of Insider and Outsider doctrines is examined here in a doubly parochial fashion. Not only are my observations largely limited to the United States in our time but they are further limited to the implications of doctrines advocated by spokesmen for certain black social movements, since these movements have often come to serve as prototypical for the others (women, youth, homosexuals, other ethnics, etc.).

Although Insider doctrines have been intermittently set forth by white elitists through the centuries, white male Insiderism in American sociology

[5] Observations on the advantaged position of the proletariat for the perception of historical and social truth are threaded throughout Marx's writings. For some of the crucial passages, see his *Poverty of Philosophy* (1847, e.g., pp. 125–26). On Marx's thinking along these lines, Georg Lukács, in spite of his own disclaimers in the new introduction to his classic work, *History and Class Consciousness*, remains of fundamental importance (1971, esp. pp. 47–81, 181–209).

during the past generations has largely been of the tacit or de facto rather than doctrinal or principled variety. It has simply taken the form of patterned expectations about the appropriate selection of specialities and of problems for investigation. The handful of Negro sociologists were in large part expected, as a result of social selection and self-selection, to study problems of Negro life and relations between the races just as the handful of women sociologists were expected to study problems of women, principally as these related to marriage and the family.

In contrast to this de facto form of Insiderism, an explicitly doctrinal form has in recent years been put forward most clearly and emphatically by some black intellectuals. In its strong version, the argument holds that, as a matter of social epistemology, *only* black historians can truly understand black history, *only* black ethnologists can understand black culture, *only* black sociologists can understand the social life of blacks, and so on. In the weaker form of the doctrine, some practical concessions are made. With regard to programs of Black Studies, for example, it is proposed that some white professors of the relevant subjects might be brought in since there are not yet enough black scholars to staff all the proliferating programs of study. But as Nathan Hare, the founding publisher of the *Black Scholar*, stated several years ago, this is only on temporary and conditional sufferance: "Any white professors involved in the program would have to be black in spirit in order to last. The same is true for 'Negro' professors."[6] Apart from this kind of limited concession, the Insider doctrine maintains that there is a body of black history, black psychology, black ethnology, and black sociology which can be significantly advanced only by black scholars and social scientists.

In its fundamental character, this represents a major claim in the sociology of knowledge that implies the balkanization of social science, with separate baronies kept exclusively in the hands of Insiders bearing their credentials in the shape of one or another ascribed status. Generalizing the specific claim, it would appear to follow that if only black scholars can understand blacks, then only white scholars can understand whites. Generalizing further from race to nation, it would then appear, for example, that only French scholars can understand French society and, of course, that only Americans, not their external critics, can truly understand American society. Once the basic principle is adopted, the list of Insider claims to a monopoly of knowledge becomes indefinitely expansible to all manner of social formations based on ascribed (and, by extension, on some achieved) statuses. It would thus seem to follow that only women can understand women—and men, men. On the same principle, youth alone is

[6] Nathan Hare as quoted by Bunzel (1968, p. 32).

capable of understanding youth just as, presumably, only the middle aged are able to understand their age peers.[7] Furthermore, as we shift to the hybrid cases of ascribed and acquired statuses in varying mix, on the Insider principle, proletarians alone can understand proletarians and presumably capitalists, capitalists; only Catholics, Catholics; Jews, Jews, and to halt the inventory of socially atomized claims to knowledge with a limiting case that on its face would seem to have some merit, it would then plainly follow that only sociologists are able to understand their fellow sociologists.[8]

In all these applications, the doctrine of extreme Insiderism represents a new credentialism.[9] This is the credentialism of ascribed status, in which understanding becomes accessible only to the fortunate few or many who are to the manner born. In this respect, it contrasts with the credentialism of achieved status that is characteristic of meritocratic systems.[10]

Extreme Insiderism moves toward a doctrine of *group* methodological solipsism.[11] In this form of solipsism, each group must in the end have a monopoly of knowledge about itself just as according to the doctrine of

---

[7] Actually, the case of age status is structurally different from that of other ascribed statuses. For although, even in this time of advanced biotechnology, a few men become transformed into women and vice versa, this remains a comparatively rare instance of the ordinarily ascribed status of sex becoming an achieved status. But in contrast to sex and other ascribed statuses, each successive age status has been experienced by suitably long-lived social scientists (within the limits of their own inexorably advancing age cohorts). On the basis of a dynamic Insider doctrine, then, it might even be argued that older social scientists are better able than very young ones to understand the various other age strata. As context, see the concept of the reenactment of complementary roles in the life cycle of scientists in Zuckerman and Merton (1972).

[8] As we shall see, this is a limiting type of case that merges into quite another type, since as a fully acquired status, rather than an ascribed one, that of the sociologist (or physician or physicist) presumably presupposes functionally relevant expertise.

[9] I am indebted to Harriet Zuckerman for these observations on the new credentialism of ascribed status. The classic source of meritocracy remains Young (1958); on the dysfunctions of educational credentialism, see Miller and Roby (1970, chap. 6).

[10] But as we shall see, when the extreme Insider position is transformed from a doctrine of assumptions-treated-as-established-truth into a set of questions about the distinctive roles of Insiders and Outsiders in intellectual inquiry, there develops a convergence though not coincidence between the assumptions underlying credentials based on ascribed status and credentials based on achieved status. In the one, early socialization in the culture or subculture is taken to provide readier access to certain kinds of understanding; in the other, the component in adult socialization represented by disciplined training in one or another field of learning is taken to provide a higher probability of access to certain other kinds of understanding.

[11] As Agassi (1969, p. 421) reminds us, the term "methodological solipsism" was introduced by Rudolf Carnap to designate the theory of knowledge known as sensationalism: "the doctrine that all knowledge—of the world and of one's own self—derives from sensation." The belief that all one *really* knows is one's subjective experience is sometimes described as the "egocentric predicament."

individual methodological solipsism each individual has absolute privacy of knowledge about him- or her-self. The Insider doctrine can be put in the vernacular with no great loss in meaning: you have to be one in order to understand one. In somewhat less idiomatic language, the doctrine holds that one has monopolistic or privileged access to knowledge, or is wholly excluded from it, by virtue of one's group membership or social position. For some, the notion appears in the form of a question-begging pun: Insider as Insighter, one endowed with special insight into matters necessarily obscure to others, thus possessed of penetrating discernment. Once adopted, the pun provides a specious solution but the serious Insider doctrine has its own rationale.

We can quickly pass over the trivial version of that rationale: the argument that the Outsider may be incompetent, given to quick and superficial forays into the group or culture under study and even unschooled in its language. That this kind of incompetence can be found is beyond doubt but it holds no principled interest for us. Foolish men (and women) or badly trained men (and women) are to be found everywhere, and anthropologists and sociologists and psychologists and historians engaged in study of groups other than their own surely have their fair share of them.[12] But such cases of special ineptitude do not bear on the Insider *principle*. It is not merely that Insiders also have their share of incompetents. The Insider principle does not refer to stupidly designed and stupidly executed inquiries that happen to be made by stupid Outsiders; it maintains a more fundamental position. According to the doctrine of the Insider, the Outsider, no matter how careful and talented, is excluded in principle from gaining access to the social and cultural truth.

In short, the doctrine holds that the Outsider has a structurally imposed incapacity to comprehend alien groups, statuses, cultures, and societies. Unlike the Insider, the Outsider has neither been socialized in the group nor has engaged in the run of experience that makes up its life, and therefore cannot have the direct, intuitive sensitivity that alone makes empathic understanding possible. Only through continued socialization in the life of a group can one become fully aware of its symbolisms and socially shared realities; only so can one understand the fine-grained meanings of behavior, feelings, and values; only so can one decipher the unwritten grammar of conduct and the nuances of cultural idiom. Or, to take a specific expression of this thesis by Ralph W. Conant (1968): "Whites are not and never will be as sensitive to the black community

---

[12] As I have noted in the first edition of this paper, the social scientists of India, for one example, have long suffered the slings and arrows of outrageously unprepared and altogether exogenous social scientists engaging in swift, superficial inquiries into matters Indian (Merton 1971, p. 456).

precisely because they are not part of that community." Correlatively, Abd-l Hakimu Ibn Alkalimat (Gerald McWorter) draws a sharp contrast between the concepts of "a black social science" and "a white social science" (1969, p. 35).

A somewhat less stringent version of the doctrine maintains only that Insider and Outsider scholars have significantly different foci of interest. The argument goes somewhat as follows. The Insiders, sharing the deepest concerns of the group or at the least being thoroughly aware of them, will so direct their inquiries as to have them be relevant to those concerns. So, too, the Outsiders will inquire into problems relevant to the distinctive values and interests which they share with members of *their* group. But these are bound to differ from those of the group under study if only because the Outsiders occupy different places in the social structure.

This is a hypothesis which has the not unattractive quality of being readily amenable to empirical investigation. It should be possible to compare the spectrum of research problems about, say, the black population in the country that have been investigated by black sociologists and by white ones, or say, the spectrum of problems about women that have been investigated by female sociologists and by male ones, in order to find out whether the foci of attention in fact differ and if so, to what degree and in which respects. The only inquiry of this kind I happen to know of was published more than a quarter-century ago. William Fontaine (1944) found that Negro scholars tended to adopt analytical rather than morphological categories in their study of behavior, that they emphasized environmental rather than biological determinants of that behavior, and tended to make use of strikingly dramatic rather than representative data. All this was ascribed to a caste-induced resentment among Negro scholars. But since this lone study failed to examine the frequency of subjects, types of interpretation, and uses of data among a comparable sample of white scholars at the time, the findings are somewhat less than compelling. All the same, the questions it addressed remain. For there is theoretical reason to suppose that the foci of research adopted by Insiders and Outsiders and perhaps their categories of analysis as well will tend to differ. At least, Max Weber's notion of *Wertbeziehung* suggests that differing social locations, with their distinctive interests and values, will affect the selection of problems for investigation (Weber 1922, pp. 146–214).

Unlike the stringent version of the doctrine which maintains that Insiders and Outsiders must arrive at different (and presumably incompatible) findings and interpretations even when they do examine the same problems, this weaker version argues only that they will not deal with the same questions and so will simply talk past one another. With the two versions combined, the extended version of the Insider doctrine can also be put in the vernacular: one must not only be one in order to understand one; one must be one in order to understand what is most worth understanding.

Clearly, the social epistemological doctrine of the Insider links up with what Sumner (1907, p. 13) long ago defined as ethnocentrism: "the technical name for [the] view of things in which one's own group is the center of everything, and all others are scaled and rated with reference to it." Sumner then goes on to include as a component of ethnocentrism, rather than as a frequent correlate of it (thus robbing his idea of some of its potential analytical power), the belief that one's group is superior to all cognate groups: "each group nourishes its own pride and vanity, boasts itself superior, exalts its own divinities, and looks with contempt on outsiders" (p. 13). For although the practice of seeing one's own group as the center of things is empirically correlated with a belief in its superiority, centrality and superiority need to be kept analytically distinct in order to deal with patterns of alienation from one's membership group and contempt for it.[13]

Supplementing the abundance of historical and ethnological evidence of the empirical tendency for belief in one's group or collectivity as superior to all cognate groups or collectivities—whether nation, class, race, region, or organization—is a recent batch of studies of what Theodore Caplow (1964, pp. 213–16) has called the aggrandizement effect: the distortion upward of the prestige of an organization by its members. Caplow examined 33 different kinds of organizations—ranging from dance studios to Protestant and Catholic churches, from skid row missions to big banks, and from advertising agencies to university departments—and found that members overestimated the prestige of their organization some "eight times as often as they underestimated it" (when compared with judgments by Outsiders). More in point for us, while members tended to disagree with Outsiders about the standing of their own organization, they tended to agree with them about the prestige of the other organizations in the same

---

[13] By introducing their useful term "xenocentrism" to refer to both basic *and* favorable orientations to groups other than one's own, Kent and Burnight (1951) have retained Sumner's unuseful practice of prematurely combining centrality and evaluation in the one concept rather than keeping them analytically distinct. The analytical distinction can be captured terminologically by treating "xenocentrism" as the generic term, with the analytically distinct components of favorable orientation to nonmembership groups (as with the orientation of many white middle-class Americans toward blacks) being registered in the term "xenophilia" and the unfavorable orientation by Pareto's term "xenophobia." The growing theoretical interest in nonmembership reference groups (a concept implying a type of Outsider) (Hyman 1968; Merton and Rossi 1950) and the intensified spread of both ethnocentrism and xenocentrism in our times have given the term xenocentrism greater relevance than ever and yet, for obscure reasons, it has remained largely sequestered in the pages of the *American Journal of Sociology* where it first appeared 20 years ago. Caplow (1964, p. 216) and Horton (1965) are the only ones I know to have made good use of the term, but their unaccustomed behavior only emphasizes its more general neglect.

set. These findings can be taken as something of a sociological parable. In these matters at least, the judgments of "Insiders" are best trusted when they assess groups other than their own; that is, when members of groups judge as Outsiders rather than as Insiders.

Findings of this sort do not testify, of course, that ethnocentrism and its frequent spiritual correlate, xenophobia, fear and hatred of the alien, are incorrigible. They do, however, remind us of the widespread tendency to glorify the ingroup, sometimes to that degree in which it qualifies as chauvinism: the extreme, blind, and often bellicose extolling of one's group, status, or collectivity. We need not abandon "chauvinism" as a concept useful to us here merely because it has lately become adopted as a vogue word, blunted in meaning through indiscriminate use as a rhetorical weapon in intergroup conflict. Nor need we continue to confine the scope of the concept, as it was in its origins and later by Lasswell (1937, p. 361) in his short, incisive discussion of it, to the special case of the *state or nation*. The concept can be usefully, not tendentiously, extended to designate the extreme glorification of *any* social formation.

Chauvinism finds its fullest ideological expression when groups are subject to the stress of acute conflict. Under the stress of war, for example, scientists have been known to violate the values and norms of universalism in which they were socialized, allowing their status as nationals to dominate over their status as scientists. Thus, at the outset of World War I, almost a hundred German scholars and scientists—including many of the first rank, such as Brentano, Ehrlich, Haber, Eduard Meyer, Ostwald, Planck, and Schmoller—could bring themselves to issue a manifesto that impugned the contributions of the enemy to science, charging them with nationalistic bias, logrolling, intellectual dishonesty and, when you came right down to it, the absence of truly creative capacity. The English and French scientists were not far behind in advertising their own brand of chauvinism.[14]

Ethnocentrism, then, is not a historical constant. It becomes intensified under specifiable conditions of acute social conflict. When a nation, race, ethnic group, or any other powerful collectivity has long extolled its own admirable qualities and, expressly or by implication, deprecated the qualities of others, it invites and provides the potential for counterethnocentrism. And when a once largely powerless collectivity acquires a socially validated sense of growing power, its members experience an intensified need for self-affirmation. Under such circumstances, collective self-glorifi-

[14] Current claims of Insiderism still have a distance to go, in the academic if not the political forum, to match the chauvinistic claims of those days. For collections of such documents, see Pettit and Leudet (1916), Duhem (1915), Kellermann (1915), Kherkhof (1933).

cation, found in some measure among all groups, becomes a predictable and intensified counterresponse to long-standing belittlement from without.[15]

So it is that, in the United States, the centuries-long institutionalized premise that "white (and for some, presumably only white) is true and good and beautiful" induces, under conditions of revolutionary change, the counterpremise that "black (and for some, presumably only black) is true and good and beautiful." And just as the social system has for centuries operated on the tacit or explicit premise that in cases of conflict between whites and blacks, the whites are presumptively right, so there now develops the counterpremise, finding easy confirmation in the long history of injustice visited upon American Negroes, that in cases of such conflict today, the blacks are presumptively right.

What is being proposed here is that the epistemological claims of the Insider to monopolistic or privileged access to social truth develop under particular social and historical conditions. Social groups or strata on the way up develop a revolutionary élan. The new thrust to a larger share of power and control over their social and political environment finds various expressions, among them claims to a unique access to knowledge about their history, culture, and social life.

On this interpretation, we can understand why this Insider doctrine does not argue for a Black Physics, Black Chemistry, Black Biology, or Black Technology. For the new will to control their fate deals with the social environment, not the environment of nature. There is, moreover, nothing in the segregated life experience of Negroes that is said to sensitize them to the subject matters and problematics of the physical and life sciences. An Insider doctrine would have to forge genetic assumptions about racial modes of thought in order to claim, as in the case of the Nazi version they did claim, monopolistic or privileged access to knowledge in these fields of science. But the black Insider doctrine adopts an essentially social-environmental rationale, not a biologically genetic one.

The social process underlying the emergence of Insider doctrine is reasonably clear. Polarization in the underlying social structure becomes reflected in the polarization of claims in the intellectual and ideological domain, as groups or collectivities seek to capture what Heidegger called the "public interpretation of reality."[16] With varying degrees of intent, groups in conflict want to make their interpretation the prevailing one of how things were and are and will be. The critical measure of success occurs when the interpretation moves beyond the boundaries of the ingroup to be

[15] This is not a prediction after the fact. E. Franklin Frazier (1949, 1957) repeatedly made the general point and Merton (1968, p. 485) examined this pattern in connection with the self-fulfilling prophecy.

[16] Heidegger (1927) as cited and discussed by Mannheim (1952, pp. 196 ff.).

accepted by Outsiders. At the extreme, it then gives rise, through identifiable processes of reference-group behavior, to the familiar case of the converted Outsider validating himself, in his own eyes and in those of others, by becoming even more zealous than the Insiders in adhering to the doctrine of the group with which he wants to identify himself, if only symbolically (Merton 1968, pp. 405–6). He then becomes more royalist than the king, more papist than the pope. Some white social scientists, for example, vicariously and personally guilt ridden over centuries of white racism, are prepared to outdo the claims of the group they would symbolically join. They are ready even to surrender their hard-won expert knowledge if the Insider doctrine seems to require it. This type of response was perhaps epitomized in a televised educational program in which the white curator of African ethnology at a major museum engaged in discussion with a black who, as it happens, had had no prolonged ethnological training. All the same, at a crucial juncture in the public conversation, the distinguished ethnologist could be heard to say: "I realize, of course, that I cannot begin to understand the black experience, in Africa or America, as you can. Won't you tell our audience about it?" Here, in the spontaneity of an unrehearsed public discussion, the Insider doctrine has indeed become the public interpretation of reality.

The black Insider doctrine links up with the historically developing social structure in still another way. The dominant social institutions in this country have long treated the racial identity of individuals as actually if not doctrinally relevant to all manner of situations in every sphere of life. For generations, neither blacks nor whites, though with notably differing consequences, were permitted to forget their race. *This treatment of a social status (or identity) as relevant when intrinsically it is functionally irrelevant constitutes the very core of social discrimination.* As the once firmly rooted systems of discriminatory institutions and prejudicial ideology began to lose their hold, this meant that increasingly many judged the worth of ideas on their merits, not in terms of their racial pedigree.

What the Insider doctrine of the most militant blacks proposes on the level of social structure is to adopt the salience of racial identity in every sort of role and situation, a pattern so long imposed upon the American Negro, and to make that identity a total commitment issuing from within the group rather than one imposed upon it from without. By thus affirming the universal saliency of race and by redefining race as an abiding source of pride rather than stigma, the Insider doctrine in effect models itself after doctrine long maintained by white racists.

Neither this component of the Insider doctrine nor the statement on its implications is at all new. Almost a century ago, Frederick Douglass (1966) hinged his observations along these lines on the distinction between collective and individual self-images based on ascribed and achieved status:

One of the few errors to which we are clinging most persistently and, as I think, most mischievously has come into great prominence of late. It is the cultivation and stimulation among us of a sentiment which we are pleased to call race pride. I find it in all our books, papers, and speeches. For my part I see no superiority or inferiority in race or color. Neither the one nor the other is a proper source of pride or complacency. Our race and color are not of our own choosing. We have no volition in the case one way or another. The only excuse for pride in individuals or races is in the fact of their own achievements. . . . I see no benefit to be derived from this ever-lasting exhortation of speakers and writers among us to the cultivation of race pride. On the contrary, I see in it a positive evil. It is building on a false foundation. Besides, what is the thing we are fighting against, and what are we fighting for in this country? What is the mountain devil, the lion in the way of our progress? What is it, but American race pride; an assumption of superiority upon the ground of race and color? Do we not know that every argument we make, and every pretension we set up in favor of race pride is giving the enemy a stick to break over our heads?

In rejecting the cause of racial chauvinism, Douglass addressed the normative rather than the cognitive aspect of Insiderism. The call to total commitment requiring one group loyalty to be unquestionably paramount is most apt to be heard when the particular group or collectivity is engaged in severe conflict with others. Just as conditions of war between nations have long produced a strain toward hyperpatriotism among national ethno-centrics, so current intergroup conflicts have produced a strain toward hyperloyalty among racial or sex or age or religious ethnocentrics. Total commitment easily slides from the solidarity doctrine of "our group, right or wrong" to the morally and intellectually preemptive doctrine of "our group, always right, never wrong."

Turning from the normative aspect, with its ideology exhorting prime loyalty to this or that group, to the cognitive, specifically epistemological aspect, we note that the Insider doctrine presupposes a particular imagery of social structure.

SOCIAL STRUCTURE OF INSIDERS AND OUTSIDERS

From the discussion thus far, it should be evident that I adopt a structural conception of Insiders and Outsiders. In this conception, Insiders are the members of specified groups and collectivities or occupants of specified social statuses; Outsiders are the nonmembers.[17] This structural concept comes closer to Sumner's usage in his *Folkways* than to various meanings assigned the Outsider by Nietzsche, Kierkegaard, Sartre, Camus (1946)

[17] This is not the place to go into the theoretical problems of identifying the boundaries of groups, the criteria of group membership, and the consequent varieties of members and nonmembers. For an introduction to the complexities of these concepts, see Merton (1968, pp. 338–54, 405–7).

Robert K. Merton

or, for that matter, by Colin Wilson (1956) just as, to come nearer home, it differs from the usages adopted by Riesman, Denny, and Glazer (1950), Price (1965, pp. 83–84), or Howard S. Becker (1963). That is to say, Insiders and Outsiders are here defined as categories in social structure, not as inside dopesters or the specially initiated possessors of esoteric information on the one hand and as social-psychological types marked by alienation, rootlessness, or rule breaking, on the other.

In structural terms, we are all, of course, both Insiders and Outsiders, members of some groups and, sometimes derivatively, not of others; occupants of certain statuses which thereby exclude us from occupying other cognate statuses. Obvious as this basic fact of social structure is, its implications for Insider and Outsider epistemological doctrines are apparently not nearly as obvious. Else, these doctrines would not presuppose, as they typically do, that human beings in socially differentiated societies can be sufficiently located in terms of a single social status, category, or group affiliation—black or white, men or women, under 30 or older—or of several such categories, taken seriatim rather than conjointly. This neglects the crucial fact of social structure that individuals have not a single status but a status set: a complement of variously interrelated statuses which interact to affect both their behavior and perspectives.

The structural fact of status sets, in contrast to statuses taken one at a time, introduces severe theoretical problems for total Insider (and Outsider) doctrines of social epistemology. The array of status sets in a population means that aggregates of individuals share some statuses and not others; or, to put this in context, that they typically confront one another simultaneously as Insiders and Outsiders. Thus, if only whites can understand whites and blacks, blacks, and only men can understand men, and women, women, this gives rise to the paradox which severely limits both premises: for it then turns out, by assumption, that some Insiders are excluded from understanding other Insiders with white women being condemned not to understand white men, and black men, not to understand black women,[18] and so through the various combinations of status subsets.

Structural analysis in terms of shared and mutually exclusive status sets will surely not be mistaken either as advocating divisions within the ranks of collectivities defined by a single prime criterion or as predicting that such collectivities cannot unite on many issues, despite their internal

[18] The conflicts periodically reported by black women—for example, the debate between Mary Mebane [Liza] and Margaret Sloan (in defense of Gloria Steinem)—between identification with black liberation and the women's liberation movement, reflect this sociological fact of crosscutting status sets. The problem of coping with these structurally induced conflicts is epitomized in Margaret Sloan's (1971) "realization that I was going to help the brothers realize that as black women we cannot allow black men to do [to] us what white men have been doing to their women all these years."

divisions. Such analysis only indicates the bases of social divisions that stand in the way of enduring unity of any of the collectivities and so must be coped with, divisions that are not easily overcome as new issues activate statuses with diverse and often conflicting interests. Thus, the obstacles to a union of women in England and North Ireland resulting from national, political, and religious differences between them are no less formidable than the obstacles, noted by Marx, confronting the union of English and Irish proletarians. So, too, women's liberation movements seeking unity in the United States find themselves periodically contending with the divisions between blacks and whites within their ranks, just as black liberation movements seeking unity find themselves periodically contending with the divisions between men and liberated women within their ranks (Chisholm 1970; LaRue 1970).

The problem of achieving unity in large social movements based on any one status when its members are differentiated by crosscutting status sets is epitomized in these words about women's liberation by a black woman where identification with race is dominant: "Of course there have been women who have been able to think better than they've been trained and have produced the canon of literature fondly referred to as 'feminist literature': Anais Nin, Simone de Beauvoir, Doris Lessing, Betty Friedan, etc. And the question for us arises: how relevant are the truths, the experiences, the findings of white women to Black women? Are women after all simply women? I don't know that our priorities are the same, that our concerns and methods are the same, or even similar enough so that we can afford to depend on this new field of experts (white, female). It is rather obvious that we do not. It is obvious that we are turning to each other" (Cade 1970, p. 9).

Correlatively, the following passage epitomizes the way in which internal differentiation works against unity of the black liberation movement where dominant identification with sex status is reinforced by further educational differentiation:

> Seems to me the Brother does us all a great disservice by telling her to fight the man with the womb. Better to fight with the gun and the mind. . . . The all too breezy no-pill/have-kids/mess-up-the-man's-plan notion these comic-book-loving Sisters find so exciting is very seductive because it's a clear-cut and easy thing for her to do for the cause since it nourishes her sense of martyrdom. If the thing is numbers merely, what the hell. But if we are talking about revolution, creating an army for today and tomorrow, I think the Brothers who've been screaming these past years had better go do their homework. [Cade 1970, pp. 167–68]

The internal differentiation of collectivities based on a single status thus provides structural bases for diverse and often conflicting intellectual and moral perspectives within such collectivities. Differences of religion or age or class or occupation work to divide what similarities of race or sex or nationality work to unite. That is why social movements of every variety that strive for unity—whether they are establishmentarian movements whipped up by chauvinistic nationals in time of war or antiestablishmentarian movements designed to undo institutionalized injustice—press for total commitments in which all other loyalties are to be subordinated, on demand, to the dominant one.

This symptomatic exercise in status-set analysis may be enough to indicate that the idiomatic expression of total Insider doctrine—one must be one in order to understand one—is deceptively simple and sociologically fallacious (just as we shall see is the case with the total Outsider doctrine). For, from the sociological perspective of the status set, "one" is not a man *or* a black *or* an adolescent *or* a Protestant, *or* self-defined and socially defined as middle class, and so on. Sociologically, "one" is, of course, all of these and, depending on the size of the status set, much more. Furthermore, as Simmel (1908, pp. 403–54; Coser 1965, pp. 18–20) taught us long ago, the individuality of human beings can be sociologically derived from social differentiation and not only psychologically derived from intrapsychic processes. Thus, the greater the number and variety of group affiliations and statuses distributed among individuals in a society, the smaller, on the average, the number of individuals having precisely the same social configuration.

Following out the implications of this structural observation, we note that, on its own assumptions, the total Insider doctrine should hold only for highly fragmented small aggregates sharing the same status sets. Even a truncated status set involving only three affiliations—WASPS, for example—would greatly reduce the number of people who, under the Insider principle, would be able to understand their fellows (WASPS). The numbers rapidly decline as we attend to more of the shared status sets by including such social categories as sex, age, class, occupation, and so on, toward the limiting case in which the unique occupant of a highly complex status set is alone qualified to achieve an understanding of self. The tendency toward such extreme social atomization is of course damped by differences in the significance of statuses which vary in degrees of dominance, saliency, and centrality.[19] As a result, the fragmentation of the capacity for understanding that is implied in the total Insider doctrine will not empirically reach this extreme. The structural analysis in terms of status sets, rather than in the fictional terms of individuals being identi-

[19] This is not the place to summarize an analysis of the dynamics of status sets that takes up variation in key statuses (dominant, central, salient) and the conditions under which various statuses tend to be activated, along lines developed in unpublished lectures by Merton (1955–71). For pertinent uses of these conceptions in the dynamics of status sets, particularly with regard to functionally irrelevant statuses, see Epstein (1970, esp. chap. 3).

fied in terms of single statuses, serves only to push the logic of Insiderism to its ultimate methodological solipsism.

The fact of structural and institutional differentiation has other kinds of implications for the effort to translate the Insider claim to solidarity into an Insider epistemology. Since we all occupy various statuses and have group affiliations of varying significance to us, since, in short, we individually link up with the differentiated society through our status sets, this runs counter to the abiding and exclusive primacy of any one group affiliation. Differing situations activate different statuses which then and there dominate over the rival claims of other statuses.

This aspect of the dynamics of status sets can also be examined from the standpoint of the differing margins of functional autonomy possessed by various social institutions and other social subsystems. Each significant affiliation exacts loyalty to values, standards, and norms governing the given institutional domain, whether religion, science, or economy. Sociological thinkers such as Marx and Sorokin, so wide apart in many of their other assumptions, agree in assigning a margin of autonomy to the sphere of knowledge[20] even as they posit their respective social, economic, or cultural determinants of it. The alter ego of Marx, for example, declares the partial autonomy of spheres of thought in a well-known passage that bears repetition here:

> According to the materialist conception of history the determining element in history is *ultimately* the production and reproduction in real life. More than this neither Marx nor I have ever asserted. If therefore somebody twists this into the statement that the economic element is the *only* determining one, he transforms it into a meaningless, abstract and absurd phrase. The economic situation is the basis, but the various elements of the superstructure—political forms of the class struggle and its consequences, constitutions established by the victorious class after a successful battle, etc.,—forms of law—and then even the reflexes of all these actual struggles in the brains of the combatants: political, legal, philosophical theories, religious ideas and their further development into systems of dogma—also exercise their influence upon the course of the historical struggles and in many cases preponderate in determining their *form*. There is an interaction of all these elements in which . . . the economic movement finally asserts itself as necessary. Otherwise the application of the theory to any period of history one chooses would be easier than the solution of a simple equation of the first degree. [Engels 1936, p. 381; see also p. 392]

We can see structural differentiation and institutional autonomy at work in current responses of scholars to the extreme Insider doctrine. They

---

[20] For a detailed discussion of the partial autonomy of subsystems in the conceptions of Marx and Sorokin, see Merton and Barber (1963, pp. 343–49; Merton 1968, pp. 521 ff.). On the general notion of functional autonomy as advanced by Gordon W. Allport in psychology, see the discussion and references in Merton (1968, pp. 15–16); on functional autonomy in sociology, see Gouldner (1958, 1959).

reject the monopolistic doctrine of the Insider that calls for total ideological loyalty in which efforts to achieve scholarly detachment and objectivity become redefined as renegadism just as ideological reinforcement of collective self-esteem becomes redefined as the higher objectivity. It is here, to continue with our case in point, that Negro scholars who retain their double loyalty—to the race and to the values and norms of scholarship —part company with the all-encompassing loyalty demanded by the Insider doctrine. Martin Kilson (1969), for example, repudiates certain aspects of the doctrine and expresses his commitment to both the institutionalized values of scholarship and to the black community in these words:

> I am opposed to proposals to make Afro-American studies into a platform for a particular ideological group, and to restrict these studies to Negro *students and teachers*. For, and we must be frank about this, what this amounts to is racism in reverse—black racism. I am certainly convinced that it is important for the Negro to know of his past—of his ancestors, of their strengths and weaknesses—and they should respect this knowledge, when it warrants respect, and they should question it and criticize it, when it deserves criticism. But it is of no advantage to a mature and critical understanding or appreciation of one's heritage if you approach that heritage with the assumption that it is intrinsically good and noble, and intrinsically superior to the heritage of other peoples. That is, after all, what white racists have done; and none of my militant friends in the black studies movement have convinced me that racist thought is any less vulgar and degenerate because it is used by black men. . . . What I am suggesting here is that the serious study of the heritage of any people will produce a curious mixture of things to be proud of, things to criticize and even despise and things to be perpetually ambivalent toward. And this is as it should be: only an ideologically oriented Afro-American studies program, seeking to propagate a packaged view of the black heritage, would fail to evoke in a student the curious yet fascinating mixture of pride, criticism and ambivalence which I think *is, or ought to be the product of serious intellectual and academic activity.* [Pp. 329–30; italics added]

Along with the faults of neglecting the implications of structural differentiation, status sets, and institutional autonomy, the Insider (and comparable Outsider) doctrine has the further fault of assuming, in its claims of monopolistic or highly privileged status-based access to knowledge, that social position wholly determines intellectual perspectives. In doing so, it affords yet another example of the ease with which truths can decline into error merely by being extended well beyond the limits within which they have been found to hold. (There *can* be too much of a good thing.)

A long-standing conception shared by various "schools" of sociological thought holds that differences in the social location of individuals and groups tend to involve differences in their interests and value orientations (as well as the sharing of some interests and values with others). Certain traditions in the sociology of knowledge have gone on to assume that these structurally patterned differences should involve, on the *average*, patterned differences in perceptions and perspectives. And these, so the convergent traditions hold—their convergence being often obscured by diversity in vocabulary rather than in basic concept—should make for discernible differences, on the average, in the definitions of problems for inquiry and in the types of hypotheses taken as points of departure. So far, so good. The evidence is far from in, since it has also been a tradition in the sociology of scientific knowledge during the greater part of the past century to prefer speculative theory to empirical inquiry. But the idea, which can be taken as a general orientation guiding such inquiry, is greatly transformed in Insider doctrine.

For one thing, that doctrine assumes total coincidence between social position and individual perspectives. It thus exaggerates into error the conception of structural analysis which maintains that there is a *tendency for, not a full determination of,* socially patterned differences in the perspectives, preferences, and behavior of people variously located in the social structure. The theoretical emphasis on tendency, as distinct from total uniformity, is basic, not casual or niggling. It provides for a range of variability in perspective and behavior among members of the same groups or occupants of the same status (differences which, as we have seen, are ascribable to social as well as psychological differentiation). At the same time, this structural conception also provides for patterned differences, *on the whole,* between the perspectives of members of different groups or occupants of different statuses. Structural analysis thus avoids what Dennis Wrong (1961) has aptly described as "the oversocialized conception of man in modern sociology."[21]

[21] Wrong's paper is an important formulation of the theoretical fault involved in identifying structural position with individual behavior. But, in some cases, he is preaching to the long since converted. It is a tenet in some forms of structural analysis that differences in social location *make for* patterned differences in perspectives and behavior *between* groups while still allowing for a range of variability *within* groups and thus, in structurally proximate groups, for considerably overlapping ranges of behavior and perspective. On the general orientation of structural analysis in sociology, see Barbano (1968); for some specific terminological clues to the fundamental distinction between social position and actual behavior or perspective as this is incorporated in structural analysis, see Merton (1968, passim) for the key theoretical expressions that *"structures exert pressures"* and structures *"tend"* to generate perspectives and behaviors. For specific examples: "people in the various occupations *tend* to take different parts in the society, to have different shares in the exercise of power, both acknowledged and unacknowledged, and to *see* the world differently"(p. 180). "Our primary aim is to discover how some *social structures exert a definite pressure upon certain persons in the society to engage in nonconforming rather than conforming conduct.* If we can locate groups peculiarly subject to such pressures, we should expect to find fairly high *rates* of deviant behavior in those groups" (p. 186). And for immediate rather than general theoretical bearing on the specific problems here under review, see Merton

Robert K. Merton

Important as such allowance for individual variability is for general structural theory, it has particular significance for a sociological perspective on the life of the mind and the advancement of science and learning. For it is precisely the individual differences among scientists and scholars that are often central to the development of the discipline. They often involve the differences between good scholarship and bad; between imaginative contributions to science and pedestrian ones; between the consequential ideas and stillborn ones. In arguing for the monopolistic access to knowledge, Insider doctrine can make no provision for individual variability that extends beyond the boundaries of the ingroup which alone can develop sound and fruitful ideas.

Insofar as Insider doctrine treats ascribed rather than achieved statuses as central in forming perspectives, it tends to be static in orientation. For with the glaring exception of age status itself, ascribed statuses are generally retained throughout the life span. Yet sociologically, there is nothing fixed about the boundaries separating Insiders from Outsiders. As situations involving different values arise, different statuses are activated and the lines of separation shift. Thus, for a large number of white Americans, Joe Louis was a member of an outgroup. But when Louis defeated the Nazified Max Schmeling, many of the same white Americans promptly redefined him as a member of the (national) ingroup. National self-esteem took precedence over racial separatism. That this sort of drama in which changing situations activate differing statuses in the status set is played out in the domain of the intellect as well is the point of Einstein's ironic observation in an address at the Sorbonne: "If my theory of relativity is proven successful, Germany will claim me as a German and France will declare that I am a citizen of the world. Should my theory prove untrue, France will say that I am a German and Germany will declare that I am a Jew."[22]

Like earlier conceptions in the sociology of knowledge, recent Insider

(1957): "In developing this view, I do not mean to imply that scientists, any more than other men [and women] are merely obedient puppets doing exactly what social institutions require of them. But I do mean to say that, like men [and women] in other institutional spheres, scientists tend to develop the values and to channel their motivations in directions the institution defines for them" (p. 640).

[22] On the general point of shifting boundaries, see Merton (1968, pp. 338–42, 479–80). Einstein was evidently quite taken with the situational determination of shifts in group boundaries. In a statement written for the London *Times* at a time (November 28, 1919) when the animosities of World War I were still largely intact, he introduced slight variations on the theme: "The description of me and my circumstances in the *Times* shows an amusing flare of imagination on the part of the writer. By an application of the theory of relativity to the taste of the reader, today in Germany I am called a German man of science and in England I am represented as a Swiss Jew. If I come to be regarded as a *'bête noire'* the description will be reversed, and I shall become a Swiss Jew for the German and a German for the English" (Frank 1963, p. 144).

doctrines maintain that, in the end, it is a special category of Insider—a category that generally manages to include the proponent of the doctrine—that has sole or privileged access to knowledge. Mannheim (1936, pp. 10, 139, 232), for example, found a structural warranty for the validity of social thought in the "classless position" of the "socially unattached intellectuals" (*sozialfreischwebende Intelligenz*). In his view, these intellectuals can comprehend the conflicting tendencies of the time since, among other things, they are "recruited from constantly varying social strata and life-situations." (This is more than a little reminiscent of the argument in the *Communist Manifesto* which emphasizes that "the proletariat is recruited from all classes of the population.")[23] Without stretching this argument to the breaking point, it can be said that Mannheim in effect claims that there is a category of socially free-floating intellectuals who are both Insiders and Outsiders. Benefiting from their collectively diverse social origins and transcending group allegiances, they can observe the social universe with special insight and a synthesizing eye.

INSIDERS AS "OUTSIDERS"

In an adaptation of this same kind of idea, what some Insiders profess as Insiders they apparently reject as Outsiders. For example, when advocates of black Insider doctrine engage in analysis of "white society," trying to assay its power structure or to detect its vulnerabilities, they seem to deny in practice what they affirm in doctrine. At any rate, their behavior testifies to the assumption that it is possible for self-described "Outsiders" to diagnose and to understand what they describe as an alien social structure and culture.

This involves the conception that there is a special category of people in the system of social stratification who have distinctive, if not exclusive, perceptions and understanding in their capacities as *both* Insiders and Outsiders. We need not review again the argument for special access to knowledge that derives from being an Insider. What is of interest here is the idea that special perspectives and insights are available to that category of Outsiders who have been systematically frustrated by the social system: the disinherited, deprived, disenfranchised, dominated, and exploited Outsiders. Their run of experience in trying to cope with these problems serves to sensitize them—and in a more disciplined way, the trained social scientists among them—to the workings of the culture and social structure that are more apt to be taken for granted by Insider social scientists drawn from social strata who have either benefited from the going social system or have not greatly suffered from it.

[23] For further discussion of the idea of social structural warranties of validity, see Merton (1968, pp. 560–62).

This reminder that Outsiders are not all of a kind and the derived hypothesis in the sociology of knowledge about socially patterned differences in perceptiveness is plausible and deserving of far more systematic investigation than it has received. That the white-dominated society has long imposed social barriers which excluded Negroes from anything remotely like full participation in that society is now known to even the more unobservant whites. But what many of them have evidently not noticed is that the high walls of segregation do not at all separate whites and blacks symmetrically from intimate observation of the social life of the other. As socially invisible men and women, blacks at work in white enclaves have for centuries moved through or around the walls of segregation to discover with little effort what was on the other side. This was tantamount to their having access to a one-way screen. In contrast, the highly visible whites characteristically did not want to find out about life in the black community and could not, even in those rare cases where they would. The structure of racial segregation meant that the whites who prided themselves on "understanding" Negroes knew little more than their stylized role behaviors in relation to whites and next to nothing of their private lives. As Arthur Lewis has noted, something of the same sort still obtains with the "integration" of many blacks into the larger society during the day coupled with segregation at night as blacks and whites return to their respective ghettos. In these ways, segregation can make for asymmetrical sensitivities across the divide.

Although there is a sociological tradition of reflection and research on marginality in relation to thought, sociologists have hardly begun the hard work of seriously investigating the family of hypotheses in the sociology of knowledge that derive from this conception of asymmetrical relations between diverse kinds of Insiders and Outsiders.

OUTSIDER DOCTRINE AND PERSPECTIVES

The strong version of the Insider doctrine, with its epistemological claim to a monopoly of certain kinds of knowledge, runs counter, of course, to a long history of thought. From the time of Francis Bacon, to reach back no further, students of the intellectual life have emphasized the corrupting influence of group loyalties upon the human understanding. Among Bacon's four Idols (or sources of false opinion), we need only recall the second, the Idol of the Cave. Drawing upon Plato's allegory of the cave in the *Republic*, Bacon undertakes to tell how the immediate social world in which we live seriously limits what we are prepared to perceive and how we perceive it. Dominated by the customs of our group, we maintain received opinions, distort our perceptions to have them accord with these opinions, and are thus held in ignorance and led into error which we parochially mistake for the truth. Only when we escape from the cave and extend our visions do we provide for access to authentic knowledge. By implication, it is through the iconoclasm that comes with changing group affiliations that we can destroy the Idol of the Cave, abandon delusory doctrines of our own group, and enlarge our prospects for reaching the truth. For Bacon, the dedicated Insider is peculiarly subject to the myopia of the cave.

In this conception, Bacon characteristically attends only to the dysfunctions of group affiliation for knowledge. Since for him access to authentic knowledge requires that one abandon superstition and prejudice, and since these stem from groups, it would not occur to Bacon to consider the possible functions of social locations in society as providing for observability and access to particular kinds of knowledge.

In a far more subtle style, the founding fathers of sociology in effect also argued against the strong form of the Insider doctrine *without turning to the equal and opposite error of advocating the strong form of the Outsider doctrine* (which would hold that knowledge about groups, unprejudiced by membership in them, is accessible only to outsiders).

The ancient epistemological problem of subject and object was taken up in the discussion of historical *Verstehen*. Thus, first Simmel and then, repeatedly, Max Weber symptomatically adopted the memorable phrase: "one need not be Caesar in order to understand Caesar."[24] In making this claim, they rejected the extreme Insider thesis which asserts in effect that one *must* be Caesar in order to understand him just as they rejected the extreme Outsider thesis that one must *not* be Caesar in order to understand him.

The observations of Simmel and Weber bear directly upon implications of the Insider doctrine that reach beyond its currently emphasized scope.

---

[24] Thanks to Donald N. Levine (1971, p. xxiii), I learn that in often attributing the aphorism, with its many implications for social epistemology, to Weber, I had inadvertently contributed to a palimpsestic syndrome: assigning a **striking** idea or formulation to the author who first introduced us to it when in fact that author had simply adopted or revived a formulation that he (and others versed in the same tradition) knew to have been created by another. As it happens, I first came upon the aphorism in Weber's basic paper on the categories of a *verstehende* sociology published in 1913. In that passage, he treats the aphorism as common usage which he picks up for his own analytical purposes: "Man muss, wie oft gesagt worden ist, 'nicht Cäsar sein, um Cäsar zu verstehen.'" Alerted by Levine's note, I now find that Weber made earlier use of the aphorism back in 1903–6 (1951, pp. 100–101) as he drew admiringly upon Simmel's *Probleme der Geschichtsphilosophie* to which he attributes the most thoroughly developed beginnings of a theory of *Verstehen*. Properly enough, Weber devotes a long, long note to the general implications of Simmel's use of the aphorism, quoting it just as we have seen but omitting the rest of Simmel's embellished version: "Und kein zweiter Luther, um Luther zu begreifen." In his later work, Weber incorporated the aphorism whenever he examined the problem of the "understandability" of the actions of others.

Robert K. Merton

The Insider argues that the authentic understanding of group life can be achieved only by those who are directly engaged as members in the life of the group. Taken seriously, the doctrine puts in question the validity of just about all historical writing, as Weber clearly saw ([1922] 1951, p. 428).[25] If direct engagement in the life of a group is essential to understanding it, then the only authentic history is contemporary history, written in fragments by those most fully involved in making inevitably limited portions of it. Rather than constituting only the raw materials of history, the documents prepared by engaged Insiders become all there is to history. But once the historian elects to write the history of a time other than his own, even the most dedicated Insider, of the national, sex, age, racial, ethnic, or religious variety, becomes the Outsider, condemned to error and misunderstanding.

Writing some 20 years ago in another connection, Claude Lévi-Strauss noted the parallelism between history and ethnography. Both subjects, he observed,

> are concerned with societies *other* than the one in which we live. Whether this *otherness* is due to remoteness in time (however slight) or to remoteness in space, or even to cultural heterogeneity, is of secondary importance compared to the basic similarity of perspective. All that the historian or ethnographer can do, and all that we can expect of either of them, is to enlarge a specific experience to the dimensions of a more general one, which thereby becomes accessible *as experience* to men of another country or another epoch. And in order to succeed, both historian and ethnographer, must have the same qualities: skill, precision, a sympathetic approach and objectivity.[26]

Our question is, of course, whether the qualities required by the historian and ethnographer as well as other social scientists are confined to or largely concentrated among Insiders or Outsiders. Simmel (1908), and after him, Schütz (1944), and others have pondered the roles of that incarnation of the Outsider, the stranger who moves on.[27] In a fashion oddly reminiscent of the anything-but-subtle Baconian doctrine, Simmel develops the thesis that the stranger, not caught up in commitments to the group, can more readily acquire the strategic role of the relatively objective inquirer. "He is freer, practically and theoretically," notes Simmel (1950), "he surveys conditions with less prejudice; his criteria for them

[25] Having quoted the Caesar aphorism, Weber goes on to draw the implication for historiography: "Sonst wäre alle Geschichtsschreibung sinnlos."

[26] The essay from which this is drawn was first published in 1949 and is reprinted in Lévi-Strauss (1963, p. 16).

[27] It is symbolically appropriate that Simmel should have been attuned to the role of the stranger as outsider. For as Lewis Coser (1965, pp. 29–39) has shown, Simmel's style of sociological work was significantly influenced by his role as "The Stranger in the Academy."

are more general and more objective ideals; he is not tied down in his action by habit, piety, and precedent" (pp. 404–5). Above all, and here Simmel departs from the simple Baconian conception, the objectivity of the stranger "does not simply involve passivity and detachment; it is a particular structure composed of distance and nearness, indifference and involvement." It is the stranger, too, who finds what is familiar to the group significantly unfamiliar and so is prompted to raise questions for inquiry less apt to be raised at all by Insiders.

As was so often the case with Simmel's seminal mind, he thus raised a variety of significant questions about the role of the stranger in acquiring sound and new knowledge, questions that especially in recent years have begun to be seriously investigated. A great variety of inquiries into the roles of anthropological and sociological fieldworkers have explored the advantages and limitations of the Outsider as observer.[28] Even now, it appears that the balance sheet for Outsider observers resembles that for Insider observers, both having their distinctive assets and liabilities.

Apart from the theoretical and empirical work examining the possibly distinctive role of the Outsider in social and historical inquiry, significant episodes in the development of such inquiry can be examined as "clinical cases" in point. Thus, it has been argued that in matters historical and sociological the prospects for achieving certain kinds of insights may actually be somewhat better for the Outsider. Soon after it appeared in 1835, Tocqueville's *Democracy in America* was acclaimed as a masterly work by "an accomplished foreigner." Tocqueville himself expressed the opinion that "there are certain truths which Americans can only learn from strangers." These included what he described as the tyranny of majority opinion and the particular system of stratification which even in that time involved a widespead preoccupation with relative status in the community that left "Americans so restless in the midst of their prosperity." (This *is* Tocqueville, not Galbraith, writing.) All the same, this most perceptive Outsider did not manage to transcend many of the deep-seated racial beliefs and myths he encountered in the United States of the time.

[28] Many of these inquiries explicitly take off from Simmel's imagery of the roles and functions of the stranger. From the large and fast-growing mass of publications on fieldwork in social science, I cite only a few that variously try to analyze the roles of the Outsider as observer and interpreter. From an earlier day dealing with "stranger value," see Oeser (1939), Nadel (1939), Merton (1947), and Paul (1953). For more recent work on the parameters of adaptation by strangers as observers, see especially the imaginative analysis by Nash (1963) and the array of papers detailing how the sex role of women anthropologists affected their access to field data (Golde 1970). On comparable problems of the roles of Insiders and Outsiders in the understanding of complex public bureaucracies, see the short, general interpretation by Merton (1945) and the comprehensive, detailed one by Frankel (1969).

Robert K. Merton

Having condemned the Anglo-Americans whose "oppression has at one stroke deprived the descendants of the Africans of almost all the privileges of humanity" (Tocqueville [1858] 1945, 1:332);

> having described slavery as mankind's greatest calamity and having argued that the abolition of slavery in the North was "not for the good of the Negroes, but for that of the whites" (ibid., 1:360–61);
> having identified the marks of "oppression" upon both the oppressed Indians and blacks *and* upon their white oppressors (ibid., vol. 1, chap. 18, passim);
> having noted "the tyranny of the laws" designed to suppress the "unhappy blacks" in the states that had abolished slavery (ibid., 1:368);
> having approximately noted the operation of the self-fulfilling prophecy in the remark that "to induce the whites to abandon the opinion they have conceived of the moral and intellectual inferiority of their former slaves, the Negroes must change; but as long as this opinion subsists, to change is impossible" (ibid., 1:358, n.);
> having also approximated the idea of relative deprivation in the statement that "there exists a singular principle of relative justice which is very firmly implanted in the human heart. Men are much more forcibly struck by those inequalities which exist within the circle of the same class, than with those which may be remarked between different classes" (ibid., 1: 373–74;
> having made these observations and judgments, this talented Outsider nevertheless accepts the doctrine, relevant in his time, that racial inequalities "seem to be founded upon the immutable laws of nature herself" (ibid., 1:358–59); and, to stop the list of particulars here, assumes, as an understandable and inevitable rather than disturbing fact that "the Negro, who earnestly desires to mingle his race with that of the European, cannot effect it" (ibid., 1:335).[29]

Without anachronistically asking, as a Whig historian might, for altogether prescient judgments from this Outsider who was, after all, recording his observations in the early 19th century, we can nevertheless note that the role of Outsider apparently no more guarantees emancipation from the myths of a collectivity than the role of the Insider guarantees full insight into its social life and beliefs.

What was in the case of Tocqueville an unplanned circumstance has since often become a matter of deliberate decision. Outsiders are sought out to observe social institutions and cultures on the premise that they are more apt to do so with detachment. Thus, in the first decade of this century, the Carnegie Foundation for the Advancement of Teaching, in

[29] Tocqueville also assumes that "fatal oppression" has resulted in the enslaved blacks becoming "devoid of wants," and that "plunged in this abyss of evils, [he] scarcely feels his own calamitous situation," coming to believe that "even the power of thought . . . [is] a useless gift of Providence" (1:333). Such observations on the dehumanizing consequences of oppression are remarkable for the time. As Oliver Cromwell Cox (1948) observes about part of this same passage, Tocqueville's point "still has a modicum of validity" (p. 369, n.).

its search for someone to investigate the condition of medical schools, reached out to appoint Abraham Flexner, after he had admitted never before having been inside a medical school. It was a matter of policy to select a total Outsider who, as it happened, produced the uncompromising Report which did much to transform the state of American medical education at the time.

Later, casting about for a scholar who might do a thoroughgoing study of the Negro in the United States, the Carnegie Corporation searched for an Outsider, preferably one, as they put it, drawn from a country of "high intellectual and scholarly standards but with no background or traditions of imperialism." These twin conditions of course swiftly narrowed the scope of the search. Switzerland and the Scandinavian countries alone seemed to qualify, with the quest ending, as we know, with the selection of Gunnar Myrdal. In the preface to *An American Dilemma*, Myrdal (1944, pp. xviii–xiv) reflected on his status as an Outsider who, in his words, "had never been subject to the strains involved in living in a black-white society" and who "as a stranger to the problem . . . has had perhaps a greater awareness of the extent to which human valuations everywhere enter into our scientific discussion of the Negro problem."

Reviews of the book repeatedly alluded to the degree of detachment from entangling loyalties that seemed to come from Myrdal's being an Outsider. J. S. Redding (1944), for one, observed that "as a European, Myrdal had no American sensibilities to protect. He hits hard with fact and interpretation." Robert S. Lynd (1944), for another, saw it as a prime merit of this Outsider that he was free to find out for himself "without any side glances as to what was politically expedient." And for a third, Frank Tannenbaum (1944) noted that Myrdal brought "objectivity in regard to the special foibles and shortcomings in American life. As an outsider, he showed the kind of objectivity which would seem impossible for one reared within the American scene." Even later criticism of Myrdal's work—for example, the comprehensive critique by Cox (1948, chap. 23)—does not attribute imputed errors in interpretation to his having been an Outsider.

Two observations should be made on the Myrdal episode. First, in the judgment of critical minds, the Outsider, far from being excluded from the understanding of an alien society, was able to bring needed perspectives to it. And second, that Myrdal, wanting to have both Insider and Outsider perspectives, expressly drew into his circle of associates in the study such Insiders, engaged in the study of Negro life and culture and of race relations, as E. Franklin Frazier, Arnold Rose, Ralph Bunche, Melville Herskovits, Otto Klineberg, J. G. St. Clair Drake, Guy B. Johnson, and Doxey A. Wilkerson.

It should be noted in passing that other spheres of science, technology,

Robert K. Merton

and learning have accorded distinctive and often related roles to both the Insider and the Outsider (Zuckerman and Merton 1972, pp. 311–14). As long ago as the 17th century, Thomas Sprat, the historian of the Royal Society, for example, took it "as evident, that divers sorts of Manufactures have been given us by men who were not bred up in Trades that resembled those which they discover'd. I shall mention Three; that of Printing, [Gun]Powder, and the Bow-Dye." Sprat goes on to expand upon the advantages of the Outsider for invention, concluding with the less-than-science-based observation that "as in the Generation of Children, those are usually observ'd to be most sprightly, that are the stollen Fruits of an unlawful Bed; so in the Generations of the Brains, those are often the most vigorous, and witty, which men beget on other Arts, and not on their own" (Sprat 1959, pp. 391–93).

In our own time, Gilfillan (1935, p. 88) reported that the "cardinal inventions are due to men outside the occupation affected, and the minor, perfective inventions to insiders." And in a recent and more exacting inquiry, Joseph Ben-David (1960) found that the professionalization of scientific research "does not in itself decrease the chances of innovation by outsiders to the various fields of science." For the special case of outsiders to a particular discipline, Max Delbrück (1963, p. 13), himself a founding father of molecular biology, notes that although "nuclear physics was developed almost exclusively within the framework of academic institutes at universities, molecular biology, in contrast, is almost exclusively a product of outsiders, of chemists, physicists, medical microbiologists, mathematicians and engineers."

The cumulative point of this variety of intellectual and institutional cases is not—and this needs to be repeated with all possible emphasis—is *not* a proposal to replace the extreme Insider doctrine by an extreme and equally vulnerable Outsider doctrine. The intent is, rather, to transform the original question altogether. We no longer ask whether it is the Insider or the Outsider who has monopolistic or privileged access to social truth; instead, we begin to consider their distinctive and interactive roles in the process of truth seeking.

INTERCHANGE, TRADE OFFS, AND SYNTHESES

The actual intellectual interchange between Insiders and Outsiders—in which each adopts perspectives from the other—is often obscured by the rhetoric that commonly attends intergroup conflict. Listening only to that rhetoric, we may be brought to believe that there really is something like antithetical "black knowledge" and "white knowledge," "man's knowledge" and "woman's knowledge," etc., of a sort that allows no basis for judging between their differing claims to knowledge. Yet the boundaries between Insiders and Outsiders tend to be far more permeable than this allows. Just as with the process of competition generally, so with the competition of ideas. Competing or conflicting groups take over ideas and procedures from one another, thereby denying in practice the rhetoric of total incompatibility. Even in the course of social polarization, conceptions with cognitive value are utilized all apart from their source. Concepts of power structure, co-optation, the dysfunctions of established institutions and findings associated with these concepts have for some time been utilized by social scientists, irrespective of their social or political identities. Nathan Hare (1967), for example, who remains one of the most articulate exponents of the Insider doctrine, made use of the notion of the self-fulfilling prophecy in trying to explain how it is that organizations run by blacks find it hard to work out.[30] As he put it, "White people thought that we could not have any institutions which were basically black which were of good quality. This has the effect of a self-fulfilling prophecy, because if you think that black persons cannot possibly have a good bank, then you don't put your money in it. All the best professors leave black universities to go to white universities as soon as they get the chance. The blacks even do the same thing. And this makes your prediction, which wasn't true in the beginning, come out to be true" (p. 65). Such diffusion of ideas across the boundaries of groups and statuses has long been noted. In one of his more astute analyses, Mannheim (1952) states the general case for the emergence and spread of knowledge that transcends even profound conflicts between groups:

> Syntheses owe their existence to the same social process that brings about polarization; groups take over the modes of thought and intellectual achievements of their adversaries under the simple law of 'competition on the basis of achievement.' . . . In the socially-differentiated thought process, even the opponent is ultimately forced to adopt those categories and forms of thought which are most appropriate in a given type of world order. In the economic sphere, one of the possible results of competition is that one competitor is compelled to catch up with the other's technological advances. In just the same way, whenever groups compete for having their interpretation of reality accepted as the correct one, it may happen that one of the groups takes over from the adversary some fruitful hypothesis or category —anything that promises cognitive gain. . . . [In due course, it becomes

[30] Elsewhere, Hare treats certain beliefs of "Negro dignitaries" as a self-fulfilling prophecy (1970, p. 44). A recent work (Hole and Levine 1971) on women's liberation movements, both new and old, also observes: "Feminists argue further that there is a self-fulfilling prophecy component: when one group dominates another, the group with power is, at best, reluctant to relinquish its control. Thus in order to keep woman in 'her place,' theories are propounded which presume that her place is defined by nature" (p. 193).

> possible] to find a position from which both kinds of thought can be envisaged in their partial correctness, yet at the same time also interpreted as subordinate aspects of a higher synthesis. [Pp. 221–23]

The essential point is that, with or without intent, the process of intellectual exchange takes place precisely because the conflicting groups are in interaction. The extreme Insider doctrine, for example, affects the thinking of sociologists, black and white, who reject its extravagant claims. Intellectual conflict sensitizes them to aspects of their subject that they have otherwise not taken into account.

Social Sadism and Sociological Euphemism

As a case in point of this sort of sensitization through interaction, I take what can be described as a composite pattern of social sadism and sociological euphemism. "Social sadism" is more than a metaphor. The term refers to social structures which are so organized as to systematically inflict pain, humiliation, suffering, and deep frustration upon particular groups and strata. This need have nothing at all to do with the psychic propensities of individuals to find pleasure in cruelty. It is an objective, socially organized, and recurrent set of situations that has these cruel consequences, however diverse its historical sources and whatever the social processes that maintain it.

This type of sadistic social structure is readily overlooked by a perspective that can be described as that of the sociological euphemism. This term does not refer to the obvious cases in which ideological support of the structure is simply couched in sociological language. Rather, it refers to the kind of conceptual apparatus that, once adopted, requires us to ignore such intense human experiences as pain, suffering, humiliation, and so on. In this context, analytically useful concepts such as social stratification, social exchange, reward system, dysfunction, symbolic interaction, etc., are altogether bland in the fairly precise sense of being unperturbing, suave, and soothing in effect. To say this is not to imply that the conceptual repertoire of sociology (or of any other social science) must be purged of such impersonal concepts and filled with sentiment-laden substitutes. But it should be noted that analytically useful as these impersonal concepts are for certain problems, they also serve to exclude from the attention of the social scientist the intense feelings of pain and suffering that are the experience of some people caught up in the social patterns under examination. By screening out these profoundly human experiences, they become sociological euphemisms.

Nor is there any easy solution to the problem of sociological euphemism. True, we have all been warned off the Whiteheadian fallacy of misplaced concreteness, the fallacy of assuming that the particular concepts we employ to examine the flow of events capture their entire content. No more than in other fields of inquiry are sociological concepts designed to depict the concrete entirety of the psychosocial reality to which they refer. But the methodological rationale for conceptual abstraction has yet to provide a way of assessing the intellectual costs as well as the intellectual gains of abstraction. As Paul Weiss (1971) has put the general issue: "How can we ever retrieve information about distinctive features once we have tossed it out?" (p. 213).

Consider some outcomes of the established practice of employing bland sociological concepts that systematically abstract from certain elements and aspects of the concreteness of social life. It is then only a short step to the further tacit assumption that the aspects of psychosocial reality which these concepts help us to understand *are the only ones worth trying to understand.* The ground is then prepared for the next seemingly small but altogether conclusive step. The social scientist sometimes comes to act as though the aspects of the reality which are neglected in his analytical apparatus *do not even exist.* By that route, even the most conscientious of social scientists are often led to transform their concepts and models into scientific euphemisms.

All this involves the special irony that the more intellectually powerful a set of social science concepts has proved to be, the less the incentive for trying to elaborate it in ways designed to catch up the humanly significant aspects of the psychosocial reality that it neglects.

It is this tendency toward sociological euphemism, I suggest, that some (principally but not exclusively black) social scientists are forcing upon the attention of (principally but not exclusively white) social scientists. No one I know has put this more pointedly than Kenneth Clark (1965): "More privileged individuals may understandably need to shield themselves from the inevitable conflict and pain which would result from acceptance of the fact that they *are* accessories to profound injustice. The tendency to discuss disturbing social issues such as racial discrimination, segregation, and economic exploitation in detached, legal, political, socio-economic, or psychological terms as if these persistent problems did not involve the suffering of actual human beings is so contrary to empirical evidence that it must be interpreted as a protective device" (p. 75).

From Social Conflict to Intellectual Controversy

Perhaps enough has been said to indicate how Insider and Outsider perspectives can converge, in spite of such differences, through reciprocal adoption of ideas and the developing of complementary and overlapping foci of attention in the formulation of scientific problems. But these intellectual potentials for synthesis are often curbed by social processes that divide scholars and scientists. Internal divisions and polarizations in the society at large often stand in the way of realizing those potentials. Under conditions of acute conflict, each hostile camp develops highly selective perceptions of what is going on in the other. Perspectives become self-confirming as both Insiders and Outsiders tend to shut themselves off from ideas and information at odds with their own conceptions. They come to see in the other primarily what their hostile dispositions alert them to see and then promptly mistake the part for the whole. The initial interaction between the contending groups becomes reduced in response to the reciprocal alienation that follows upon public distortions of the others' ideas. In the process, each group becomes less and less motivated to examine the ideas of the other, since there is manifestly small point in attending to the ideas of those capable of such distortion. The members of each group then scan the outgroup's writings just enough to find ammunition for new fusillades.

The process of increased selective inattention to ideas of the other produces rigidified all-or-none doctrines. Even intellectual orientations that are not basically contradictory come to be regarded as though they were. *Either* the Insider *or* the Outsider has access to the sociological truth. In the midst of such polarized social conflict, there is little room for the third party uncommitted in the domain of knowledge to, for them, situationally irrelevant group loyalties, who try to convert that conflict into intellectual criticism. Typically, these would-be noncombatants are caught in the crossfire between hostile camps. Depending on the partisan vocabulary of abuse that happens to prevail, they are tagged as intellectual mugwumps, pharisees or renegades, or somewhat more generously, as "mere eclectics" with the epithets making it unnecessary to examine the substance of what is being asserted or to consider how far it holds true. Perhaps most decisively, they are defined as mere middle-of-the-roaders who, through timidity or expediency, will not see that they try to escape the fundamental conflict between unalloyed sociological good and unalloyed sociological evil.[31]

When a transition from social conflict to intellectual controversy is achieved, when the perspectives of each group are taken seriously enough to be carefully examined rather than rejected out of hand, there can develop trade offs between the distinctive strengths and weaknesses of Insider and Outsider perspectives that enlarge the chances for a sound and relevant understanding of social life.

[31] The foregoing two paragraphs are drawn almost verbatim from a not easily accessible source: Merton 1961, pp. 21–46.

Insiders, Outsiders, and Types of Knowledge

If indeed we have distinctive contributions to make to social knowledge in our roles as Insiders or Outsiders—and it should be repeated that all of us are both Insiders and Outsiders in various social situations—then those contributions probably link up with a long-standing distinction between two major kinds of knowledge, a basic distinction that is blurred in the often ambiguous use of the word "understanding." In the language of William James (1932, pp. 11–13), drawn out of John Grote (1865, p. 60), who was in turn preceded by Hegel (1961 [1807]),[32] this is the distinction between "acquaintance with" and "knowledge about." The one involves direct familiarity with phenomena that is expressed in depictive representations; the other involves more abstract formulations which do not at all "resemble" what has been directly experienced (Merton 1968, p. 545). As Grote noted a century ago, the distinction has been imbedded in contrasting pairs of terms in various languages as shown below.

"Acquaintance with"	"Knowledge about"
noscere	scire
kennen	wissen
connaître	savoir

These interrelated kinds of understanding may turn out to be distributed, in varying mix, among Insiders and Outsiders. The introspective meanings of experience within a status or a group may be more readily accessible, for all the seemingly evident reasons, to those who have shared part or all of that experience. But authentic awareness, even in the sense of acquaintance with, is not guaranteed by social affiliation, as the concept of false consciousness is designed to remind us. Determinants of social life —for an obvious example, ecological patterns and processes—are not necessarily evident to those directly engaged in it. In short, sociological understanding involves much more than acquaintance with. It includes an empirically confirmable comprehension of the conditions and often complex processes in which people are caught up without much awareness of what is going on. To analyze and understand these requires a theoretical and technical competence which, as such, transcends one's status as Insider or Outsider. The role of social scientist concerned with achieving knowledge about society requires enough detachment and trained capacity to know how to assemble and assess the evidence without regard for what the analysis seems to imply about the worth of one's group.

[32] Hegel catches the distinction in his aphorism: "Das Bekannte überhaupt ist darum, weil est bekannt is, nicht erkannt." Polanyi (1959, 1967) has made a significant effort to synthesize these modes of understanding, principally in his conception of "tacit knowing."

41

Robert K. Merton

Other attributes of the domain of knowledge dampen the relevance of Insider and Outsider identities for the validity and worth of the intellectual product. It is the character of an intellectual *discipline* that its evolving rules of evidence are adopted *before* they are used in assessing a particular inquiry. These criteria of good and bad intellectual work may turn up to differing extent among Insiders and Outsiders as an artifact of immediate circumstance, and that is itself a difficult problem for investigation. But the margin of autonomy in the culture and institution of science means that the intellectual criteria, as distinct from the social ones, for judging the validity and worth of that work transcend extraneous group allegiances. The acceptance of criteria of craftsmanship and integrity in science and learning cuts across differences in the social affiliations and loyalties of scientists and scholars. Commitment to the intellectual values dampens group-induced pressures to advance the interests of groups at the expense of these values and of the intellectual product.

The consolidation of group-influenced perspectives and the autonomous values of scholarship is exemplified in observations by John Hope Franklin who, for more than a quarter-century, has been engaged in research on the history of American Negroes from their ancient African beginnings to the present.[33] In the first annual Martin Luther King, Jr., Memorial Lecture at the New School for Social Research, he observes in effect how great differences in social location of both authors and audiences can make for profound differences in scholarly motivation and orientation. Franklin notes that it was the Negro teacher of history, "outraged by the kind of distorted history that he was required to teach the children of his race," who took the initiative in the 19th century to undo what one of them described as "the sin of omission and commission on the part of white authors, most of whom seem to have written exclusively for white children" (1969, p. 4). The pioneering revisionist efforts of W.E.B. DuBois and others found organized expression in the founding in 1915 of the Association for the Study of Negro Life and History and, a year later, of the *Journal of Negro History* by Carter G. Woodson and his associates. This institutionalization of scholarship helped make for transfer and interchange of knowledge between Insiders and Outsiders, between black historians and white. In Franklin's words, the study of Negro history became "respectable. Before the middle of the twentieth century it would entice not only a large number of talented Negro scholars to join in the quest for a revised and more valid American history, but it would also bring into its fold a considerable number of the ablest white historians who could no longer tolerate biased, one-sided American history. Thus, Vernon Wharton's *The Negro in Mississippi*, Kenneth Stampp's *The Peculiar Institution*, Louis Harlan's *Sepa-*

[33] Perhaps the best known of Franklin's many writings is *From Slavery to Freedom*, now in its third edition.

rate But Unequal and Winthrop Jordan's *White Over Black*—to mention
only four—rank among the best of the efforts that any historians, white or
black, have made to revise the history of their own country. In that role
they, too, became revisionists of the history of Afro-Americans" (1969,
pp. 5–6).

These efforts only began to counter the "uniformed, arrogant, un-
charitable, undemocratic, and racist history [which] . . . spawned and per-
petuated an ignorant, self-seeking, superpatriotic, ethnocentric group of
white Americans who can say, in this day and time, that they did not
know that Negro Americans had a history" (1969, p. 9). But much
needed counterdevelopments can induce other kinds of departure from
scholarly standards. Franklin notes that the recent "great renaissance" of
interest in the history of Negro Americans has found proliferated and
commercialized expression. "Publishers are literally pouring out handbooks,
anthologies, workbooks, almanacs, documentaries, and textbooks on the
history of Negro Americans. . . . Soon, we shall have many more books than
we can read; indeed, many more than we should read. Soon, we shall have
more authorities on Negro history than we can listen to; indeed, many more
than we should listen to" (1969, pp. 10–11).

Franklin's application of exacting, autonomous and universalistic standards culminates in a formulation that, once again, transcends the statuses
of Insiders and Outsiders:

> Slavery, injustice, unspeakable barbarities, the selling of babies from their
> mothers, the breeding of slaves, lynchings, burnings at the stake, discrimi-
> nation, segregation, these things too are a part of the history of this
> country. If the Patriots were more in love with slavery than freedom, if
> the Founding Fathers were more anxious to write slavery into the Con-
> stitution than they were to protect the rights of men, and if freedom was
> begrudgingly given and then effectively denied for another century, these
> things too are a part of the nation's history. It takes a person of stout
> heart, great courage, and uncompromising honesty to look the history of
> this country squarely in the face and tell it like it is. But nothing short of
> this will make possible a reassessment of American history and a revision
> of American history that will, in turn, permit the teaching of the history
> of Negro Americans. And when this approach prevails, the history of the
> United States and the history of the black man can be written and taught
> by any person, white, black, or otherwise. For there is nothing so irrelevant
> in telling the truth as the color of a man's skin. [1969, pp. 14–15]

Differing profoundly on many theoretical issues and empirical claims,
Cox (1948; also introduction to Hare 1970) and Frazier (1957, 1968) are
agreed on the relative autonomy of the domain of knowledge and, spe-
cifically, that white scholars are scarcely barred from contributing to what
Frazier described as a "grasp of the condition and fate of American
Negroes." Recognition of what has been called "the mark of oppression,"

Robert K. Merton

Frazier notes, "was the work of two white scholars that first called attention to this fundamental aspect of the personality of the American Negro. Moreover, it was the work of another white scholar, Stanley M. Elkins, in his recent book on *Slavery*, who has shown the psychic trauma that Negroes suffered when they were enslaved, the pulverization of their social life through the destruction of their clan organization, and annihilation of their personality through the destruction of their cultural heritage" (Frazier 1968 p. 272). And Cox, in his strong criticism of what he describes as "the black bourgeoisie school" deriving from Frazier's work, emphasizes the distorting effects of the implicitly black nationalist ideology of this school on the character of its work (Cox 1970, pp. 15–31).

It should now be evident that structural analysis applied to the domain of knowledge provides an ironically self-exemplifying pattern. For just as the union of any other collectivity based on a single status—of Americans or of Nigerians, of blacks or of whites, of men or of women—is continuously subject to the potential of inner division owing to the other statuses of its members, so with the collectivities often described as the scientific community and the community of scholars. The functional autonomy of science and learning is also periodically subject to great stress, owing in part to the complex social differentiation of the population of scientists and scholars that weakens their response to external pressures. The conditions and processes making for the fragility or resiliency of that autonomy constitute one of the great questions in the sociology of knowledge.

It is nevertheless that autonomy which still enables the pursuit of truth to transcend other loyalties, as Michael Polanyi (1959), more than most of us, has long recognized: "People who have learned to respect the truth will feel entitled to uphold the truth against the very society which has taught them to respect it. They will indeed demand respect for themselves on the grounds of their own respect for the truth, and this will be accepted, even against their own inclinations, by those who share these basic convictions" (pp. 61–62).[34]

A paper such as this one needs no peroration. Nevertheless, here is mine. Insiders and Outsiders in the domain of knowledge, unite. You have nothing to lose but your claims. You have a world of understanding to win.

REFERENCES

Agassi, Joseph. 1969. "Privileged Access." *Inquiry* 12 (Winter): 420–26.
Barbano, Filippo. 1968. "Social Structures and Social Functions: The Emancipation of Structural Analysis in Sociology." *Inquiry* 11:40–84.
Becker, Howard S. 1963. *Outsiders: Studies in the Sociology of Deviance*. New York: Free Press.

34 I have taken the liberty of modifying Polanyi's pronouns in this passage in order to preserve his meaning within the context of the subject of this paper.

Ben-David, Joseph. 1960. "Role and Innovations in Medicine." *American Journal of Sociology* 65 (May): 557–68.

Berger, Peter L., and Thomas Luckmann. 1966. *The Social Construction of Reality.* Garden City, N.Y.: Doubleday.

Bunzel, John H. 1968. "Black Studies at San Francisco State." *Public Interest* 13 (Fall): 22–38.

Cade, Toni, ed. 1970. *The Black Woman: An Anthology.* New York: New American Library.

Campbell, Donald T. 1969. "Ethnocentrism of Disciplines and the Fish-Scale Model of Omniscience." In *Interdisciplinary Relationships in the Social Sciences,* edited by Muzafer Sherif and Carolyn W. Sherif. Chicago: Aldine.

Camus, Albert. 1946. *The Outsider.* London: Hamilton.

Caplow, Theodore. 1964. *Principles of Organization.* New York: Harcourt Brace Jovanovich.

Chisholm, Shirley. 1970. "Racism and Anti-Feminism." *Black Scholar* 1 (January–February): 40–45.

Clark, Kenneth. 1965. *Dark Ghetto.* New York: Harper & Row.

Conant, Ralph W. 1968. "Black Power in Urban America." *Library Journal* 93 (May 15): 1963–67.

Coser, Lewis A. 1965. *Georg Simmel.* Englewood Cliffs, N.J.: Prentice-Hall.

Cox, Oliver Cromwell. 1948. *Caste, Class and Race.* New York: Doubleday.

Curtis, James E., and John W. Petras. 1970. *The Sociology of Knowledge.* New York and Washington: Praeger.

Delbrück, Max. 1963. "Das Begriffsschema der Molekular-Genetik." *Nova Acta Leopoldina* 26:9–16.

Douglass, Frederick. 1966 (1889). "The Nation's Problem." Speech delivered before the Bethel Literary and Historical Society in Washington, D.C. In *Negro Social and Political Thought,* edited by Howard Brotz. New York: Basic.

Duhem, Pierre. 1915. *La science allemande.* Paris: Hermann.

Engels, Friedrich. 1936 (1890). "Letter to Joseph Block." In *Karl Marx: Selected Works,* edited by V. Adoratsky. Vol. 1. Moscow: Cooperative Publishing Society.

Epstein, Cynthia. 1970. *Woman's Place: Options and Limits in Professional Careers.* Berkeley: University of California Press.

Fontaine, William T. 1944. " 'Social Determination' in the Writings of Negro Scholars." *American Journal of Sociology* 49 (Winter): 302–15.

Frank, Philipp. 1963. *Einstein: His Life and Times.* New York: Knopf.

Frankel, Charles. 1969. *High on Foggy Bottom: An Outsider's Inside View of the Government.* New York: Harper & Row.

Franklin, John Hope. 1967. *From Slavery to Freedom: A History of Negro Americans.* 3d ed. New York: Knopf.

———. 1969. *The Future of Negro American History.* New York: New School for Social Research.

Frazier, E. Franklin. 1949. *The Negro in the United States.* New York: Macmillan.

———. 1957. *Black Bourgeoisie.* New York: Free Press.

———. 1968. "The Failure of the Negro Intellectual." In *E. Franklin Frazier on Race Relations,* edited by G. Franklin Edwards. Chicago: University of Chicago Press.

Friedrichs, Robert W. 1970. *A Sociology of Sociology.* New York: Free Press.

Gilfillan, S. C. 1935. *The Sociology of Invention.* Chicago: Follett.

Golde, Peggy, ed. 1970. *Women in the Field.* Chicago: Aldine.

Gouldner, Alvin W. 1958. "Reciprocity and Autonomy in Functional Theory." In *Symposium on Social Theory,* edited by L. Z. Gross. Evanston, Ill.: Row, Peterson.

———. 1959. "Organizational Analysis." In *Sociology Today,* edited by Robert K. Merton, Leonard Broom, and L. S. Cottrell, Jr. New York: Basic.

———. 1970. *The Coming Crisis of Western Sociology.* New York: Basic.

Grote, John. 1865. *Exploratio Philosophica.* Cambridge: Deighton, Bell & Co.

Gurvitch, Georges, and Wilbert E. Moore, eds. 1945. *Twentieth Century Sociology.* New York: Philosophical Library.

Robert K. Merton

Hare, Nathan. 1967. "Interview with Nathan Hare." *U.S. News and World Report* 22 (May): 64–68.
———. 1970. *The Black Anglo-Saxons*. London: Collier-Macmillan.
Hegel, Georg. 1961 (1807). *The Phenomenology of Mind*. 2d rev. ed. New York: Macmillan.
Heidegger, Martin. 1927. *Sein und Zeit*. Halle: Max Niemeyer.
Hole, Judith, and Ellen Levine. 1971. *Rebirth of Feminism*. New York: Quadrangle.
Horton, Paul B. 1965. *Sociology and the Health Sciences*. New York: McGraw-Hill.
Hyman, Herbert H. 1968. "Reference Groups." *International Encyclopedia of the Social Sciences*. Vol. 13. New York: Macmillan and Free Press.
Ibn Alkalimat, Abd-l Hakimu (Gerald McWorter). 1969. "The Ideology of Black Social Science." *Black Scholar* (December): 28–35.
James, William. 1932 (1885). *The Meaning of Truth*. New York: Longmans Green.
Kellermann, Hermann. 1915. *Der Krieg der Geister*. Weimar.
Kent, Donald P., and Robert G. Burnight. 1951. "Group Centrism in Complex Societies." *American Journal of Sociology* 57 (November): 256–59.
Kherkhof, Karl. 1933. *Der Krieg gegen die Deutsche Wissenschaft*. Halle.
Kilson, Martin. 1969. "Black Studies Movement: A Plea for Perspective." *Crisis* 76 (October): 327–32.
Krieck, Ernst. 1935. *Nationalpolitische Erziehung*. Leipzig: Armanen Verlag.
La Rue, Linda. 1970. "The Black Movement and Women's Liberation." *Black Scholar* 1 (May): 36–42.
Lasswell, Harold D. 1937. "Chauvinism." *Encyclopedia of the Social Sciences*. Vol. 3. New York: Macmillan.
Levine, Donald N. 1971. *Georg Simmel: On Individuality and Social Forms*. Chicago: University of Chicago Press.
Lévi-Strauss, Claude. 1963. *Structural Anthropology*. New York: Basic.
Lukács, Georg. 1971 (1923). *History and Class Consciousness: Studies in Marxist Dialectics*. Cambridge, Mass.: M.I.T. Press.
Lynd, Robert S. 1944. "Prison for Our Genius." *Saturday Review*, April 22, pp. 5–7, 27.
Mannheim, Karl. 1936. *Ideology and Utopia*. New York: Harcourt Brace Jovanovich.
———. 1952. *Essays on the Sociology of Knowledge*. New York: Oxford University Press.
Marx, Karl. 1847 (n.d.). *The Poverty of Philosophy*. Moscow: Foreign Languages.
Merton, Robert K. 1945. "Role of the Intellectual in Public Bureacracy." *Social Forces* 23 (May): 405–15.
———. 1947. "Selected Problems of Field Work in the Planned Community." *American Sociological Review* 12 (June): 304–12.
———. 1957. "Priorities in Scientific Discovery: A Chapter in the Sociology of Science." *American Sociological Review* 22 (December): 635–59.
———. 1961. "Social Conflict in Styles of Sociological Work." *Transactions, Fourth World Congress of Sociology* 3:21–46.
———. 1968. *Social Theory and Social Structure*. Rev. ed. New York: Free Press.
———. 1971. "Insiders and Outsiders." In *Essays on Modernization of Underdeveloped Societies*, edited by A. R. Desai. Bombay: Thacker.
Merton, Robert K., and Bernard Barber. 1963. "Sorokin's Formulations in the Sociology of Science." In *Pitirim A. Sorokin in Review*, edited by Philip J. Allen. Durham, N.C.: Duke University Press.
Merton, Robert K., and Alice Kitt Rossi. 1950. "Contributions to the Theory of Reference Group Behavior." In *Continuities in Social Research*, edited by R. K. Merton and P. F. Lazarsfeld. New York: Free Press. [Now out of print and reprinted in Merton, *Social Theory and Social Structure*, 1968.]
Miller, S. M., and Pamela A. Roby. 1970. *The Future of Inequality*. New York: Basic.
Myrdal, Gunnar, with the assistance of Richard Steiner and Arnold Rose. 1944. *An American Dilemma: The Negro Problem and Modern Democracy*. New York and London: Harper & Bros.
Nadel, S. F. 1939. "The Interview Technique in Social Anthropology." In *The Study*

of Society, edited by F. C. Bartlett, M. Ginsberg, E. J. Lindgren, and R. H. Thouless. London: Kegan Paul.

Nash, Dennison. 1963. "The Ethnologist as Stranger: An Essay in the Sociology of Knowledge." *Southwestern Journal of Anthropology* 19:149–67.

Oeser, O. A. 1939. "The Value of Team Work and Functional Penetration as Methods in Social Investigation." In *The Study of Society*, edited by F. C. Bartlett, M. Ginsberg, E. J. Lindgren, and R. H. Thouless. London: Kegan Paul.

Paul, Benjamin D. 1953. "Interview Techniques and Field Relationships." In *Anthropology Today*, edited by A. L. Kroeber. Chicago: University of Chicago Press.

Pettit, Gabriel, and Maurice Leudet. 1916. *Les allemands et la science*. Paris.

Polanyi, Michael. 1958. *Personal Knowledge*. London: Routledge & Kegan Paul.

———. 1959. *The Study of Man*. London: Routledge & Kegan Paul.

———. 1964. *Science, Faith and Society*. Chicago: University of Chicago Press.

———. 1967. *The Tacit Dimension*. London: Routledge & Kegan Paul.

Price, Don K. 1965. *The Scientific Estate*. Cambridge, Mass.: Harvard University Press.

Redding, J. S. 1944. "Review." *New Republic*, March 20, pp. 384–86.

Riesman, David, with Reuel Denny and Nathan Glazer. 1950. *The Lonely Crowd*. New Haven: Yale University Press.

Schütz, Alfred. 1944. "The Stranger: An Essay in Social Psychology." *American Journal of Sociology* 49 (May): 499–507.

Simmel, Georg. 1905. *Die Probleme der Geschichtsphilosophie: eine erkenntnistheoretische Studie*. 2d ed. Leipzig: Duncker und Humblot.

———. 1908. *Soziologie*. Leipzig: Duncker und Humblot.

———. 1950. *The Sociology of Georg Simmel*. Translated, edited, and with an introduction by Kurt H. Wolff. New York: Free Press.

Sloan, Margaret. 1971. "What We Should Be Doing, Sister." *New York Times*, December 8. Op-Ed.

Sprat, Thomas. 1959 (1667). *History of the Royal Society*, edited by Jackson I. Cope and Harold W. Jones. London: Routledge & Kegan Paul.

Stark, Werner. 1958. *The Sociology of Knowledge*. London: Routledge & Kegan Paul.

Sumner, William Graham. 1907. *Folkways*. Boston: Ginn.

Tannenbaum, Frank. 1944. "An American Dilemma." *Political Science Quarterly* 59 (September): 321–40.

Tiryakian, Edward A., ed. 1971. *The Phenomenon of Sociology*. New York: Appleton-Century-Crofts.

Tocqueville, Alexis de. 1945 (1835). *Democracy in America*. New York: Knopf.

Weber, Max. 1913. "Ueber einige Kategorien der verstehenden Soziologie." *Logos* 4:254.

———. 1951 (1922). *Gesammelte Aufsätze zur Wissenschaftslehre*. Tubingen: J. C. B. Mohr.

Weiss, Paul A. 1971. "One Plus One Does Not Equal Two." In *Within the Gates of Science and Beyond*. New York: Hafner.

Wilson, Colin. 1965. *The Outsider*. Boston: Houghton Mifflin.

Wolff, Kurt H. 1965. "Ernst Grünwald and the Sociology of Knowledge: A Collective Venture in Interpretation." *Journal of the History of the Behavioral Sciences* 1:152–64.

Wrong, Dennis. 1961. "The Oversocialized Conception of Man in Modern Sociology." *American Sociological Review* 26 (April): 183–93.

Young, Michael. 1958. *The Rise of Meritocracy 1870–2033*. London: Thames & Hudson.

Ziman, John. 1968. *Public Knowledge*. Cambridge: Cambridge University Press.

Zuckerman, Harriet A., and Robert K. Merton. 1972. "Age, Aging and Age Structure in Science." In *Aging and Society*, edited by Matilda W. Riley, Marylin Johnson, and Ann Foner. New York: Russell Sage Foundation. Vol. 3, *A Theory of Age Stratification*.

Radical Politics and Sociological Research: Observations on Methodology and Ideology

Howard S. Becker
Northwestern University

Irving Louis Horowitz
Rutgers University

With the increasing polarization of political opinions and positions in the United States, sociologists have become increasingly concerned about the political import of their work. Until recent years, most sociologists probably believed that sociology was somehow above politics, even though sociologists had often engaged in political activity, and political and sociological discussion had often overlapped. Events have now made it impossible to leave that belief uninspected. The disclosure that social scientists have undertaken research designed to further the interests of the powerful at the expense of those of the powerless (e.g., riot control at home and "civic action" abroad) showed how even apparently innocent research might serve special political interests. Prison research has for the most part been oriented to problems of jailers rather than those of prisoners; industrial research, to the problems of managers rather than those of workers; military research, to the problems of generals rather than those of privates. Greater sensitivity to the undemocratic character of ordinary institutions and relationships (ironically fostered by social scientists themselves) has revealed how research frequently represents the interests of adults and teachers instead of those of children and students; of men instead of women; of the white middle class instead of the lower class, blacks, chicanos, and other minorities; of the conventional straight world instead of freaks; of boozers instead of potheads. Wherever someone is oppressed, an "establishment" sociologist seems to lurk in the background, providing the facts which make oppression more efficient and the theory which makes it legitimate to a larger constituency.

The belief that members of the sociological discipline are guilty as charged helps to account for the way many sociologists have responded to the attacks. They have not dismissed the charges. On the contrary, professional associations, scientific societies, the periodical literature, and foundations from Ford to Russell Sage have reviewed the political tenor of sociological work. Younger men have debated whether it was moral to be affiliated with the sociological enterprise. Older sociologists have searched their work and their consciences to see if, far from being the political liberals they imagined themselves, they were in fact lackeys of capitalist repression.

In the midst of these reconsiderations, positions hardened. The language of scholarly journals became increasingly polemical. Meetings thought to be scientific were disrupted by political protest and discussion. Presidential addresses at national and regional meetings were interrupted. All this was accompanied by, and in some cases was intimately connected with, political uprisings on entire campuses, in more than one of which sociology students played a key role. Some teachers found themselves unable to bear the discourtesies of their radical students. Some professors saw attempts to change the hierarchical relations of a department as an attack on the very idea of scholarship. They assumed that a student who called their ideas "bullshit" was attacking rational thought, and not simply using in public a critical rhetoric usually reserved for private meetings. Sometimes they were right, for some students seemed intent on cutting off debate and substituting for the free play of intellect a vocabulary designed exclusively to conform to a political position. The distinction was not always easy to make, and those making affronts were often as unsure of what they were about as those receiving them.

In situations of collective upheaval, persons and groups move to maximize their private interests. In this case, some sociologists tried to further their professional careers by judiciously taking one side or the other. Groups moved to secure power within professional associations. Some radicals seriously discussed taking over professional associations or university departments, having convinced themselves that worthwhile political goals might be served by such acts—though the resemblance of such maneuvers to similar careerist actions by doctrinaire groups of quite different persuasions in the same associations and departments was obvious. Elder sociological statesmen of every political stripe appeared, trying to gather "unpredictable youth" into their own sphere of influence. The rhetoric of radicalism appeared in every area of sociology.

Participants in these events found themselves confused. Members of the older "straight" factions, however, failed to note the confusion. They saw the actions as concerted expressions of radical or left sentiment. They could not see the conflicts of interests among radicals, blacks, chicanos, women, and other "liberation" groups. The persistent emergence of differences among these groups made it obvious that the mere assertion of radical sympathies guaranteed neither concerted political action nor a uniform style of sociological analysis. The differences and confusions demonstrate the need for a clearer analysis of the political meaning and relevance of sociology.

Howard S. Becker and Irving Louis Horowitz

Good sociology is often radical. A sociology which is not good, however, cannot be radical in any larger sense. But moral sentiments do not determine scientific quality. The reverse is more often true: the quality of sociological work determines the degree to which it has a radical thrust.

We insist on the isomorphism between radical sociology and good sociology in order to dissuade those who think political sloganeering can substitute for knowledge based on adequate evidence and careful analysis; to persuade others that their work has suffered from a conventional social and political attitude, expressed in the way they frame problems and in the methods of research they choose; and to demonstrate that there is a tradition of good sociology worth preserving, that the expression "good sociology" has meaning, and that the possibility of doing good sociology is not tied irrevocably to contemporary academic institutions.

GOOD SOCIOLOGY

Good sociology is sociological work that produces meaningful descriptions of organizations and events, valid explanations of how they come about and persist, and realistic proposals for their improvement or removal. Sociology based on the best available evidence should provide analyses that are likely to be true in the linguistic sense of not being falsifiable by other evidence, and also in the ontological sense of being "true to the world."

In the first sense, generations of methodologists have developed procedures and techniques by which approximate truth can be reached. The sociologist achieves partial truths, always open to correction. While methodologists have dealt only with a small part of the problem of arriving at propositions and inferences likely to be true, the techniques they recommend as warranted are all we have; we will have to use them until we invent something better. With all their faults, interviews, participant observation, questionnaires, surveys, censuses, statistical analysis, and controlled experiments can be used to arrive at approximate truth. While the results to date are modest, some things are known because sociologists have employed these techniques.

Sociologists have done less well by truth in the second sense. While they know some things well, they can predict few things with accuracy. Humanists and scientists alike complain that sociology tells them only a tiny part of what they really want to know. Men want to know how the world is; sociologists give them correlation coefficients. Coefficients do help us know how the world is, and one need not accept the humanistic contention that unless sociology can reproduce the world in full living color it is worthless. Nonetheless, the charge stings. Sociologists' knowledge about real problems in society does not take them far.

50

If essentials are left out, the work cannot pass the tests that science poses for itself. The work cannot, to use the language of statistical analysis, account for much of the variance in the phenomena under study. In addition, sociological work loses its potential practical importance if it does not encompass the major processes and actors involved in those parts of the world to be changed. Therefore, work that is not true to the world has neither scientific nor practical value.

Why does so much sociological work fail to be true both to its own scientific standards and to the larger world? Some radical sociologists have insisted that political ideologies blind us to the truth because our political masters have paid us to produce research that will be useful in a different direction, or (more subtly) because our standard methods and concepts, reflecting political biases and pressures, prevent us from seeing what would be politically inconvenient. Many failures in sociological research result from simple ignorance, having little to do with either ideological bias or utopian fantasy. But we should examine those instances in which sociological research has been severely blemished not so much by ignorance as by bias.

Consider the charge that the concept of "accommodation," applied to racial relations, had a conservative effect (Myrdal 1944). It implied that blacks accepted their lower position in American society and that therefore, because blacks did not complain, the situation was not unjust. But to say that racial relations in a given place at a given time were accommodative means only that the racial groups involved had achieved a modus vivendi and does not imply that the actors were happy or the system just. Whether any or all actors considered the system pleasant or righteous is a matter for empirical investigation. If the description of the situation as accommodative were true to the world, no evidence of conflict and resistance could be discovered because none would exist. To assume consensus would be bad sociology insofar as it assumed that, since there is evidence of accommodation, we can rule out the possibility of conflict. The concept of accommodation can be objectionable only if we insist that its use will necessarily cause sociologists to overlook or ignore conflict, exploitation, or resistance to change where they occur. But a full exploration of possibilities, as in Robert Park's description of the race relations cycle (Park and Burgess 1921), applied evenhandedly, should spare sociologists such errors.

Much contemporary sociology is not true even in the narrow scientific sense. It is falsifiable by evidence contained in its own data or by evidence that could have been obtained had the investigator bothered to look for it. Sociologists tend to ignore the degree to which they fail to abide by their own methodological standards and consequently fail to achieve the sci-

51

entific rationality to which they pretend. Where sociology allows political biases and generalized expressions of wishful thinking to affect its conclusions, it lacks truth in either of the two meanings discussed.

RADICAL SOCIOLOGY

An immense variety of political positions have been announced as radical. Since the actual consequences of the label are so important to all the people involved, one cannot expect any definition to go undisputed. But most arguments over definitions turn on questions of the means by which agreed-on goals can be achieved or of the correct diagnosis of the ills that afflict society, rather than on the goals that radicals ought to strive for. Thus, most radicals will agree that a key feature of any radical political program is the reduction and eventual removal of inequalities in society, whether the inequality is of power, economic resources, life chances, or knowledge. Likewise, most radicals will agree that a radically reconstructed society should maximize human freedom, especially when that is conceived as dialectically related to social order.

Radicals may not so universally agree on the necessity of permanent change and revolution as an ideal. We ourselves believe that every society and every set of social arrangements must be inspected for their potential inequalities and interferences with freedom, even those which seem to conform to one or another blueprint for a socialist utopia. The radical, so defined normatively, is never satisfied, never prepared to abandon the struggle for an even more egalitarian and free society. At the least, the better is the critic of the good.

Where circumstances compel a choice between individual interests, self-expression, and personal welfare, on the one hand, and social order, stability, and the collective good, on the other, such a radical politics acts for the person as against the collectivity. It acts to maximize the number and the variety of options people have open to them, at the expense of neatness, order, peace, and system. It regards conflict as a normal concomitant of social life and a necessary element in political action. Clearly, some definitions of radicalism are based precisely on collectivism. While we look for the convergence of personal and public goals, when we are compelled to make a choice, it is on behalf of persons.

The radical sees change as permanent and inevitable, but he need not accept all changes as good. Rather, he sides with the powerless against the powerful, and renounces coercion, terror and control as methods of establishing truths about the world.

The posture of a radical sociology overlaps considerably with that of a radical politics. Radical sociology also rests on a desire to change society in a way that will increase equality and maximize freedom, and it makes a distinctive contribution to the struggle for change. On the one hand, it provides the knowledge of how society operates, on the basis of which a radical critique of inequality and lack of freedom can be made. On the other hand, it provides the basis for implementing radical goals, constructing blueprints for freer, more egalitarian social arrangements, the working plans for radical utopias. These constructive aspects are rooted in the positivist tradition, just as the critical aspects are rooted in the Marxist tradition. Both involve an explanation of radical goals, and both involve a repudiation of all forms of mystical, theological, and supernaturalist interpretations of events.

A radical sociology thus looks for explanations of social life and theories of society which assume that radical change is at least possible, and resists those theories which root inequality in "inescapable facts" of biology or social structure (Horowitz 1968). Since such assumptions are seldom subjected to empirical test, a radical sociology can just as reasonably assume possibilities that more conservative or pessimistic sociologies do not.

In the controversy between Davis and Moore (1945, pp. 242–49) and Tumin (1953, pp. 387–93), the real difference of opinion was not over the fact of social stratification in American life, or even over the existence of inequality. There were indeed differences of opinion at the factual level, but the core controversy concerned the tendencies of American society: whether the direction of the democratic society carried with it as a central agenda item the reduction and finally the elimination of inequality. If inequality is rooted in the nature of man, with only the forms of inequality changing and the types of oppressors shifting, then the goal of equality is itself suspect. Any radical sociology must explore the nature of inequality fully, and beyond that must assume the possibility of abolishing inequality and describing the machinery necessary to implement a more egalitarian social order (Dumont 1969).

It might be objected that this equation of radicalism and the search for equity itself represents a liberal "bourgeois" model rather than a radical paradigm, that true radicalism must uphold the banner of a particular social system, such as socialism. While this formulation is abstractly appealing and in fact is often employed by radical theorists, it omits the most important fact of our times: the need for a social scientific judgment of *all* available political systems. Any equation of radical perspectives with the demand for equity implies the universal claim to priority of equality in socialist systems such as the Soviet Union, no less than in capitalist systems such as the United States. To demand allegiance to any social system as the mark of a radical perspective is to ignore the 100-year history of inequality within what has passed for socialism, as well as the far longer history of inequality under capitalism.

But the search for equity is only one side of the radical thrust. At least equal in importance is the investigation of the ability of society, as presently organized, to deliver equity. It is the assessment of that ability that divides radical and liberal analysts. The ability of established society to absorb new social demands of disenfranchised groups becomes a major concern of the radical. The historic concern of radicalism with problems of revolution expresses a pessimistic view of the present social and economic order's ability to absorb change.

No matter which of these several tasks a radical sociology undertakes, it finds itself providing the facts, theories, and understandings that a radical politics requires for its implementation. For a radical political posture without reliable facts and analyses is no more than insurrectionary art incapable of predicting its own successes or failures. Radical sociology provides relevant and trustworthy data, intellectual resources for measuring costs as well as benefits in realizing the insurrectionary act.

CONFLICT BETWEEN RADICAL SOCIOLOGY AND RADICAL POLITICS

Radical sociology may create a tension with radical politics, pure and simple, by indicating the high cost of some desired act. For example, it may analyze the special features of the Cuban-Castro revolution and produce an explanation of why guerrilla insurgency was successful in Cuba in 1959 but tragically unsuccessful in Bolivia in 1969. It is by no means a simple matter to counsel the gathering of evidence instead of performing a revolutionary act. But the gathering of evidence distinguishes a radical sociology from a radical politics, without necessarily destroying the basis for their mutual interaction.

A radical sociology will base itself either explicitly or implicitly on the premises of a radical politics. In either case, it will produce knowledge that serves the purposes of radical politics, in any of a variety of ways.

Every group in power is bent on the protection of privilege. Therefore, every radical sociology must expose the nature of such privilege, unmasking forms of domination. This unmasking process creates dilemmas. It implies a ruthless stripping away of all mystery and cant, not just that of the Department of Defense but also that of the Nation of Islam. One task of a radical sociology is thus to persuade the oppressed and radicals of the need for as total a dedication to what is true as to what they may deem good. It is here too that the issue between most contemporary forms of radical sociology and radical political action becomes enmeshed in controversy, since many forms of radical politics are themselves bound to canons of secrecy, perhaps more benign than conservative politics but ultimately no less destructive of the search for truth in society.

Every status quo—societal, organizational, or factional—thrives on myth and mystification. Every group in power—in a nation, a government, an economy, a political party, or a revolutionary cadre—tells its story as it would like to have it believed, in the way it thinks will promote its interests and serve its constituencies. Every group in power profits from ambiguity and mystification, which hide the facts of power from those over whom power is exerted and thus make it easier to maintain hegemony and legitimacy. A sociology that is true to the world inevitably clarifies what has been confused, reveals the character of organizational secrets, upsets the interests of powerful people and groups. And while uncovering error does not necessarily aid the interests of those exploited by an organization or society, it does at least permit equal access to the evidence upon which action must be based. Only if sociological work is good in the sense of explaining actual relationships of power and authority can it provide a force for change. Thus, work which is true to the world and explains the actual relations of power and privilege that envelop and determine what goes on in society will be politically useful to radicals, even though (importantly) those who do such work may not themselves be committed to radical political goals.

Sociologists already know the difficulties that come from doing work which exposes the operations of powerful groups in society (see the various accounts in Vidich, Bensman, and Stein 1964). In operating explicitly in behalf of radical goals and in cooperation with people engaged in radical political action, the sociologist will experience other characteristic difficulties. For instance, a good sociological analysis, explored fully for its political implications, may undermine one's own position of superiority and privilege. Thus, a radical sociological analysis of universities entails exposing the myths by which the professor who makes the analysis supports his own privileged position of tenure and income. Similarly, white sociologists find themselves producing work which undermines their unequal privileges vis-à-vis blacks; men undermine the bases of their social superiority to women; and so on. This is why the poor and downtrodden are never "radical"—what they do is "natural," in keeping with their "interests." The radical violates the canon of self-interest or group interest. The good sociologist carries radicalism a step further: he makes it a principle to transcend parochialism and patriotism in investigating the social context.

The radical sociologist will also find that his scientific "conservatism"— in the sense of being unwilling to draw conclusions on the basis of insufficient evidence—creates tension with radical activists. This results from the differing time scales of the two activities. The social scientist takes time to collect evidence, but the political activist must often make decisions prior to the compilation of adequate evidence. Under such circumstances, the political man will act; the sociologist can give him the best available evidence. Radical activism is not the same as the know-nothing-

55

ism underlining the irrationalist "will to act," but rather a recognition that action may be induced by needs that cannot possibly await the supply of the social scientist's information. The lag between action and information explains, in part, the peculiar tension between the political man and the social scientist, a tension that often leads the activist to disregard the sociologist's advice and, correspondingly, often leads the sociologist to an overconservative estimate of the potential success of a dramatic political action.

Since radical politics and radical sociology are not the same, the two may conflict. What is the relation between political radicalism and sociological radicalism? Rosa Luxemburg acted as a revolutionist and as a leader of the Spartacists of the German Left Socialist movement, but at the same time she functioned as a radical, as a critic of Lenin and of the dogma of proletarian dictatorship. She did this at a moment of revolutionary euphoria when serious thinking was at a premium. It is her criticism which is now best remembered. The same can be said of Eugene V. Debs, whose importance in the Socialist movement lay precisely in his being above the fratricidal struggles for control of the Socialist party apparatus. Debs, the radical man, had little organizational power in American socialism. Far less concerned with organization than DeLeon, Debs alone emerged as the ecumenical figure for the Socialists (see Ginger 1949.)

Radicalism, then, entails a critique of organizational constraints. Yet revolution can only be made on the basis of a theory of organization. This is why the roles of radical sociologist and revolutionary activist, while they may coexist, cause considerable tension within the person and between the organization and the individual. If the activist joins forces with other advocates for rapid change, the sociologist points out how limited the practical effects of these changes may be. The activist, achieving his goals, seeks to enjoy the fruits of his victory; the radical sociologist looks for new sources of inequality and privilege to understand, expose, and uproot.

The difference between political radicalism and sociological radicalism deserves further elaboration. While the two can be linked, they can also occur independently and may be quite distinct. Radical action and rhetoric are one thing, and a radically informed sociology is another. Confusing the two opens leftism to any professional opportunism of the moment. Political sloganeers can easily tailor their doctrine to the changing fortunes of political sects. Serious sociologists find it much harder to change their sociological practice to match their changing political beliefs. To teach the same courses in theory and method one taught 20 years ago, while shifting from support for the government to opposition, does little to change the political thrust of contemporary social science. One can use radical rhetoric and engage in radical political action while one's sociology, because of its failure to be good, leaves established myths and institutions untouched. This is only the radical manifestation of the dualist distinction between "fact" and "value" adhered to by most conservatives. The "values" shift and become anti-establishment rather than pro-establishment. But the world of "fact," or, as is more nearly true, the fantasy that passes for sociological fact, remains unaltered.

RADICALISM AND CAUSAL ANALYSIS

The intersection of sociological and political analysis, the common ground which allows a characterization of various kinds of sociology as having one or another political cast, lies in their mutual concern with causes of events. It seems clear that any necessary condition for the occurrence of an event may be considered a cause of that event, at least in the limited sense that if the condition were not present, the event would not occur. From this point of view, there is an infinite or at least a very large number of causes of any event. To use a *reductio ad absurdum*, the presence of oxygen in the atmosphere is a cause of class exploitation, since without oxygen there would be no people, and without people there could be no exploitation. All such physical conditions of human action are, in this extended and vacuous sense, causes. In a more restricted and less trivial way, the actions of every person and group that contribute, however remotely, to a social event occurring in the way it did can be seen as a contributing cause of the event, since in their absence things would have occurred differently. To take a not-so-absurd example, the actions of slaves constitute one of the causes of slavery, since they could (and sometimes did) refuse to act as slaves (even though the price might be death).

Even though there are a multitude of causes of any event, both scientific and political analysis concentrate on only a few of them—different analyses emphasizing different causes. How do sociologists choose from among the many possible causes those they will emphasize in their political analysis or investigate in their research? Sometimes they look for those potential causes which vary, or might vary, in the specific cases observed. Thus, social scientists ignore the presence of oxygen as a cause of social events, since it is a constant in human affairs (except, of course, for those rare situations in which its presence becomes problematic, as in a recent study of social relationships among the men who climbed Mount Everest [Emerson 1966]). Sometimes they choose causes for investigation with an eye to the "usefulness" of results. Insofar as analysis is meant to be useful as a guide to someone's action, sociologists look to causal analysis for the clues as to how things might be changed, how they might be kept the same, and what the cost of either course is.

These guidelines help somewhat but do not go far enough in cutting down the number of causes the analyst pays attention to. On further inspection, we can see that the assignment of causes to events has a political aspect. The way sociologists assign causes, both in setting up hypotheses to be studied and in announcing conclusions, exhibits the influence of a political point of view, however implicit or hazy.

When sociologists link a cause to an event or a state of affairs, they at the same time assign blame for it. An event occurred because certain actors did something that helped to make it occur; had they acted differently, the event would not have occurred as it did. If the event is judged to be morally or politically reprehensible, the sociological analysis, by isolating those actors as the cause of the event, blames them for its occurrence.

An analysis may also implicitly or explicitly place the blame for events on impersonal forces beyond personal control—human nature, the human condition, or the social system—and thus excuse the people whose actions appeared to be morally suspect by suggesting that they could not help doing what they did. Deterministic sociologies of every description perform this service for the villains they identify.

If sociology allows for choice on the part of human actors, then it can blame, by the way it assigns causes, any of the people involved, since they could have chosen not to do what they did. This has consequences for the political character of a sociological analysis. Volitional sociologies perform this service for the heroes they identify.

The sociological analysis of causes has practical importance. When some object or action is labeled as the cause of the event or situation, the analysis suggests what would have to be influenced or altered in order to make a significant change in that event or situation. Some things will be easier to change than others. The analysis may suggest that, under the circumstances, it is virtually impossible to change what must be changed in order to affect the situation. Alternatively, the analysis may focus on things easily changed in themselves but which have little chance of changing the situation. Every combination of the feasibility of intervention and of the magnitude of the expected effect can occur in a particular analysis.

When sociologists, in their investigation of causes, implicitly or explicitly assign blame for events and when they suggest what must be done to cause meaningful social change, they speak of matters that are also the subject of political analyses. Their analyses can be judged to be radical, liberal, or conservative by the same criteria used to judge political analyses.

In general, radicals will judge a sociological analysis as radical when its assignment of causes, and thus of blame, coincides with the preferred demonology of the political group making the judgment. Radicals will denounce analyses as conservative (and conservatives will denounce analyses as radical) when the assignment of causes blames people who "don't deserve it." Similarly, radicals may criticize analyses that suggest causes which, when we take action, are too easily influenced and will not produce sufficiently profound results (right-wing reformism or opportunism), or are too difficult to influence, thus leading to disillusionment and low morale (left adventurism).

Since radical political positions are more "unusual" and thus more visible in contemporary social science, it is radical sociologists who are most aware of these political connotations of sociological work. Most discussions of the problem have therefore been conducted by sociologists who conceive of themselves, or would like to conceive of themselves, as radical and who therefore focus on ferreting out the political implications of work that is not politically self-conscious. Both because of our own political position and for the sake of congruence with current discussions, we will take the same tack. It should be understood, however, that in a society where some version of radical politics was more common and dominated research in an unselfconscious way, a similar critique might be mounted from the center or right. In our own society, political judgments of the results of sociological work could as easily be made from those positions, though they could scarcely be designed to uncover hidden radical assumptions, since radical sociologists tend to make these quite explicit.

Examples of the political import of causal analysis are easily available. It is common knowledge that most black Americans live less well than most white Americans. Something ought to be done about it; people mostly agree on that as well. What causes this situation? Some explanations explicitly blame the victims themselves, by finding, for instance, that their own inherited defects lead to all their trouble (see the critique in Ryan 1971, pp. 3–30). Many people found fault with Moynihan's explanation that some of the trouble lay in the disorganization of the black family (Rainwater and Yancey 1967). That explanation seemed implicitly to blame blacks for their own troubles by suggesting that they need not have been so disorganized. It did not emphasize the causes of that disorganization, which, when revealed, placed the blame on their oppression by the white community. The same analysis further suggested that it would be difficult to change things because it is quite difficult to change family patterns. The Moynihan analysis might thus be interpreted as having a conservative political thrust.

Consider the rash of ideological interpretations of student protest movements. Investigators may locate the causes of those protests in some characteristic of students themselves (e.g., Shils 1969; Feuer 1969), and thus implicitly suggest that it is the actions of students which, without the help of any of the other involved parties, produce all the trouble. Students are to blame while, by implication, others whose behavior we do not regard as a cause are not to blame. Alternatively, we can interpret campus disorders as political phenomena which arise in the same way as other political phenomena, and serve as a mechanism by which subordinate groups make hierarchical superiors pay attention to their demands for change (e.g., Becker 1970; Horowitz and Friedland 1970). In such a case, the difficulty can be located in the disparity between what one group wants and what the other group is willing to give, and it becomes equally possible to blame those who refuse to give students what they want, since that refusal is one of the necessary conditions for the occurrence of the disorderly events.

Political and sociological analyses both operate under a potent constraint, which is that actions based on them should have the anticipated consequences. That remains a major test of any *scientific* proposition. If an analysis is factually incorrect, then political predictions will not come to pass and strategies will be discredited. Science will not validate propositions just because they appear ethically worthwhile; the propositions must be correct in the real world. In this sense, radicalism is a necessary, but not a sufficient, condition of good sociology.

The production of factually correct analyses involves a paradox. What sociologists need to know about any institution or organization in order to achieve radical goals is usually similar to what they must know to achieve conservative ends as well. Consider research on consumer behavior. Advertising and marketing experts, presumably lackeys of the capitalist system, have done research to discover how to make advertising more effective, that is, how to manipulate people so that they will buy what they might not have bought otherwise. Simultaneously, radicals have complained, though they have not done research on the topic, that advertising makes people desire commodities they do not need. Radicals agree that advertising works the way marketing people say it does. Radical sociologists presumably want to know how to lessen the impact of advertising and make people's choices free; they might be interested in how the process of choice would work in a situation devoid of the artificial influence of advertising.

Apart from the difference in the moral animus of the language used by opposing groups, both conservative businessmen and radical activists need, to further their opposing ends, the same knowledge about the process by which consumers choose products. If we had a decent theory of consumer behavior, empirically validated, then the radical, knowing how advertising works, would know where to intervene so that it would not work, and the marketing expert would know why his techniques fail and how to improve them. An adequate analysis of how things stay the same is thus at the same time an analysis of how to change them. Conventional, presumably conservative, analyses often fail to take into account matters radicals think important. If those matters are indeed important, then the conservative analysis which ignores them will be faulty and its predictions will not prove true.

Political commitment is revealed by the kind of causes sociologists include in their analyses, by the way blame is assigned and the possibilities of political action evaluated. It is revealed most clearly by ignoring causes conceived of as incapable of change when in fact they could be changed under certain conditions, and by regarding a situation as easily subject to change when in fact there are substantial forces perpetuating it. Such false assumptions make it likely that plans of action resting on them will fail. In fact, although it is often charged that American social science is (presumably successfully) engaged in helping oppressors keep subject populations in their place, the actions which are supposed to be based on these analyses often fail, precisely because they have failed to take into account important causes suggested by more radical sociological analyses.

OBSTACLES TO RADICAL SOCIOLOGY

If the foregoing analysis of causality is correct, it ought to be no more difficult to create radical sociology than other varieties already available. Yet, for all the stated need for a more radical sociology, we find mostly programmatic statements and little substantive work that could reasonably be so labeled. It cannot be that there are no radical sociologists, for they have made their presence known. Indeed, as we have suggested, even those who call themselves radical have trouble knowing what their sociology ought to look like; in fact, we can see that it often differs in no observable way from nonradical sociology.

Some radicals in sociology claim that there is no truly radical sociology because most sociologists, being liberals or worse, are on the take from the establishment and naturally do not wish to make analyses that will subvert their own material interests. These radicals further suggest that the organizations which distribute research funds and control publication are so dominated by liberals and conservatives that radical work cannot be supported or published. If we accept such statements as radical sociological work, the ease with which they too achieve publication and professional recognition suggests that they are not true (see Nicolaus 1969).

Those who conceive of themselves as radical sociologists find it hard to do identifiably radical research, while politically neutral sociologists do research useful for radical goals (in the sense that they discover causal relationships which can be used as guides for radical political action).

That demands explanation. There seem to be three chief reasons for this lack of connection between radical sociology and radical politics: (1) the conservative influence of conventional technical procedures, (2) common-sense standards of credibility of explanations, and (3) the influence of agency sponsorship. Each of these, in its own way, deters the sociologist's full exploration of the range of necessary conditions that ought to be considered as potential causes of the situation he studies.

Most commonly used research techniques require the investigator to have worked out his hypotheses fully before he begins gathering data. If we conceive research as testing deductions made from existing theories (wherever those theories come from), then the data one gathers must be suitable for making such tests. One restricts what he finds out to what will be relevant to those hypotheses. Experiments, surveys, and paper-and-pencil testing necessarily restrict the range of causes eventually considered, by the simple technical fact of confining inquiry to what the researcher has in mind when he plans his research. But in doing research, we often find that we have failed to take into account many variables and causes that, on the basis of early findings, we see we should take into account.

With respect to the possibility of a radical sociology, what we leave out may not be important for the allocation of blame. But if what has been neglected, or made impossible to locate, is necessary to effect change, such research becomes less useful for radical political purposes by virtue of that gap. Even committed political radicals find themselves constrained by the research techniques they are familiar with. These techniques often leave out some things they would think important if they knew about them. Some techniques, indeed, require sociologists to leave out things they *know* might be important. Thus, it is difficult, though not altogether impossible, to study certain kinds of power relationships and many kinds of historical changes by the use of survey research techniques. If that is what one knows how to do, then he is stuck with what he can discover by that technique.

Another barrier to a radical sociology lies in common-sense conceptions of credibility. Every theoretical stance, including those defined as radical, makes assumptions about the character of the world. In particular, the sociological view of the world usually assumes that some people are more believable than others, that their stories, insights, notions, and theories are more worthy of being taken seriously than those of others. One of the chief reasons conventional sociology fails to uncover some important causes of events and situations is that it accepts the common-sense notion that the people who run organizations and are highly placed in communities know more about those organizations and communities than others, and therefore ought to be taken more seriously. The immediate effect of assuming the veracity of highly placed people is to leave out of consideration questions and problems that appear foolish from an elitist viewpoint (Becker 1967).

Conventional sociologists might, for instance, find it reasonable to ask why some schools are more effective in teaching their students than others. But it violates common sense to suggest, even though research might show it to be true, that schools actually prevent people from learning what they are supposed to learn. We have similar official versions and analyses of most social problems. When we study those problems, we find it hard to free ourselves from official analyses sufficiently to consider causes not credited in those versions. This is not to say that other causes are necessarily operative, but only that sociologists often fail to look at them because they seem unlikely or bizarre.

Radical politics has its own set of official explanations, its own set of preferred causes, and one can err as badly by taking these for granted as he can by taking conventional causes for granted. Of course, radically oriented research will seldom leave out of account what conventional sociologists include, if only because it wishes to demonstrate that those analyses are wrong. Therefore, research organized on radical lines will probably be more inclusive and therefore more useful.

Agency sponsorship tends to put conservative limits on the search for necessary conditions (Blumer 1967). Although research is most commonly funded and sponsored by the government or foundations politically suspect from some radical point of view, the trouble does not necessarily arise from the political character of the sponsors. Rather, it occurs because, whatever their political persuasion, when agencies purchase research they are concerned with answers to particular questions, questions which arise for them as operational difficulties. They do not wish to spend their money on meandering investigations of God knows what. Therefore, the agreement between researcher and agency typically specifies a limited area of research, the limits set by the agency's conception of what the problem is and where its causes lie. Ordinarily, the agency will not see its own operations as one of the causes of the problem, and thus those operations will not be included in the area the researcher agrees to study; by implication, he agrees not to study them (see Platt 1971).

This discussion of barriers to unconventional radical sociological analyses allows us to look critically at some common notions of what constitutes radical sociology. Most of the common definitions of a radical style in sociology bear some relation to making the kinds of analyses we have now identified as radical. In every case, however, the connection is contingent rather than necessary. We need to understand the circumstances under which the phenomenon in question actually leads to radical analysis and when it does not.

When one does research for a government agency, that agency will want the questions to be studied in a way that makes it difficult to come up with unconventional and radical conclusions. But refusing to accept government funds does not guarantee a radical analysis, nor is all research paid for by the government by definition conservative. If a federally funded researcher has arranged conditions so that he has maximum freedom, he may very well produce radical findings. Having done so, he may find it difficult to get further research funds from the same or similar sources. The remedy for that is to travel light, to avoid acquiring the obligations and inclinations that make large-scale funds necessary.

Studying radical groups from a sympathetic point of view, though one need not be particularly sympathetic with them to do so, may be of great use. Those groups might be exceptions to sociological wisdom, based on more conventional cases, and might make us aware of causal connections sociologists had not seen before. Thus, the study of communal living groups might allow sociologists to see certain possibilities of social organization that are ordinarily masked if we examine only longer-lasting and more stable institutions.

The influence of the sociologist's life style on his work becomes especially important in an era of theatrical politics. Wearing a Viet Cong button does not make one a radical any more than living in a suburb makes one a conservative. Nevertheless, wearing buttons, beads, or otherwise looking "freaky" may cause the person to have experiences (with police, fellow sociologists, or others) which will force him or her to question assumptions that might otherwise have been left uninspected. In the same way, living in a middle-class suburb might insulate the sociologist from some experiences and so lead him to incorrect assumptions about some matters of fact.

Personal involvement in political radicalism or affiliation with an organization that champions radical programs and positions does not necessarily lead one to do radical sociology. Such a political commitment might dispose a sociologist to search for causes and possible modes of intervention other analyses had left out. On the other hand, a radical sociologist might do research for his political allies which was no different in its style from the research other sociologists do for General Electric or Standard Oil. Such research might produce no more profound analysis of causes and would thus be no more useful to the movement than market research and an investigation of how to keep the native labor force happy have been for industry.

A radical rhetoric or ideological posture does not inevitably result in politically useful sociological work. Ideologically "correct" analyses cannot substitute for cogent, empirically verified knowledge of the world as a basis for effective action. Ideological radicalism cannot provide a workable understanding of the relative roles of China and India in the developmental process of Asia. Ideological radicalism cannot tell us how long it takes to make the transition from rural to urban life. Ideological radicalism cannot prove the merits or demerits of one or another form of economic investment. When radicalism without sociology is employed as a surrogate for truth, it becomes fanaticism—a foolish effort to replace substance with style. But when these limits are understood and expressed, sociological radicalism can help us measure the distance between where people are and where they want to go—between the society and the utopia.

In a period of railing and ranting against the social sciences, it is perhaps time once again to raise the matter of priorities for our age. It is the purpose of a meaningful sociology to demonstrate how it is that society and its institutions are on trial, and how it is that society and its organizations are undergoing crisis. When we keep this in mind and remember that sociology is part of society, and that sociology in itself means very little apart from the larger social tasks, then perhaps the sense and style of radical sociology will be enhanced, adding flesh and blood to its current programmatics and calling us back once again *first* to the criticism of society and only *second* to the criticism of other sociologists.

REFERENCES

Becker, Howard S. 1967. "Whose Side Are We On?" *Social Problems* 14 (Winter): 239–48.
———. 1970. "Introduction: The Struggle for Power on Campus." In *Campus Power Struggle,* edited by Howard S. Becker. Chicago: Aldine.
Blumer, Herbert. 1967. "Threats from Agency-Determined Research: The Case of Camelot." In *The Rise and Fall of Project Camelot,* edited by Irving Louis Horowitz. Cambridge, Mass.: M.I.T. Press.
Davis, Kingsley, and Wilbert E. Moore. 1945. "Some Principles of Stratification." *American Sociological Review* 10 (April): 242–49.
Dumont, L. 1969. "Caste, Racism and 'Stratification': Reflections of a Social Anthropologist." In *Social Inequality: Selected Readings,* edited by André Béteille. Baltimore: Penguin.
Emerson, Richard M. 1966. "Mount Everest: A Case Study of Communication Feedback and Sustained Group Goal-Striving." *Sociometry* 29 (September): 64–70.
Feuer, Lewis S. 1969. *The Conflict of Generations.* New York: Basic.
Ginger, Ray. 1949. *The Bending Cross.* New Brunswick, N.J.: Rutgers University Press.
Horowitz, Irving Louis. 1968. *Professing Sociology: Studies in the Life Cycle of a Social Science.* Chicago: Aldine-Atherton.
Horowitz, Irving Louis, and William H. Friedland. 1970. *The Knowledge Factory: Student Power and Academic Politics in America.* Chicago: Aldine-Atherton.
Myrdal, Gunnar. 1944. *An American Dilemma.* New York: Harper & Bros.
Nicolaus, Martin. 1969. "The Professional Organization of Sociology: A View from Below." *Antioch Review* 29 (Fall): 375–87.
Park, Robert E., and Ernest W. Burgess. 1921. *Introduction to the Science of Sociology.* Chicago: University of Chicago Press.
Platt, Anthony M. 1971. *The Politics of Riot Commissions.* New York: Collier.
Rainwater, Lee, and William L. Yancey. 1967. *The Moynihan Report and the Politics of Controversy.* Cambridge, Mass.: M.I.T. Press.

Howard S. Becker and Irving Louis Horowitz

Ryan, William. 1971. *Blaming the Victim*. New York: Pantheon.
Shils, Edward. 1969. "Plentitude and Scarcity." *Encounter* 32 (May): 37–48.
Tumin, Melvin W. 1953. "Some Principles of Stratification: A Critical Analysis." *American Sociological Review* 18 (August): 387–93.
Vidich, Arthur J., Joseph Bensman, and Maurice R. Stein. 1964. *Reflections on Community Studies*. New York: Harper & Row.

The Politics of American Sociologists

Seymour Martin Lipset
Harvard University

Everett Carll Ladd, Jr.
University of Connecticut

Sociology has recently been subject to a severe critique by Alvin Gouldner (1970), who has repeated and sought to document the charge that the theoretical orientations fostered by Talcott Parsons carry conservative implications and have been dominant within the field. Such arguments now fall on fertile soil. A large number, especially among the younger and more left-wing sociologists, echo the claim that the major trends in the field sustain a conservative view of society and are basically biased against radical social change. The caucus of left-wing sociologists, the Sociology Liberation Movement, has been perhaps the most aggressive and critical among those leftist academics within various professional associations (Brown 1970; Roach 1970; Nicolaus 1969).

At the same time, however, as Gouldner himself has noted, one observes "the prominent role of young sociologists in current student rebellions" (Gouldner 1970, p. 10). Sociology has provided more support for student militancy than any other discipline. Daniel Cohn-Bendit, who was himself a student of sociology at the University of Paris-Nanterre (one of the few institutions at the time in France which had a full-blown sociology department), asserts that "student agitation since 1960, abroad as in France, has been rife among sociologists far more than among other social scientists and philosophers. . . . The case was similar in the U.S.A., in France, in Germany, and also in Poland and Czechoslovakia" (Cohn-Bendit and Cohn-Bendit 1968, p. 47). On the other "side," David Riesman has lamented that "the field is becoming so politicized it's hard to bring sober people into it. Sociology is the soft underbelly [of the academy which is] the soft underbelly of society. It is interesting that all over the world student revolutionists have been led by sociologists; from Tokyo to the Free University of Berlin, sociologists have been the vanguard" (Riesman and Harris 1969, p. 63).

Long before the rise of the contemporary New Left, moreover, German sociology stood out as a leftist discipline amidst the general conservatism and even right-wing sentiment of professors in the Weimar period (Eschenburg 1965). There is, then, at least a superficial conflict between Gouldner's charge of ascendant conservative orientations in sociology and the picture of the field as the most activist and change oriented in academe. We shall here try to unravel the sources of this contradiction by examining

the impressive body of survey data that explores the actual political views
of sociologists.

ATTITUDES TOWARD NATIONAL POLITICS

In the 1950s and 1960s, a number of surveys of the views of social scientists—on civil liberties, party identification and voting behavior, and
on politics generally—showed sociology to be among the most liberal fields
in academe. The national survey of social scientists (1955) under the
direction of Paul Lazarsfeld and Wagner Thielens found sociologists to be
more disposed to vote for liberal and left candidates such as Truman,
Wallace, and Thomas in 1948, and Stevenson in 1952 (Lazarsfeld and
Thielens 1958). Along with social psychologists, sociologists were the most
opposed to firing faculty for membership in the Communist party and were
most likely to think of themselves as left of the rest of the faculty (table
1).

Another series of studies made between 1959 and 1964 found sociologists
in the vanguard on several different measures of liberalism. Spaulding and
Turner reported that sociologists (78%) identified as Democrats slightly
more often than political scientists, historians, and psychologists, and
much more than physical and biological scientists (for example, botanists
50%) and the applied fields (engineers, 27%) (Spaulding and Turner
1968). This support of Democrats reflects a generally liberal to left orientation. Using a 14-item index to measure the liberal-conservative dimension,
only 12% of sociologists emerged as conservatives compared with 51%
of botanists, 61% of geologists, and 66% of engineers. Similar findings
which placed sociologists in the forefront of other disciplines were reported
by Ladd in a study of academics who signed newspaper statements opposed
to the Vietnam War and in questionnaire responses of a small sample of
social scientists who signed such advertisements. The sociologists among
them were most disposed to favor student activism (Ladd 1969, 1970).

This picture of the politics of sociologists, based on limited samples,
may now be elaborated through an analysis of data from a comprehensive
survey of 60,000 academics.[1] The questionnaire contained more than 300
items of information covering social background, professional activities
and achievements, and opinions about issues and controversies ranging
from those exclusively within the academy to matters of national and

[1] This is a massive survey of college faculty conducted in the spring of 1969 with the
financial support of the Carnegie Commission and the United States Office of Education, Department of Health, Education, and Welfare. We wish to acknowledge our
debt to Dr. Clark Kerr, chairman of the Carnegie Commission, Professor Martin Trow
of the University of California, Berkeley, who directed the administration of the
survey, and to their colleagues. The interpretations expressed in this publication are,
of course, solely our responsibility.

TABLE 1

Political Positions of American Social Scientists, by Discipline
(Lazarsfeld-Thielens Data; as Percentages of N)*

	All Fields (N = 2,451)	Sociology (N = 405)	Social Psychology (N = 141)	Political Science (N = 384)	History (N = 681)	Economics (N = 565)	Geography (N = 160)
Are you more liberal or more conservative than most of the faculty here [respondent's university]?							
More liberal	39	49	43	42	37	37	22
Same	39	36	38	33	39	41	50
More conservative	12	6	10	15	12	13	17
Don't know	9	8	9	9	11	9	11
Should an admitted Communist teaching in a college be fired?							
Yes	46	38	38	46	51	43	61
No	36	42	48	32	31	39	23
Don't know	18	19	14	22	18	17	16
1948 Vote†							
Dewey	28	19	24	27	32	28	28
Truman	63	70	62	66	59	66	63
Wallace	4	6	9	2	3	4	4
Thurmond	1	1	...	1	1	...	1
Other (mainly Socialist)	4	5	5	4	4	2	4
1952 Vote†							
Eisenhower	34	26	42	27	33	36	61
Stevenson	65	73	55	73	67	63	39
Others	1	1	3	...	...	...	...

* The data in this table were obtained from a secondary analysis of the data set made available to us by the Bureau of Applied Social Research of Columbia University.

† Nonvoters excluded from the computations.

international affairs. Just 1.7% (1,036 persons) of the respondents are sociologists, which is about 20% of those teaching full time in sociology in American colleges and universities.[2]

In general, these data indicate that while liberal to left propensities are characteristic of all social scientists, there is a progression to the right from the social sciences to the humanities to the natural sciences, and an even stronger progression to the right by the applied fields with a close connection to economic enterprises—business administration, engineering, and agriculture. While they closely resemble their associates in the other social sciences on national questions, sociologists are almost invariably somewhat to the left. For example, only 6% describe their political views as conservative, as do 12% of all social scientists, 27% of the entire faculty, 41% in engineering, and 50% in agriculture.[3] In the 1968 election, only 13% of the sociologists voted for Nixon, and in 1964 only 6% opted for Goldwater. Among all social scientists, support for these candidates was slightly higher, 19% in 1968 and 10% in 1964. On the other hand, Nixon received the votes of 41% in the natural sciences, 45% in medical schools, 56% in business administration, 58% in engineering, and 62% in agriculture.

When the survey was conducted in early 1969, about one-third of the sociologists supported the immediate withdrawal of American troops from Vietnam while another half believed the government should decrease its involvement and encourage the formation of a coalition government in South Vietnam (83% for both), compared with 26% and 49% for all social scientists. These figures should be contrasted with others who favored either immediate withdrawal or the encouragement of a coalition government: 73% in English, 67% in physics, 58% in chemistry, 55% in education, 44% in business, and 36% in agriculture.

The extent to which sociologists differ even from other social scientists in commitment to a liberal-left position is pointed up by the data in table 2. Three scales—"Liberalism-Conservatism," "Campus Activism," and "Black Support"—comprise pertinent items that cover an immense amount of ground, from Vietnam to the hiring of black faculty, yet it is striking that the various disciplines occupy the same relative position in each.[4]

---

[2] Sample and weighting procedures allow us to generalize from the survey's respondents to the entire full-time faculty in the United States. For a complete description of the sampling and weighting procedures and for a copy of the questionnaire with marginals, see Bayer (1970).

[3] The question to which they responded was: "How would you characterize yourself politically at the present time?" The alternatives posed were "left," "liberal," "middle of the road," "moderately conservative," and "strongly conservative."

[4] The dimensions used for analysis were derived from a factor analysis and orthogonal rotation. The basis for the scales is described briefly elsewhere (Ladd and Lipset 1971b, pp. 137–38). The texts of the questions in the scales, and the construction of

TABLE 2

FACULTY POSITIONS ON CAMPUS ACTIVISM, BLACK SUPPORT, STUDENT ROLE,
AND LIBERALISM-CONSERVATISM SCALES BY FIELD (AS PERCENTAGES OF N)

Field	Liberalism-Conservatism Scale— Percentage Very Liberal and Liberal	Campus Activism Scale—Percentage Strongly Supportive and Moderately Supportive*	Black Support Scale—Percentage Strongly Supportive and Moderately Supportive
Sociology (1,033)	72	72	58
Social work (510)	71	60	62
Political science (1,267)	61	63	49
Psychology (2,103)	62	59	48
Anthropology (421)	64	55	41
Economics (1,490)	57	52	40
All social sciences (7,122)	63	61	48
Humanities (9,546)	55	52	42
Law (611)	51	46	38
Fine arts (3,475)	45	43	41
All fields† (52,364)	41	40	34
Education (3,277)	32	39	37
Physical sciences (7,599)	38	35	28
Medicine (2,384)	38	34	31
Biological sciences (4,403)	35	34	28
Business (2,080)	20	25	21
Engineering (4,165)	24	24	21
Agriculture (1,348)	13	16	19

NOTE.—N in parentheses.
* Includes the percentage of the field with scores in the range of the two most supportive (liberal) quintiles for the faculty as a whole.
† Some 7,664 respondents did not answer the question, "What is your principal teaching field?" and are excluded from the total. Included in the total are some fields not shown in this table.

RELEVANCE OF SURVEY ANALYSIS TO
THE GOULDNER CRITICISM

Some radical critics of sociology, who are generally impatient with the use of survey data to deal with political questions, may argue that these data do not bear on the central theoretical emphases in the discipline. They contend that the dominant theme of sociology since World War II has been functional analysis (an approach inherently concerned with problems of system maintenance), that adherents of functional analysis have controlled the major positions in the field and led it away from social problems and involvement in social change. These criticisms have been most

each scale are available on request. We computed the raw scores for all 60,000 faculty members in the Carnegie sample on each of the scales—from most liberal to most conservative or from the most supportive of student activism and of the demands of blacks, to the most opposed—and then collapsed the raw scores into five approximately equal categories: that 20% of the faculty with the most liberal (supportive) responses, on down to the 20% most conservative (opposed). If the percentage in a field classified as very liberal exceeds 20%, then a larger proportion of this field is very liberal than of the whole professoriate.

definitively set forth in Professor Gouldner's book, *The Coming Crisis of Western Sociology.*

Therefore, in seeking to evaluate the worth of surveys as a means of understanding "domain assumptions," it should be noted that the largest single such survey of American sociologists was conducted by Gouldner and his then doctoral student, J. T. Sprehe, in 1964. They collected data from 3,400 members of the American Sociological Association (ASA) on 89 attitude items plus assorted other questions dealing with politics and the profession. Gouldner (1970) has defended investigations such as his in terms we would second completely:

> Some methodological purists might object that such questions cannot be answered, or are "meaningless," or are lacking in specificity. Basically, however, such an objection either rests on the assumption that sociologists are fundamentally different from other human beings and do not hold the same kind of vague and "unproven" beliefs that others do, or else it wishes to blur the issue, which is an empirical one, with the irrelevant notion that sociologists *should* not have such beliefs. But, if our approach needs any defense, it was one of the elemental findings of our research that sociologists seem to have no more difficulty than anyone else in answering such broad questions, and, like other men, they do indeed hold the kind of beliefs that I have characterized as domain assumptions. [P. 36]

Gouldner relies heavily on the responses to one of the 89 attitude items to justify his contention that the work of Talcott Parsons has been predominant:

> In the United States, where I believe Parsons' influence has reached its apogee, his work retains a considerable audience, and its standpoint still commands considerable respect. Thus, in the 1964 survey that Timothy Sprehe and I conducted among American sociologists . . . we asked these men to express their views on the following statement: "Functional analysis and theory still retain great value for contemporary sociology." Some eighty percent of the responding sociologists expressed agreement with it in varying degrees of intensity. We must thus center our discussions of the present state of Academic Sociology on Talcott Parsons' theory. [P. 168]

It is unfortunate that although the Gouldner-Sprehe survey is the largest ever conducted of sociologists, very little from it has ever been published. Apart from the one variable that Gouldner mentions, the only publication was a short article which appeared soon after the data were collected, reporting mainly on the marginals for most of the attitude items (Gouldner and Sprehe 1965). In Sprehe's dissertation (1967), he factor analysed the 89 attitude items. An examination of the marginals for various indices measuring these factors supports the conclusions of other surveys that, as a group, sociologists hold leftist positions. For example, he finds the "sample as a whole scored towards the radical side on the Index of Conservatism-Radicalism" (p. 321). Respondents were asked to list the three most pressing social problems facing the United States and whether "the solution would require basic change in American social structure and values." As of 1964, race relations was perceived as the most pressing issue, followed by unemployment, mental health, and urban problems. "Only 13.3% felt little change in basic structure or values would be necessary to solve these problems; 10% were at the midpoint, 76.7% scored on the side of 'Basic Change in Structure and Values'" (pp. 264–65).

Replies to statements about sociology suggest, moreover, that despite agreement by 82% that "functional analysis and theory still retain great value for contemporary sociology," the large majority of sociologists do not accept a Parsonian view of the world or of sociology, nor do they define functionalism in conservative terms.

From the data in table 3 it appears that most sociologists in 1964 found merit in functional analysis, in focusing on social problems, in the use of mathematics, and in humanistic approaches. Over three-quarters of them also looked for basic changes in the "structure and values" of society to solve major social problems. Contradicting what one might assume would

TABLE 3

OPINIONS OF AMERICAN SOCIOLOGISTS (GOULDNER-SPREHE STUDY, 1964)
(%)

Item	Agree	Uncertain	Disagree
Functional analysis and theory still retain great value for contemporary sociology	82.4	7.7	9.9
Some of the most powerful theories in sociology have emerged from the study of social problems	75.6	12.5	11.9
Emphasis on methodology too often diverts sociologists from a study of society to the problem of how to study society	61.0	10.4	28.6
The coming generation of sociologists will need much more training in the use of higher mathematics	80.0	7.5	12.5
Sociology should be as much allied with the humanities as with the sciences	58.0	9.9	32.1
The problems of modern society are so complex that only planned change can be expected to solve them	62.2	11.4	26.4
By and large, social problems tend to correct themselves without planned intervention	7.7	6.4	85.9
Many modern social institutions are deeply unstable and tensionful	61.0	14.8	24.2
The sociologist, like any other intellectual, has the right and duty to criticize contemporary society	91.1	4.4	4.5
One part of the sociologist's role is to be a critic of contemporary society	70.6	10.0	19.4

SOURCE.—Sprehe 1967, pp. 235, 236, 241, 247, 258, 259, 221.

be the beliefs of professionals committed to Gouldner's image of functionalism, a large majority thought that many modern social institutions "are deeply unstable and tensionful," and that a sociologist should be "a critic of contemporary society." If Parsonian sociology has indeed been as conservative (system-maintenance oriented) as Gouldner argues, how could it have been so influential in a profession so concerned with system instabilities and tensions and with the need for radical change?

One possible answer is that the dominant sociologists—those who controlled the prestigious departments, who secured the largest research funds, who led the ASA—were indeed adherents of Parsonian sociology, did hold conservative functionalist beliefs, and did oppose a political activist, social change orientation. Dominant minorities clearly wield much more social power than does majority opinion as recorded in opinion polls. And the Gouldner-Sprehe survey did make this assumption about sociology. Sprehe observed that "there [is] a group of persons who informally dominate any social system." He sought to identify "dominant groupings within sociology and to examine their ideological leanings" (p. 150). Respondents were classified as members of the "dominant group" by such criteria as whether they came from a prestigious department, were employed in a large secular university, were tenured, had significant sums of research money, published often in professional journals, held office in professional associations. Sprehe states that the study began with the hypothesis that "dominant" sociologists would show positive orientations toward an emphasis on "Scientific Method," "Value Freeness" in social research, "Professionalization," and "Self-Image." Conversely, the "dominants" would tend "to score low on Optimism and Radicalism." That is, the more prestigious and highly rewarded sociologists should be more conservative, less optimistic about the possibilities of social reform, more supportive of a scientistic view of the discipline, of the idea that social science research can and should be value free, and for establishing formal professional criteria for membership in the discipline. The dominants also "were expected to score low on Societal Roles" (involvement in action groups) because "those espousing the ideology of dominant sociology [should] engage principally in the work of sociology itself and not personally concern themselves with political or social action" (pp. 151–54).

Unfortunately, the results of the analysis did not confirm these hypotheses. The one indicator of "dominance" which was most frequently correlated with conservative academic and political views was academic rank, but, as Sprehe noted, this variable is strongly associated with age. Repeatedly, the precise opposite of what the investigators predicted occurred: As some of Sprehe's conclusions make clear, the dominants held the more left-of-center positions:

> Respondents from smaller schools tended to hold the concept of applied sociology in disfavor while those from larger schools scored higher on Societal Role. . . . In general, it appeared that the more research funds a respondent claimed to be responsible for, the higher he scored on Societal Role. . . . Those who participated heavily in professional associations tended to score high on Societal Role. . . The higher the score on Societal Role, the lower the predicted score on dominance measures. For the variables, Prestige School of Origin, Size of School, Research Funds Responsible for, and the Indexes of Periodical Publication and Professional Participation, the . . . hypothesis appears disconfirmed. For the first three variables named immediately above, the relationship is apparently opposite to that predicted. . . . In summary, as regards general, diffuse beliefs concerning the role of sociology in solving society's problems, the over-all relationships seem to be: the higher the score on dominance measures the . . . higher the factor score. [Pp. 301–3]

The factors of "Value Freeness" and "Pure Sociology" were related inconsistently or inconclusively to the indicators of dominance, but "the more research funds a respondent is responsible for, the more likely he was to score low on Value Freeness. The statistical relationship was the strongest for any considered of this factor" (Sprehe 1967, p. 305). The investigators had posited that professionalization, that is, desire to limit membership in the ASA and set up formal qualifications, would be correlated with indicators of dominance within the profession. Again, Sprehe says "the . . . hypothesis . . . was largely disconfirmed." There was, in fact, some indication that low-status and aspiring sociologists ("respondents from non-prestige schools" and "nontenured faculty") were "more in favor of professionalizing sociology," while curiously, "the greater the amount of research funds a respondent had, the more likely he was to score low on Professionalization" (p. 314). "The . . . hypothesis for the Index of Radicalism stipulated that the dominant sociologists would be low scorers." This was also "largely disconfirmed" (pp. 312–13). The only measure of dominance which correlated positively with radicalism was the age-related factor of academic rank. With respect to possession of research grants, "radicalism tended to increase . . . as the amount of research funds grew larger, except for the very highest category" (pp. 327–33).

Since increasing age was generally accompanied by a more conservative position on academic and political issues, controlling for age should reduce any association of the dominance indicators with a conservative position and enhance the relationships with a liberal, radical, or activist position. In the body of his dissertation, Sprehe did not deal with the age variable, but in a later brief chapter some age-controlled relationships were presented. For the most part, these relationships strengthened the associations between dominance and an activist, reformist view of sociology and society —particularly among sociologists over 40 (pp. 446–51).

These unpublished results of the Gouldner-Sprehe study present a picture of sociology that is consistent with other surveys, including the recent Carnegie one. At the same time, their findings sharply contradict many of the assumptions about dominant trends within the discipline which Gouldner uses to justify his detailed polemical criticisms of Parsons.[5]

The 1964 survey was explicitly designed to locate the "domain assumptions" of sociologists. Yet all through *The Coming Crisis of Western Sociology* (1970) Gouldner continues to identify as the "domain assumptions" of sociology positions which, in 1964, he had found were not adhered to by the majority of sociologists and were particularly rejected by the most productive and most rewarded scholars.

It may be worth noting that a much smaller "survey" of "30 outstanding sociologists at . . . Columbia, Harvard, Boston, Brandeis, Chicago, University of Michigan in Ann Arbor, and University of California in Berkeley" who were interviewed in depth in 1963–64 by a Yugoslav sociologist, Mihailo Popovich, yielded results highly congruent with the Gouldner-Sprehe findings. Twenty-two of the 30 who presumably were all among Gouldner's dominants did not think that there is any "general theory which is dominating or prevailing in today's American sociology." When asked "which problems are among the most important in contemporary sociology," the largest number (10) mentioned "social change"; next in order of frequency (five) was "social problems of economic development." Only three mentioned "problems of social integration." Most strikingly, when these 30 "outstanding sociologists" were asked, before the recent wave of campus activism and revived left ideology, about the relationship of Marxism to other sociological theories, most found a considerable overlap in approach and concerns. As Popovich (1966) reported, "it is a significant fact that almost all of the interviewed sociologists think that there are some 'common points' between Marxist theory and non-Marxist sociological theories. These common points concern not only certain categories or principles, but also some problems. As is pointed out above, problems of social change and economic development are mentioned the most as *the* important issues of modern sociology. Are not they the problems with which Marxist sociologists mainly deal, at least on a theoretical level?" (p. 135).

[5] Some readers may think that we are unfair in identifying Gouldner with a study whose primary product is an unpublished (though publicly available) manuscript written by J. T. Sprehe. We should note, therefore, that Gouldner refers to this study in the following terms in his book: "In a study of the American Sociological Association, Timothy Sprehe and I polled its 6,762 members"; "the national opinion survey of American sociologists conducted by Timothy Sprehe and myself"; "Thus in the 1964 survey that Timothy Sprehe and I conducted among American sociologists, . . . we asked . . . the following"; "The findings of the national survey of American sociologists that Timothy Sprehe and I conducted in 1964. In this survey we sought"; "As previously mentioned, the national survey of American sociologists conducted by Timothy Sprehe and myself asked them" (Gouldner 1970, pp. 24, 36, 168, 247, 377).

OTHER COMPONENTS OF THE GOULDNER CRITICISM

Since the Gouldner-Sprehe survey did not inquire directly about the influence of Talcott Parsons or of any other sociologist, Gouldner sought indirect measures of Parsons's impact to justify his criticism of the work of a man whom he considers "more Delphically obscure, more Germanically opaque, more confused and confusing by far than . . . any other sociologist considered here or, indeed . . . any whom I know" (p. 200). In fact, statistical data on the scholarly influence of Parsons and other leading functionalists do exist in studies of the frequency with which various individuals are cited in the literature of the field. All such surveys indicate that Parsons and Merton are invariably the two most cited modern sociologists (Oromaner 1969, 1970; Bain 1962). Though these indicators of intellectual influence are ignored by Gouldner, other supposed evidence of Parsons's organizational or political control are given, namely that some of his students have played "dominant roles as officers of the American Sociological Association and as editors of its journals" (Gouldner 1970, p. 168). In fact, an examination of the editors of the *American Sociological Review* and of the contests for president of the ASA since World War II suggests that Gouldner is mistaken. Only one editor, Neil Smelser, was a student of Parsons or any other exponent of functionalism. Most, in fact, were severe critics of the functionalist approach, as the following list indicates:

> 1946–48, Robert C. Angell
> 1948–51, Maurice R. Davie
> 1952–55, Robert E. L. Faris
> 1955–57, Leonard Broom
> 1958–60, Charles H. Page
> 1960–62, Harry Alpert
> 1963–65, Neil Smelser
> 1966–68, Norman B. Ryder
> 1969–present, Karl F. Schuessler

The results of the contests for the presidency of the association also challenge the view that the rank-and-file membership followed Parsons. The first two times he ran for the presidency he was defeated by Louis Wirth and by Franklin Frazier, both of whom represented a clear social-problems, nonfunctionalist viewpoint. Parsons defeated Thorstein Sellin, the criminologist, in his third effort. His close friend and Harvard colleague, Samuel Stouffer, was beaten on his first try by Robert Cooley Angell but was elected in 1953 over Florian Znaniecki. A direct confrontation in 1953 between a functionalist, Robert Merton, and an SSSP (Society for Study of Social Problems) proponent, Herbert Blumer, produced a victory for Blumer. Merton was elected the following year, followed in succession by two other students of Parsons, Robin Williams and Kingsley Davis. These contests, from 1954 to 1957, were the high point for the functionalists of the Columbia-Harvard school. Then Paul Lazarsfeld, regarded by critics as an exponent of a value-free or "scientistic" approach, was twice defeated, by Howard Becker and Ellsworth Faris. Lazarsfeld won on his third try against the same Thorstein Sellin who had been beaten by Parsons. Another prominent functionalist student of Parsons, Wilbert Moore, also had two electoral defeats, from Everett Hughes and Pitirim Sorokin, before finally winning against Philip Hauser in 1964. However one interprets these results, they certainly do not add up to domination of the field by Parsons and the "pure sociology" approaches allegedly represented by Harvard and Columbia sociologists.

In spite of the fact that Parsons's students and collaborators have not played "dominant roles as officers of the American Sociological Association and as editors of its journals, "there can be no question that Parsons has had more impact on sociology than any other modern scholar. Yet the Gouldner-Sprehe survey and our own findings in the Carnegie study sharply challenge Gouldner's conclusions that a commitment to functionalism, and particularly to Parsons's version of it, has served to conservatize the discipline. It might even be reasonable, with the needed research, to question Gouldner's contention that as a result of lifelong antisocialist orientations, Parsons occupied himself with undermining Marxist and other radical thought. Unfortunately, Gouldner has done little or no serious research on Parsons's early academic career and seriously misinterprets some of his initial publications and scholarly activities.

Far from being an apolitical or conservative student, at Amherst College Parsons was a member of the Student League for Industrial Democracy (SLID), a direct ancestor of the Students for a Democratic Society (SDS) —a membership which various histories of the league and of its student affiliates have proudly noted over the years. Both SLID and SDS were formed as affiliates of the adult league. Parsons published his first article in what was the major left student magazine of the 1920s, *The New Student* (Cutler and Parsons 1923). In a joint article with another Amherst undergraduate, Addison Cutler (later a Communist intellectual who published frequently in the Marxist magazine, *Science and Society*), Parsons discussed the factors related to the firing of Alexander Meiklejohn, the liberal academic and reformist president of Amherst. He noted that "there was a very definite split in the faculty . . . [among] Old Guard, New Guard, middle ground men" (Cutler and Parsons 1923, pp. 6–7). Parsons subsequently went abroad to study at the London School of Economics (LSE) in part because of its image as a center of socialist scholarship.

It is interesting that although Gouldner does not refer to Parsons's undergraduate activities or his choice of the LSE for study, he does analyze in some detail Parsons's first scholarly paper as part of his effort to show that Parsons was always fighting socialism. To demonstrate that Parsons's early interest in three "anticapitalist" thinkers (Marx, Sombart, and Weber) represented a defense of the established order, Gouldner (1970, pp. 178–84) says that "Parsons believed modern society could be gradually perfected *within* the framework of capitalism: that is 'on the basis which we now have'" (p. 183). It is clear from the original article of Parsons that this is not so. In the context of criticizing Sombart and agreeing with Marx, Parsons (1928) wrote: "There seems to be little reason to believe that it is not possible *on the basis which we now have* to build by a continuous process something more nearly approaching an ideal society. In any case the process of social change is certainly neither so radically discontinuous nor so radically determined by any 'principles' as Sombart would have us believe. *In the transition from capitalism to a different social system* surely many elements of the present would be built into the new order. This is precisely *what socialism wishes to do*, retaining all the technical progress of capitalism" (p. 653) (italics ours).

In his effort to identify the conservatism of the sociological interests of the young Parsons, Gouldner discusses his membership in the Pareto Circle, a seminar of faculty and graduate students which met regularly at Harvard from 1932 to 1934. Gouldner (1970, pp. 148–51) uses selective "guilt by association" to demonstrate that membership in the circle implied conservatism. By citing statements of L. J. Henderson, the chairman of the group, George Homans, and Crane Brinton, he presumably shows that each became interested in Pareto as an outgrowth of a conservative philosophy, and attributes their supposed motivations to Parsons as well.[6] But while Henderson and Homans were political conservatives, other members of the circle were involved in liberal and even left-wing activities and associations. Brinton, for example, was an early member of the Harvard Teachers' Union, then under heavy attack as allegedly controlled by the Communists. Gouldner does not refer to the membership or politics of Henderson's senior colleague in the seminar, Charles P. Curtis, Jr., who subsequently wrote a book with Homans about Pareto. Although Curtis was a member of the Harvard Corporation (its governing board), he was quite surprisingly a "liberal and New Dealer," according to his coauthor. In his discussion of the circle, Gouldner notes that "also attending were R. K. Merton, Henry Murray, and Clyde Kluckholn," but says nothing

[6] Gouldner relies heavily for his information and quotations referring to the Pareto Circle on an article by Barbara S. Heyl (1968). This article is taken from a master's thesis written at Washington University which we have not read. It should be noted that Miss Heyl carefully differentiated the influence of Pareto on Henderson, Homans, and Brinton, from that on Parsons. She noted that Parsons "did not embrace the Paretan social system and equilibrium concepts as immediately or as completely as did the others" (p. 333)

about their politics. Since all of them have been close collaborators of Parsons and belonged to the circle, an inquiry about their politics might have been fruitful.

The record seems clear that Robert Merton, as a young faculty member at Harvard, was deeply interested in assorted left-wing causes and ideas. One aspect of his Cambridge friendship pattern is reported in an autobiographical work by Granville Hicks, then a close friend of Merton's, a member of the English department, and deeply and publicly involved in the Communist party as its chief literary spokesman (Hicks 1965, pp. 170, 172, 174, 175). Merton and Hicks had been active in the Harvard Teachers' Union. Merton published one of his early papers on science in the Marxist journal, *Science and Society*, in 1939, and a subsequent eulogy of the magazine's longtime editor, Bernhard J. Stern, in 1957. As executive officer of the Columbia sociology department during the early 1950s, Merton played a major role in defending Stern against attacks stemming from Senator Joseph McCarthy. In 1952, the New York *Daily News* attacked Merton together with other Columbia sociologists, Robert Mac-Iver and Paul F. Lazarsfeld, as "reds" and "pinks." Clyde Kluckholn also had liberal to left sympathies, according to those who knew him. This may be seen from the fact that, among other things, he wrote two highly sympathetic reviews (1946, 1955) of books by Marxist scholars, Vernon Venable and Herbert Marcuse. His description of *Eros and Civilization* as a "stirring" and "significant" book brought Marcuse's work to general intellectual attention at a time (1955) when such praise of the work of Marxists in the mass media was rare. Henry Murray reports that as a young student of psychology he was totally "apolitical."

In citing some of the "leftist" links of some members of the Pareto Circle to counter Gouldner's attempt at "guilt by association," we are not trying to substitute a form of "absolution by association" that would be equally illogical and irrelevant. But the kind of quick imputation of political orientation by affiliation or friendships can be seen as meaningless by demonstrating how easy it is to find contradictory evidence of the kind on which the imputation is based. The conservative or leftist views of members of the Pareto Circle have no bearing on an attempt to characterize Talcott Parsons, nor do they help to explain why he joined George Homans and Robert Merton in the seminar.

It is worth noting in this connection that the principle of "guilt by association" was applied in the fifties to Samuel Stouffer, who was told when he appealed a denial of clearance by a federal agency that one of the negative facts on his record was his close personal association with Talcott Parsons. Lest this article become an exercise in correcting errors about Parsons's biography, we will leave things here in the hope that we have demonstrated that Gouldner's inferences from Parsons's career display the same weakness as those he drew from survey data and the history of the leadership of the ASA. (Parenthetically, we would note that Gouldner was also in error [1970, p. 15] when he reported that C. Wright Mills "never became a full professor" as evidence that a radical outlook has blocked chances for academic rewards. As a matter of easily accessible fact, Mills became a full professor at Columbia in 1956.)

LEFT-OF-CENTER POLITICS OF THE INTELLECTUAL ELITE

In beginning their research with the assumption that the "dominants" would be more supportive of left views than the "rank and file" sociologists, Gouldner and Sprehe had apparently been unaware of earlier surveys which found that the most successful academics were seldom "conservative" in any accepted sense but were rather the most liberal or left-oriented faculty. The earliest studies of faculty religious beliefs conducted by James Leuba, a psychologist (1921, 1950) in 1913–14 and again in 1933 revealed that the more distinguished professors, both among natural and social scientists, were much more irreligious than their less eminent colleagues. Leuba sampled members of the ASA both times and found that academic members were more inclined to atheism or "liberal" religious beliefs than the nonacademic, and that the most creative sociologists (as judged by a panel) were the least religious. Only 19% of the "greater" sociologists reported a belief in God in 1913, by contrast to 29% of the "lesser" and 55% of the nonacademic members of the ASA (Leuba 1921, pp. 262–63). Although religious and political beliefs are clearly different, many investigations have shown that, among Americans, religious unbelief is associated with liberal to left political values.

The Lazarsfeld-Thielens study of social science opinion mentioned earlier found a clear relationship between scholarly productivity and propensity to vote Democratic, and to see themselves as further left in their views. Moreover, "the proportion of productive scholars rises as we move from the very conservative to the very . . . [liberal] respondents, with respect to opinions on academic freedom" (Lazarsfeld-Thielens 1958, pp. 17, 144–46). Secondary analysis of the data shows that the more productive sociologists are clearly to the left of those less involved with research and lower on indicators of achievement (table 4).

More recent studies support the same conclusion. Eitzen and Maranell (1968), in their national survey of party affiliation, found a comparable relationship (p. 150). Ladd (1969) showed that the signers of anti–Vietnam War petitions were quite disproportionately academics of higher rank and status. His findings for the faculty generally, have been confirmed for sociology in a study of the characteristics of the 1,300 who signed the

Seymour Martin Lipset and Everett Carll Ladd, Jr.

TABLE 4

POLITICAL POSITIONS OF SOCIOLOGISTS, BY ACADEMIC STANDING AND ACHIEVEMENTS
(LAZARSFELD-THIELENS STUDY; AS PERCENTAGES OF N)

Achievement of the Sociologist	Disagrees That a College Professor Who Is an Admitted Communist Should Be Fired	Considers Himself More Liberal than Most Faculty at His University
Number of publications:		
None (104)	33	42
Three or more (239)	46	50
Number of books published:		
None (258)	39	46
Some (145)	45	52
Number of papers delivered at professional meetings:		
None (109)	36	41
Three or more (185)	44	48
Index of personal academic status:*		
Low (131)	38	42
Medium (198)	41	47
High (76)	51	53

NOTE.—N in parentheses.
* The index is based upon highest degree held, whether dissertation was published, whether the respondent had held office in a professional society, and whether he had served as a consultant.

"Open Letter to President Johnson and Congress" in November 1967 opposing the Vietnam War: "The overrepresented signer is male, an ASA Fellow with a Ph.D., primarily engaged in research or teaching at an academic institution located in the Northeast. These characteristics hardly describe the younger, less professionally socialized, and more alienated member of the profession. Rather, they point to a signer who is well integrated into the profession and who signs from at least an objective position of security and strength" (Walum 1970, p. 163).

Our own 1969 Carnegie survey of the politics of academics, not surprisingly, reinforces the findings of previous investigations. The more scholarly and highly achieving faculty appear significantly more disposed to left-liberal views than the professoriate generally (Lipset and Ladd 1970, 1971a; Lipset 1972a). In addition, sociologists who had, in the 12 months preceding the 1969 survey, served as paid consultants to some federal agency or who had held federal grants were much more opposed to United States policies in Vietnam and more supportive of an immediate U.S. withdrawal than were the rank and file of the profession. Those receiving federal research grants gave more support in 1968 for left-wing third-party candidates than their colleagues who had not received grants and furnished much less backing for Richard Nixon's candidacy. The reason for such

TABLE 5

POLITICAL POSITIONS OF SOCIOLOGISTS, BY ACADEMIC STANDING AND ACHIEVEMENTS
(1969 CARNEGIE SURVEY; AS PERCENTAGES OF N)

	VERY LIBERAL AND LIBERAL, LIBERALISM-CONSERVATISM SCALE	FOR IMMEDIATE U.S. WITHDRAWAL FROM VIETNAM (SPRING 1969)	1968 VOTE		
			Left Candidates*	Humphrey	Nixon
Achievers (140)	85	48	8	90	2
Consultants (173)	80	40	8	85	7
All sociologists (1,036)	72	32	7	79	14
Research support:					
Received federal grants during last year (287)	82	43	8	86	5
No federal grants (722)	70	30	6	77	16
Teaching vs. research:					
Primarily committed to research (484) ..	83	39	9	82	8
Primarily committed to teaching (532) ..	68	28	6	77	17

NOTE.—N in parentheses.
* Includes Dick Gregory, Eldridge Cleaver, and the established minor parties of the left.

"curious" findings, of course, is that the federal government appoints as consultants and awards grants to a disproportionate number of high achievers—that segment of the academic community most disposed to left views. Achievers in sociology (defined in table 5 as those with five or more scholarly publications in the preceding two years and holding positions at major universities) are predominantly to the left of the general membership of the discipline on all measures of opinion on important issues.

Findings of a relationship between academic achievement and liberal social and academic views are all the more impressive if we recall the high correlation between age and opinions. More so than in extramural society, younger academics are much more liberal politically than their elders (table 6). Since older sociologists are more likely to have achieved "positions of dominance," the older dominants should show up as even more liberal when compared with their age peers who have been less productive or less involved in research—as indeed is the case. Thus, according to the Carnegie data, among sociologists 50 years of age and older, of those who received a federal research grant during the year prior to the survey, 70% rate as liberal or very liberal by contrast to 48% of those who did not have a grant. Sixty-four percent of the older members who had five or more publications in the previous two years were liberal compared with 43% of

83

Seymour Martin Lipset and Everett Carll Ladd, Jr.

TABLE 6

POLITICAL POSITIONS OF SOCIOLOGISTS, BY AGE STRATA
(1969 CARNEGIE SURVEY; AS PERCENTAGES OF N)

Scale	Over 50 Years of Age ($N = 205$)	Aged 40–49 ($N = 294$)	Aged 30–39 ($N = 358$)	Under 30 Years of Age ($N = 179$)
Liberalism-conservatism:				
Very liberal and liberal	50	58	80	85
Conservative and very conservative	28	13	9	12
Percentage liberal minus percentage conservative	+22	+45	+71	+73
Campus activism:				
Strongly supportive and moderately supportive	54	70	77	86
Moderately opposed and strongly opposed	23	24	6	6
Percentage supportive minus percentage opposed	+31	+46	+71	+80
Black support:				
Strongly supportive and moderately supportive	24	56	58	70
Moderately opposed and strongly opposed	35	21	26	16
Percentage supportive minus percentage opposed	−11	+35	+32	+54

those who had not published. Older recipients of federal grants were more likely (36%) than those who had no government funds (24%) to favor immediate U.S. withdrawal from Vietnam, as of spring 1969. Clearly the "dominants," the men who supposedly controlled the field, were to the left of those who had lesser publication accomplishments and research resources.[7]

The association between academic status, left views, and propensity to be used as consultants or to receive grants from the federal government has affected the pattern of participation in assorted government-funded projects which have been under severe criticism from the left. Thus the ill-fated notorious Project Camelot (financed by the Department of the

[7] It should be noted that the pattern varies somewhat with respect to opinion on campus controversies, relationships discussed in detail for the social sciences elsewhere. Many who are liberal or leftist on national and international issues, and who reject the idea that social science can be neutral, are not supportive of student activism or the demands for intramural student power. The antiestablishment-disposed, research-oriented faculty may be troubled by activist attacks on the research complex. But whatever factors are involved, it remains true that the correlations between academic achievement and left views do not hold up for campus issues (Ladd and Lipset 1971a).

Army to study "internal conflict" or revolution) was headed by the late Rex Hopper, a serious student and partisan of revolutions in Latin America, a man who was a strong public admirer of C. Wright Mills (Hopper 1964). Many of the sociologists who served the project have been active in assorted activist causes, a fact implicitly attested to by C. Wright Mills's literary executor, who reports his concern about whether to deal with the subject because so many of those involved with Camelot "were former students of mine, while yet others were and remain colleagues and warm acquaintances" (Horowitz 1967, p. vi). (Parenthetically, it may be worth noting that three of the best-known radical spokesmen at Berkeley, Harvard, and M.I.T. have been long-term recipients of personal grants from the defense department. It is "bad form" to mention such facts about the far left, but seemingly proper for some on the left to invent such items about those they seek to discredit or intimidate.)

THE INTELLECTUAL AS SOCIAL CRITIC

The relative liberalism of the dominant in academe must be viewed as a manifestation of the general tendency of achieving intellectuals to support a politics of social criticism (Lipset and Dobson 1972). What factors, then, inherent in the social role of intellectuals result in their persistent position as critics of the larger society, in their fostering what Lionel Trilling (1965) has perceptively called the "adversary culture"?

Thomas Hobbes, writing in the *Behemoth* in the mid-17th century about the English revolution, noted that "the core of the rebellion as you have seen by this, and read of other rebellions, are the universities." Whitelaw Reid, American abolitionist leader, in an essay on "The Scholar in Politics" (1873) described behavior in a variety of Western countries that led him to conclude that "exceptional influence eliminated, the scholar is pretty sure to be opposed to the established. . . . Wise unrest will always be their [the scholars'] chief trait. We may set down . . . the very foremost function of the scholar in politics, *to oppose the established*" (pp. 613–14) (italics ours).

Intellectuals, as distinct from professionals, are concerned with the creation of knowledge, art, or literature. Status within the occupation accrues from creation, innovation, from being in the avant-garde. Inherent in the obligation to create, to innovate, is the tendency to reject the status quo, to oppose the existing or the old as philistine. Intellectuals are also more likely to be partisans of the ideal, of the theoretical, and thus to criticize reality from this standpoint. The need to express the inner logic of their discipline, of their art form also presses them to oppose the powers —the patrons—who seemingly are philistines, who prefer continuity rather than change.

85

A similar argument was made over half a century ago by Thorstein Veblen (1934) in an attempt to account for "the intellectual pre-eminence of Jews":

> The first requisite for constructive work in modern science and indeed for any work of inquiry that shall bring enduring results, is a skeptical frame of mind. The enterprising skeptic alone can be counted on to further the increase of knowledge in any substantial fashion. This will be found true both in the modern sciences and in the field of scholarship at large. ... For [the intellectually gifted Jews] as for other men in the like case, the skepticism that goes to make him an effectual factor in the increase and diffusion of knowledge among men involved a loss of that peace of mind that is the birthright of the safe and sane quietist. He becomes a disturber of the intellectual peace. [Pp. 226-27]

In their effort to explain why faculty at high-quality schools had the most liberal and left views, Lazarsfeld and Thielens (1958) pointed out that such institutions "attract more distinguished social scientists," and they pointed out that creativity is associated with "unorthodox views" about society (pp. 161–63).

The pressure to reject the status quo, is, of course, compatible with a conservative or right-wing position as well as with a liberal or left-wing one. In some European countries, intellectual opposition to the status quo has often taken the form of right-wing extremist critiques of democracy because it fostered a mass society in which the vulgar taste of the populace destroyed creative culture and in which populist demagogues undermined national values. Although right-wing intellectual criticism remains vital, it is clear that since the 1920s, in the United States and increasingly in other Western countries, intellectual politics have become left-wing politics. The American value system, with its stress on egalitarianism and populism, fosters challenges to the polity for not fulfilling the ideas inherent in the American creed.

This stress on the critical antiestablishment role of the intellectuals may imply more support for reformist and radical social objectives than actually exists within the professoriate. Obviously, only a small minority of American intellectuals are radicals or revolutionists, as is even more true in the polity generally. In a country where 1% or less of the electorate call themselves "radicals" and where leftist parties secure but a handful of votes, we cannot expect that intellectuals, no matter how much farther left they are than other groups, will contain a dominant revolutionary segment.

Of course, most of the opinions voiced in our Carnegie survey and in the Gouldner-Sprehe study can be classified as liberal, not radical or revolutionary. Yet evidence definitely suggests that there is a much higher proportion of radicals among sociologists than among any other occupational group. In 1948, 11% of sociologists favored Henry Wallace and Norman Thomas, in contrast with 8% among social scientists generally, and only 2% among the American electorate. More strikingly, perhaps, in 1968, left-wing third-party candidates were on the ballot in considerably less than half the states, and went unmentioned in most discussions of the election. Yet 7% of sociologists reported voting for them, compared with 4% among other social scientists, 2% among professors generally, and well under half of 1% in the electorate. Wherever the choices offered by the larger American political system are extended, sociologists have disproportionately supported the most left-of-center alternatives. In 1968, a larger proportion of sociologists than of any other discipline preferred McCarthy (66%) to Humphrey for the Democratic nomination.

In other countries, where there are more radical alternatives, sociology is in the forefront of academic backing for them. This has generally been true in eastern Europe, where sociology has stood out as the discipline most identified with opposition to Marxist orthodoxy and regime politics.

The one survey of sociologists in a non-Communist country with strong radical movements, Japan, reinforces our conclusion (Suzuki 1970, p. 368). This study indicated that most sociologists voted for the Left Socialists (pro-Peking), with the Communists receiving the next highest support. Only one in 10 voted for the "bourgeois" Liberal Democrats, the majority party in the country, while less than 10% chose the Democratic Socialists (pro-Western). Yet these predominantly radical Japanese scholars, when asked to name non-Japanese sociologists worthy of considerable attention, listed Talcott Parsons more frequently than anyone else (24%), with Robert Merton in second place (19%) (Suzuki, p. 383).

Even more striking in the Japanese results is the fact that preference for radical politics and for the sociology of Talcott Parsons and Robert Merton was strongest among the youngest scholars. Sociologists under 30 years of age gave more backing to the Communists (35%) than did any other age group, and they did not supply a single vote for either the Liberal Democrats or the Democratic Socialists. Conversely, those aged 54 and over were the most conservative—35% Liberal Democratic—with not one Communist voter among them. Yet endorsement of the two leading American exponents of functionalism (31% for both Parsons and Merton) was most frequent among the sociologists under 30, none of whom mentioned Karl Marx. The others who received the remaining endorsements from this youngest cohort were Dahrendorf, Fromm, Homans, Lipset, and Weber. Support for Parsons and Merton generally declined with age, and was lowest in the oldest age group.

A comparable link between support for socialist politics and praise for functionalist sociology may be found in British data. The 1964 sample survey of the British academic profession, conducted by A. H. Halsey and

Martin Trow (1971), indicated a relationship between discipline categories and political orientation very similar to that in the United States. Two-thirds of the social scientists (66%) reported supporting the Labour party, while 70% defined their politics as "left." Other fields showed much less backing for Labour: arts, 47%; natural science, 36%; technology, 32%; and medicine, 26% (p. 430). The Halsey-Trow sample was too small to permit specification within disciplines, but our guess that a larger survey would also show British sociologists to be to the left of their colleagues is given weight by the findings of a survey of students at the LSE in 1967, during a student boycott and sit-in. This study found much higher percentages of sociology students, both undergraduate and graduate, giving "support" to and participating in the sit-in. The same pattern occurred with respect to political allegiance; sociologists were more preponderantly socialist, with higher percentages backing groups to the left of the Labour party than those in other social sciences (Blackstone et al. 1970, pp. 212–15, 277). Though American sociologists are involved in "liberal" politics and the British, like the Japanese, back "socialist" or "left" causes, English-speaking scholars on both sides of the Atlantic agree in citing Parsons, Merton, and Durkheim, major theorists of functionalism, most frequently in their literature (Oromaner 1970, p. 329). Clearly, the Japanese and British data indicate that there is no incompatibility between adherence to radical and socialist politics and positive attitudes toward American functionalism.

There are, of course, sharp differences in social and political outlooks among academics, but we suggest that they result, in part, from different levels of commitment to intellectual and hence critical functions. Most faculty are, in fact, primarily teachers, dedicated to the passing on of existing traditions, not to the enlargement or critical rejection of it. And, of course, many faculty, even those who are doing research, are not concerned with "basic" work, with the core of ideas centered in the so-called liberal arts faculties.

WHY SOCIOLOGY?

It is obviously necessary at last to ask why sociology has been the most liberal-left field in academe. What makes those who practice it, particularly the more successful and scholarly among them, more favorable to basic social change than those in other fields, even in the other social sciences? What factors produce the Gouldner-Sprehe finding that 77% of the sociologists in 1964 affirmed the need for "basic change in structure and values" to accomplish necessary social reforms?

First we should note that neither the greater liberalism of sociologists nor the distribution of political orientations among the various disciplines

TABLE 7

SOCIAL BACKGROUND OF FACULTY, BY FIELD

	Father's Education (Percentage Having Attended College)	Father's Occupation (Percentage Manual)	Father's Occupation (Percentage High Status)*	Religious Background (Percentage Jewish)
Sociology	34	25	18	13
Social work	34	26	23	16
Political science	48	22	26	13
Psychology	41	22	20	17
All social sciences	42	22	21	15
Anthropology	53	16	30	12
Economics	43	18	21	15
Humanities	43	21	24	8
Law	50	14	32	25
Education	30	32	14	6
All fields	40	23	22	9
Medicine	57	10	39	22
Physical sciences	41	25	21	8
Biological sciences	42	23	22	10
Business	32	27	13	8
Engineering	39	26	19	9
Agriculture	25	21	9	1

* Working with the Duncan occupational prestige scale, occupations were classified as high status, middle status, and low status.

can be attributed to differences in the social origins of their members. The academic fields do contain different mixes of social backgrounds, and at the extremes these are quite substantial. The percentage of those of Jewish parentage (table 7) ranges from 25 in law and 22 in medicine to 15 in the social sciences—the most Jewish of the liberal arts and sciences groups—down to less than 1% among the faculties of agriculture. Professors of law and medicine also come, on the whole, from families of much higher socioeconomic status than the faculty as a whole: fathers of nearly 60% of the medical school faculty, for example, attended college, and only 10% were blue-collar workers—compared with 23% in the whole professoriate and 60% in the country's male labor force in 1950. Sociology, contrary to some speculation, has a slightly smaller proportion of Jewish faculty members than the social sciences collectively, and indeed it is not much more Jewish than the faculty at large. Sociologists and their colleagues in social work come from families of lower socioeconomic status than other social scientists; the contrast with political science and anthropology is quite striking.

Interesting as these data on social origins are, they do not account for differences in political orientations. Whether a faculty member was brought up in a working-class family with parents who only attended grade school

Seymour Martin Lipset and Everett Carll Ladd, Jr.

or was the child of a college-trained professional shows little effect on his present political opinions. Class position of parents is not closely correlated with any of the scales or with any political-opinion variable included in the Carnegie questionnaire. This holds for all fields.

Religious background is another matter. Faculty members of Protestant and Catholic parentage do not, as groups, differ much in their politics, but Jewish faculty members are much more liberal-left (Lipset and Ladd 1971*b*). The liberalism of social sciences, however, is not a function of Jews "bringing up the average." Jews in the social sciences are very liberal, but so are the others. Indeed, the more liberal the field, the smaller the differences between Jews and non-Jews. In such conservative disciplines as business or engineering, professors of Jewish backgrounds are much more liberal than their non-Jewish colleagues: in engineering, for example, 54% are very liberal or liberal on the liberalism-conservatism scale, compared with just 20% of the faculty of Protestant and Catholic parentage; in business, 51% of the Jews but only 17% of the Gentiles are in the two most liberal quintiles. Those factors which have operated to make American Jews disproportionately liberal-left operate as well among Jewish academics, and, in conservative fields, Jews are thereby sharply distinguished. But in the liberal fields, Protestant and Catholic faculty are—contrasted with their religious peers in the general public—distinctly liberal, and the Jew-non-Jew differences are not large. Besides this, sociology is less Jewish than any of the social sciences except anthropology.

To understand the political commitments of sociologists, we should begin with the fact that academe as a profession has recruited heavily through the years from the more left-inclined segment of undergraduates (Rosenberg 1957; Davis 1965). For example, a study of the Berkeley undergraduates in 1959–61 found that those who "realistically considered" becoming a college professor were more likely to have a left political self-identification. A large majority of those describing themselves as "socialists" (62%) considered becoming professors, followed by liberal Democrats (34%), liberal Republicans (20%), conservative Democrats (14%), and conservative Republicans (15%). "Other findings which [independently] support this conclusion are that those who give liberal responses to questions concerning the Bill of Rights, labor unions, and minority groups are more likely than illiberal responders to have considered college teaching" (Currie et al. 1968, p. 541). Studies of student images of various occupations give professors "a high score on radicalism" and on "power in public affairs" (Beardslee and O'Dowd 1962; Knapp 1962).

If academe attracts more left-disposed students, then social science should have the most appeal to those who would combine an academic career with a concern for social problems. As Alain Touraine (1971) put it, "It is normal that those who have chosen to study society should be

The Politics of American Sociologists

most aware of social problems" (p. 312). The 1969 Carnegie surveys of undergraduate and graduate students found that a higher proportion in the social sciences were oriented to social reform.

And if social science intrinsically appeals to the more politically oriented and reform-minded among students, it may be anticipated that sociology should be even more attractive to students with left predispositions than the other social sciences, concerned as it is with topics which remain a focus for discontent—race, stratification, urbanism, power, crime, delinquency, etc. It differs from the two directly policy-relevant social sciences, political science and economics, in having less focus on government as a source of social change. Charles Page (1959) has explicitly suggested that the view of sociology as "an ameliorative enterprise . . . fairly widespread in academic faculties and among college students, draws many of the latter to classes in sociology" (p. 586).

The Carnegie faculty questionnaire permits a limited test of these assumptions since it asked about the politics of the respondents while they were seniors in college. The results (table 8) seem to generally confirm

TABLE 8

PERCEPTION OF FACULTY MEMBERS OF THEIR POLITICS
AS COLLEGE SENIORS, BY CURRENT DISCIPLINE

Field	Left	Liberal	Middle of the Road	Moderately Conservative	Very Conservative
Social work	15	51	20	12	2
Anthropology	15	42	26	16	1
Sociology	12	48	21	16	3
Political science	10	50	22	16	3
All social sciences	10	46	23	18	3
Economics	9	44	24	19	4
Psychology	7	46	26	18	3
Humanities	6	41	25	22	5
Law	6	41	26	20	7
Medicine	5	35	26	28	6
All fields	5	34	29	27	6
Biological sciences	4	32	30	29	6
Physical sciences	4	31	30	30	6
Education	3	32	31	28	6
Business	2	26	30	34	9
Engineering	2	24	33	33	8
Agriculture	1	16	33	41	9

the "selective ideological recruitment" thesis. Fifty-six percent in the liberal social sciences remember their undergraduate politics as "left" or "liberal," compared with just 28% of the faculty in business, 26% in engineering, and 17% in agriculture. The differences, however, among the various social sciences are much too small to validate the hypothesis that sociology has been more attractive as a career to reform or left-minded students than political science, for example. Clearly, sociologists as faculty members are further to the left of those in the other social sciences than they were as students. These impressions are reinforced by the results of the Carnegie surveys of undergraduates and graduate students, which show smaller differences between sociologists and other social scientists on the student than on the faculty level. If we compare the retrospective findings of table 8 with the current views of scholars in different disciplines (table 2), it becomes evident that postgraduate activities of sociologists have had a more radicalizing or less conservatizing effect on their political views than have the experiences of those in the other social sciences.

Much of the grand (and petty) tradition in sociology has fostered the "distrust of reason," through the effort to explain opinion and behavior as motivated by hidden private drives, by concealed self-interest and by the system needs of societies. Methodologically, the sociologist is cautioned against accepting rational manifest explanations for human activity (Bendix 1951, 1970). Robert Merton (1968) has effectively pointed out that functionalism does not differ from Marxism in this respect. As an example, he outlined the similarities between the functionalist and Marxist analyses of religion, that both see it "as a *social mechanism* for 'reinforcing the sentiments most essential to the institutional integration of the society' " (p. 98). Elsewhere, one of us (Lipset 1970) has analyzed the fact that the three major approaches to social stratification—those of Marx, Weber, and functionalism (Durkheim)—each assumed a form of alienation, of self-estrangement, as a consequence of inequality. Thus no "school" of sociology believes that social hierarchy can constitute a stable system accepted fully by the lowly. As Lipset noted, "Functionalist sociology . . . like the Marxist and Weberian forms of analysis . . . points to ways in which the demands of a stratification system press men to act against their own interest, and alienate them from autonomous choice. However, the focus in functionalism on means-ends relationships reveals the conflict-generating potential of stratification systems, in which goals are inherently scarce resources. Hence, functional analysis, like the other two, locates sources of consensus and cleavage in the hierarchical structures of society" (p. 184).

Sociology also has a "debunking" effect on belief in basic assumptions through its production of empirical data which invariably "disprove" the validity of collective self-images. Research which is relevant to social stratification conclusively indicates the existence of sharp inequities with respect not only to income, status, and power, but also to education, health, housing, treatment before the law, and many other values. Whether it is sociological research on social mobility and education in the Soviet Union and Poland, on the skin color of people in differentially rewarded positions in Yugoslavia, on infant mortality or job possibilities in the United States, on the factors related to job satisfaction in many countries, the evidence all points to punitive character of social systems on the personalities and life chances of those segments of the population who are the offspring of the lowly valued. And given the legitimation of authority in most "advanced" societies, whether communist or capitalist, on the basis of populist and egalitarian values, the findings of sociology reinforce the position of left antiestablishment critics. Whether these results affect the views of many outside the discipline is debatable, but that they are known to most sociologists can hardly be doubted.

What the relevant factors are that press sociology to greater support for leftist views and social activism may not be decided here. It is clear, however, that sociology must be rated as most socially critical, or at the very least, "less conservative" in its dominant ideological orientations or "domain assumptions" in university life. This would seem to support Merton's (1968) thesis that "the fact that functional analysis can be seen by some as inherently conservative and by others as inherently radical suggests that it may be *inherently* neither one or the other" (p. 93).

Moreover, this conclusion throws considerable doubt on the effort to create a politically linked dichotomy between functional analysis and supposed radical sociology—in which the latter is differentiated by its prophetic image of potentialities of society, compared with the preoccupation with things as they are in functional systems analysis. Though Gouldner seeks to present Parsonian sociology as a conservative ahistorical approach to social analysis, a decade ago he saw it in terms which are not antagonistic to an emphasis on the concrete historical sources of maintenance and change: "Both Merton and Parsons agree that in any accounting for any social or cultural pattern an effort must be made to relate this to the context in which it occurs, so that it may not be understood in isolation but must be analyzed in relation to other patterns" (Gouldner 1959). He concluded his earlier comparison of functionalist and Marxist theory by insisting that the real distinction among sociological theories was not, as some critics of functionalism then argued, between system and factor theories (those which emphasize the primacy of certain factors such as the economic) but rather "between implicit [Marxist] and explicit [functionalist] system theories" (1959, p. 211). And he suggested that functionalists, unable to specify the causal weight of particular factors possibly "because they then lacked the mathematical tools for a rigorous resolution of the problem," might soon be able to deal with it given "mathematical and statistical developments."

Two East European Marxists, Helmut Steiner of the Academy of Sciences of the German Democratic Republic and Owsej I. Schkaratan of the

Academy of Sciences of the USSR, presented a paper at the 7th World Congress of Sociology in Varna (1970) in which they also argued that with all its major deficiences from their point of view, Parsons's "functional system theory is preferable to most of other mentioned [western sociological] concepts because it tries to understand the social structure as a social organism. That makes it possible to conceive the social structure not only as a complex of statistical variables but as a system of social interrelations. . . . The Marxist understanding of society as a social system is based on the idea that the most important social processes are determined by socio-economical factors. It must be emphasized that in most cases the forms of the socio-economic determinations are extremely interrelated— the more so as a great number of misunderstandings of the Marxist concept derive from neglecting this fact" (p. 3).

Gouldner's earlier position has recently been reiterated by the Marxist sociologist, Pradeep Bandyopadhyay (1971), who observes that "Marxian sociology is often just as concerned [as functionalism] with the analysis of system, structure and equilibrium" (p. 19). And though he has sharp disagreements with the Parsonian theory, Bandyopadhyay points out that the issue between the two approaches is not, as some radical sociologists argue, one of alternative paradigms of analysis. He criticizes many of the contemporary radicals for attacking those objectives which Marxism shares with functional analysis when they seek to show that since all thought has some ideological referent, scientific analysis is, in effect, impossible. Bandyopadhyay notes that this position is not a radical one, but one which has been argued against sociology by conservatives in order "to deprive radicals of their justification for social change" (p. 21).

Given the predisposition to the left of most sociologists, including inevitably most functionalists, much that has been written by functionalist sociologists supports a left ideological position. However one interprets the relevance of the empirical findings to the ideological concomitants of given theoretical approaches, the fact remains that data collected by scholars of different political persuasions over six decades indicate the following: (1) Those involved in intellectual pursuits, including academics, have been farther to the left than any other occupational group on religious and political issues. (2) Within academe, those who possess dominant characteristics (particularly when age is held constant), who have done more as scholars and have been more rewarded, are to the left of the nondominants; and those who emphasize research are to the left of those who focus on teaching. (3) Sociology has been the most critical and change oriented of all academic disciplines. And since the dominants within sociology are more critical of the status quo than others in the field, the leading scholars in sociology are as a group the most antiestablishment. Even the anarchist leader of the French student revolt of May 1968, Daniel Cohn-Bendit

(1968), though convinced that universities inherently serve the needs of capitalism, notes that "sociology professors like to pose as Leftists, in contrast to the heads of other departments who apparently still hanker after the good old times" (p. 39).

Perhaps the reason that there is so much literature in sociology attacking other sociologists for their alleged "conservatism" is that the left is more heavily represented in this field than in any other, and that within a "left discipline" (as within a radical political party) the question of who is the "most revolutionary" becomes salient. The extremity of such criticism may be seen in the manifesto put out by the sociology students of Nanterre, "Tuer les sociologues," in which they called for boycotts of "reactionary" sociology courses. They bitterly attacked American sociology for, among other things, reacting to riots in the ghetto by taking government funds to "study the movements of mobs and furnish recipes for repression." In their judgment, sociology in France and at Nanterre is equally bad since "all current sociology in France is imported from the US, with a few years' delay." The task is "to unmask the false arguments, throw light on the generally repressive meaning of a career in sociology, and to dispel illusions on this subject" (Cohn-Bendit et al. 1969, pp. 374–75, 378).

To appreciate fully the politics of this manifesto by sociology students who were among the principal leaders of student activism in Nanterre, it is necessary to recognize that, in general, there has been considerable sympathy for Marxist and dialectic approaches in French sociology.[8] The major figure at the Sorbonne, and in French sociology until his death in 1965, was Georges Gurvitch who "was able to effect in France his own highly original synthesis of Marxism, phenomenology and empirical sociology" (Birnbaum 1971, p. 16). As René Lourau (1970) notes: "Among the principal representatives of French sociology are professors and research workers who have been members of the Communist party for periods of a few months to several years" (p. 228). The most important of these former Communists, Henri Lefebvre, was the first sociologist appointed at Nanterre. He was followed by Alain Touraine, also a radical sociologist. Though hostile to each other, both men have been strong critics of American empirical and functional sociology. They were instrumental

[8] A national survey of French university students in the faculties of letters and the human sciences (May–June 1965), three years before the "events" of 1968 and in a period of relative quiescence in university politics, found that the sociology students were more active in syndicalist or political groupings and much more supportive of Marxism than were those in any other field. When asked to which school of thought they adhered, 35% of the sociology students replied, "Marxism," more than mentioned any other approach (Delsaut 1970, p. 53). Student views, of course, need have no relationship to the opinions of the faculty, but there is some indication that they did in the French case.

in appointing almost all the junior faculty ("assistants") still at Nanterre in 1968. Radical sociology dominated Nanterre even though the next two professors appointed there, François Bourricaud and Michel Crozier, could not be described in these political terms (Crouzet 1969). These men, however, were much less influential, since the assistants (lecturers) who dominated communications with the students were largely unsympathetic to them.

In Germany, where sociology students and assistants have also played a major role in university-based radical protest, the leading leftist sociologist of the postwar era, Jürgen Habermas—as a student and later a member of the Frankfurter school of Marxist sociology made famous by men like Horkheimer, Adorno, and Marcuse—has also been denounced as a conservative by younger sociologists. Adorno, the most creative of the senior members of the Frankfurt Institute, died in 1969 soon after his class was disrupted by students. His long-time friend, Carla Henius, has recently written that these events had so "hurt him and broken him that they probably caused his death." Habermas, admired by many American "critical sociologists," has given up teaching at Frankfurt for a full-time research appointment at the Max-Planck Institute near Munich (Lasky 1971, p. 64). Norman Birnbaum (1971), a self-described "revisionist Marxist" and disciple of C. Wright Mills, could not restrain his astonishment at such charges by German and French student radicals: "These were students taught *inter alla* by Alain Touraine and Henri Lefebvre: depicting them as agents of the oppression is as grotesque as the curious belief manifested by some German students that Jürgen Habermas is reactionary. . . . [This] suggests the discipline has been unable to assimilate the self-critique administered by radical professors like Habermas, Lefebvre, and Touraine" (p. 230).

The division within the Left which plagues sociology has, on the one hand, those protagonists who are primarily concerned with social action and who want the discipline to be its handmaiden, and on the other, those oriented toward traditional forms of scholarship. The latter include many who consider themselves as radicals. In an effort to defend himself from the radical attacks on *The Coming Crisis of Western Sociology* Gouldner (1971) has made it clear that the issue is largely one of a commitment to basic scholarship versus activism, rather than radicalism or other forms of politics. He states explicitly: "Sociology today does not need a Karl Marx or an Isaac Newton; it needs a V. I. Lenin," that is, a theorist concerned with political action (p. 96).

The activist, whether student or young faculty member—and our data indicate that age is by far the most important correlate of activist orientations within the American professoriate generally and sociology in particular—is inherently more of an advocate than a scholar. An activist must seek to simplify problems if he is to help the movement. Scholarship, on the other hand, and functionalist theory in particular, seems to emphasize an opposite style. Stressing interrelationships and the fact that, in the absence of a key factor theory of change, harmful "unanticipated consequences" may result from "purposive social action," functional analysis implicitly argues for some caution in radical social change. The functionalist, in effect, tells the young (or old)activist that he should move—carefully. And his course of "action" is usually a request for more research, more consideration of the interrelationship of assorted factors.

The concentration on functional interrelationships and the consequent concern for "unanticipated consequences" does have political or ideological implications, then, to the extent that it stresses the complexities involved in social change. Still, as Irving Horowitz (1968) argues in a sophisticated analysis of functionalist ideology, men committed to sharply different political values may employ functional analysis in their scholarship. Thus, Tawney was able to conclude that "profits extracted from industry which serve the cause of conspicuous consumption; and in general, ownership divorced from production," were dysfunctional from a larger system point of view. Functional analysis supported his socialist beliefs (Horowitz 1968, p. 240). Or if we consider the two classic theorists of functionalism, Horowitz continues, "there is no more a 'functionalist imperative' for Malinowski's individualism than there is for Durkheim's socialism" (p. 243). The same can be said about the more recent controversy concerning the functions of systems of stratification between Kingsley Davis and Melvin Tumin. Davis sought to demonstrate that unequal rewards are necessary to motivate people to take on various "responsible" positions and to associate jobs with talent. Tumin countered with evidence that many highly rewarded positions do not in fact require scarce talent, prolonged training, or tension-breeding tasks, and that alternative systems of motivation can be envisaged. Yet both men saw themselves engaging in functional analysis. A recent methodological critique of functionalism by a Polish scholar, Piotr Sztompka (1971), lists the following scholars as functionalists: "R. K. Merton and T. Parsons, as well as some other writers like K. Davis, W. E. Moore, A. Gouldner, G. Sjoberg, M. Tumin, M. Levy" (p. 369).

To assert, as we do, that academic social science generally has an in herent built-in gradualist bias because of the scholarly dictum to consider all relevant hypotheses, factors, and possible evidence before coming to definitive conclusions is not to argue that political activists must draw policy conclusions from these inherent methodological considerations. It is simply to say again that scholarship and politics are different areas of human activity, even though some individuals are involved in both. A scholar is duty bound to report all evidence which challenges his basic assumptions and to stress the limitations of his results, their tentative and uncertain character. A politician, on the other hand, is an advocate and an organizer. He is expected to make the best possible case for his point of view, to ignore contradictory materials, to make up his mind on the basis of the limited information he can secure before the deadlines imposed on him by his role, and then to act in a self-assured fashion. The worst thing that can be said about a politician is that he is as indecisive as an intellectual, an image held of Adlai Stevenson, to his sorrow. Conversely, an academic will be subjected to criticism for publishing before all the evidence is in, or for oversimplifying what is inherently a complicated phenomenon (Lipset 1972*b*).

Once these distinctions are made, it should be clear that the two roles, scholarly analyst and political actor, must be separated. The scholar who seeks to serve directly political ends does both scholarship and politics a disservice, unless he keeps the two roles as distinct as possible. One reason that Max Weber was so insistent on the need to keep politics out of the classroom and research was that he was an active politician. Those dedicated to politics, particularly to reform or revolution, should, of course, seek relevant information or scholarly knowledge, but only as advice relevant to the attainment of precise ends. There are times when revolutions are necessary; any scholarly assessment of the probabilities that they will attain the goals they seek can only serve to undermine the commitment of the rebels to risk all. Our conclusion that social science is inherently gradualist is based on this logic: the implications of an analysis that can only claim to explain part of the variance, that admits any conclusion may be very wrong in a specific case, can only be to move slowly and carefully.

The case may be made that social scientists are more likely to contribute to the "solution" of many social problems if they separate themselves from policy-relevant matters to be free to look for more abstract levels of generalization. This point has been urged effectively by radical historian Christopher Lasch (1969), who finds the work of Erving Goffman on stigma and "spoiled identity" particularly useful in analyzing leadership behavior among blacks and other socially oppressed groups: "Goffman deliberately excludes the race problem from his analysis of 'spoiled identity,' on the grounds that established minorities do not provide the best objects for an analysis of the delicate mechanisms surrounding the management of stigma. . . . At the same time an understanding of face-to-face relationships drawn from quite a different perspective throws unexpected light on certain aspects of race relations—notably on the role of 'professionals' " (p. 21).

These sources of difference between the orientation of the committed scholar and those primarily concerned with political reform or revolution are real and should be regarded in a noninvidious fashion. As noted earlier, many students and young faculty enter sociology because they seek ways of enhancing their political objectives. Hence, the interest of many of them is not that of the scholar but of the activist or politician. Such an interest is both valid and necessary. Insofar as it is also academic, it resembles that of the engineer or physician more than of the physicist or biochemist. Some individuals in science and social science successfully combine both the activist and the scholarly roles. A difficulty arises, however, when the activist in social science sees a concern with scholarship alone as reactionary, as necessarily serving the interests of the status quo.

Similar controversies, of course, have appeared in many other disciplines with comparable arguments, although the "activist" faction tends to be weaker. As in sociology, the debate is often conducted within the left between those who emphasize the obligation of the politically concerned academic to the canons of scholarship and those who would place activism first. In history, for example, the three major leaders of the "scholarly" faction which has been dubbed "rightist" by its opponents have been H. Stuart Hughes, who has a record of third-party involvement dating back to the Henry Wallace Progressive party, who ran as an "Independent" peace candidate for senator in Massachusetts in 1962, and who has been the head of the antiwar group SANE; C. Vann Woodward, a participant in the Socialist Scholars Conference; and Eugene Genovese, a self-described Marxist historian who was pressured to resign from Rutgers University in 1965 for his public advocacy of a victory for the NLF in Vietnam and his praise for Mao and Communist China. Genovese (1971) has written eloquently concerning the tensions faced by the leftist academic. He concludes, however, that he must concentrate on his academic work, that it cannot be done well by anyone who considers it a "substitute for the more exciting vocation of street fighting or organizing" (pp. 7–8).

To emphasize the validity and importance of the scholarly undertaking is not to suggest, of course, that value-free scholarship, in any absolute sense, is possible. Personal values, variations in life experiences, differences in education and theoretical orientation, strongly affect the kind of work men do and their results. Max Weber, long ago, pointed out that the concept of ethical neutrality was spurious, that those who adhered to it were precisely the ones who manifested "obstinate and deliberate partisanship." He stated unequivocally that all "knowledge of cultural reality, as may be seen, is always knowledge from particular points of view" (1949, p. 81).

Weber wrote both as a scholar and a political activist. As scholar, he also argued that verifiable knowledge was possible given the communism of science, the exposure of findings to the community at large. Any given scholar may come up with erroneous results stemming, in part, from the way in which his values have affected his work. But the commitment of scientists to objective methods of inquiry, the competition of ideas and concepts, will increase the possibility of finding analytic laws which hold up regardless of who does the investigation. "For scientific truth is precisely what is valid for all who seek the truth" (1949, p. 84).

A similar argument has recently been made by the Marxist sociologist, Pradeep Bandyopadhyay (1971), writing in the oldest continuous journal of Marxist scholarship in English, *Science and Society*. He strongly challenges the contention of contemporary university activists that a Marxist sociology of knowledge would deny the possibility of objective knowledge in the social sciences and cites various comments by Marx himself which are directly relevant (pp. 17, 18, 22).

The increase in efforts to inject into sociology tests of ideological purity has made the discipline perhaps the only one in which "professional" reviews of books can take the form not of evaluating the evidence for the validity of the hypotheses enunciated but solely of seeking to demonstrate that the author reflects a "conservative" bias; and in which a scholar like Talcott Parsons, who has supported a great variety of programs designed to foster social welfare policies, racial equality, equal opportunity, and peaceful and friendly relations with the Communist world, becomes a symbol of conservatism.

The effort to denigrate intellectual work by labeling it in terms which are deemed opprobrious by the audience to which they are addressed can only serve to prevent intellectual dialogue. A recent review of Gouldner's work states the problem vividly. "A central idea . . . is that when we pit an ideological tag on a theory by calling it repressive, prophetic, or whatnot, we say something about the validity of the theory. This notion is alarming, for it would turn sociology into substandard moral philosophy with the resonating of sentiments replacing reason and observation as the basis for constructing and judging theories. Thus . . . Gouldner . . . [has] attacked more than one brand of sociological theory . . . [he has] attacked the rational underpinnings of the entire discipline, without which it cannot and should not be taken seriously as an intellectual enterprise" (Simpson 1971, p. 664). How are we to evaluate Gouldner's earlier work if we recognize, as Jackson Toby (1972) has pointed out, that in his textbook (Gouldner and Gouldner 1963), written presumably to introduce students to the best thought in sociology, Gouldner has "only respectful references to Parsons? Indeed, the 15 references to Parsons in his textbook dwarfed the three to Karl Marx and indicated intellectual debts on a variety of subjects in a straightforward fashion."

This point of view is not limited to defenders of the academic profession. A Marxist also finds that such efforts undermine the radical's effort to gain acceptance for his theory. "To judge theories in terms of the values they promote is to mistake good intentions for knowledge. . . . By using our values for the acceptable or rejection of theories, we do no more than provide crutches for ourselves. . . . To criticize a sociologist for the values he holds when unable objectively to demonstrate the error of holding those values is to allow him to get off lightly" (Bandyopadhyay 1971, pp. 22–23, 26).

Efforts to judge scholars and theories by the presumed political consequences of their work produces curious amalgams. Thus, for some years the radical sociologists adopted Pitirim Sorokin, White Russian emigré bitterly denounced by Lenin and militant anti-Communist, as a hero, presumably because he was a severe critic of the sociological "establishment," and in his older years a strong peace advocate. Similarly, Alvin Gouldner sees conservative implications in the work of Parsons, but has much more praise for that of his colleague, George Homans, a self-proclaimed conservative who (as Gouldner acknowledges) has taken a variety of conservative positions on domestic, international, and university issues. Gouldner also prefers the sociology of Erving Goffman, as comprehensive an advocate of an apolitical, nonproblem, "pure sociology" as exists in the field today. We suspect that the unifying theme which makes sense of these positions is that Parsons, together with others identified with him—Merton, Lazarsfeld, and the late Samuel Stouffer—became identified as the "Sociology Establishment" from the late 1940s on, an establishment defined by scholarly achievement and influence.

Applying the class-interest theory of politics to academe, as reflected in the hypotheses of the Gouldner-Sprehe study, those who see themselves outside the "Establishment" attribute an inherent social and academic conservatism to those they identify as within it, and a more left-oriented posture to those outside it. But, in fact, whatever the politics of a given individual, statistically speaking the "dominants" within sociology have been and remain considerably to the left of the "nondominants," a finding that should be analyzed by the radical critics of the university.

REFERENCES

Bain, R. 1962. "The Most Important Sociologists?" *American Sociological Review* 27:746–48.
Bandyopadhyay, P. 1971. "One Sociology or Many: Some Issues in Radical Sociology." *Science and Society* 35:1–26.
Bayer, A. E. 1970. *College and University Faculty: A Statistical Description.* Washington, D.C.: American Council on Education.
Beardslee, D. C., and D. D. O'Dowd. 1962. "Students and the Occupational World." In *The American College,* edited by N. Sanford. New York: Wiley.
Bendix, R. 1951. *Social Science and the Distrust of Reason.* Berkeley: University of California Press.
———. 1970. "Sociology and the Distrust of Reason." *The American Sociological Review* 35:831–43.
Berger, B. 1965. "Review of *Sociology on Trial.*" *American Journal of Sociology* 70:724–27.
Birnbaum, N. 1971. *Toward a Critical Sociology.* New York: Oxford University Press.

Seymour Martin Lipset and Everett Carll Ladd, Jr.

Blackstone, T., K. Gales, R. Hadley, and W. Lewis. 1970. *Students in Conflict*. London: Weidenfeld & Nicolson.

Brown, C. 1970. "A History and Analysis of Radical Activism in Sociology, 1967–1969, with Special Reference to the Sociology Liberation Movement, the Black Caucus, the Executive Council, the War in Vietnam and a Few Other Things." *Sociological Inquiry* 40:27–33.

Cohn-Bendit, D., and G. Cohn-Bendit. 1968. *Obsolete Communism: The Left-Wing Alternative*. New York: McGraw-Hill.

Cohn-Bendit, D., J. P. Duteull, B. Gerard, and B. Granutier. 1969. "Tuer les sociologues," translated as "Why Sociology?" In *Student Power*, edited by R. Blackburn and A. Cockburn. Harmondsworth: Penguin.

Crouzet, F. 1969. "A University Besieged: Nanterre 1967–1969." *Political Science Quarterly* 84:328–50.

Currie, I. D., H. C. Finney, T. Hirschi, and H. C. Selvin. 1968. In *Sociology of Education*, edited by R. M. Pavalko. Itasca, N.Y.: Peacock.

Cutler, A., and T. Parsons. 1923. "A Word from Amherst Students." *The New Student* 3 (October 20): 6–7.

Davis, J. A. 1965. *Undergraduate Career Decisions*. Chicago: Aldine.

Delsaut, Y. 1970. "Les opinions politique dans le systeme des attitudes: les étudiants en lettres et la politique." *Revue française de sociologie* 11:45–64.

Eitzen, D. S., and G. M. Maranell. 1968. "The Political Party Affiliations of College Professors." *Social Forces* 47:145–53.

Eschenburg, T. 1965. "Aus dem Universitatsleben vor 1933." In *Deutsches Geistesleben and Nationalsozialismus*, edited by Andreas Flitner. Tubingen: Wunderlich.

Genovese, E. D. 1971. *In Red and Black: Marxian Explorations in Southern and Afro-American History*. New York: Pantheon.

Gouldner, A. 1959. "Reciprocity and Autonomy." In *Symposium on Sociological Theory*, edited by L. Gross. Evanston: Row, Peterson.

———. 1970. *The Coming Crisis of Western Sociology*. New York: Basic.

———. 1971. "Sociology Today Does Not Need a Karl Marx or an Isaac Newton; It Needs a Lenin." *Psychology Today* 5 (September): 53–57.

Gouldner, Alvin W., and Helen P. Gouldner. 1963. *Modern Sociology: An Introduction to the Study of Human Interaction*. New York: Harcourt, Brace & World.

Gouldner, A., and J. T. Sprehe. 1965. "Sociologists Look at Themselves." *Trans-action* 2 (May–June): 42–44.

Halsey, A. H., and M. Trow. 1971. *The British Academics*. Cambridge: Harvard University Press.

Heyl, B. S. 1968. "The Harvard 'Pareto Circle.'" *Journal of the History of the Behavioral Sciences* 4:316–34.

Hicks, G. 1965. *Part of the Truth*. New York: Harcourt, Brace & World.

Hopper, R. 1964. "Cybernation, Marginality and Revolution." In *The New Sociology: Essays in Social Science and Social Theory in Honor of C. Wright Mills*, edited by I. L. Horowitz. New York: Oxford University Press.

Horowitz, I. L. 1967. *The Rise and Fall of Project Camelot*. Cambridge, Mass.: M.I.T. Press.

———. 1968. "Functionalist Sociology and Political Ideologies." *Professing Sociology*. Chicago: Aldine.

Kluckhohn, C. 1946. "Marxism and Modern Anthropology." *Kenyon Review* 8:149–54.

———. 1955. "A Critique of Freud." *New York Times Book Review*, November 27, 30.

Knapp, R. H. 1962. "Changing Functions of the College Professor." In *The American College*, edited by N. Sanford. New York: Wiley.

Ladd, E. C., Jr. 1969. "Professors and Political Petitions." *Science* 163:1425–30.

———. 1970. "American University Teachers and Opposition to the Vietnam War." *Minerva* 8:542–56.

Ladd, E. C., Jr., and S. M. Lipset. 1971a. "American Social Scientists and the Growth of Campus Political Activism in the 1960's." *Social Science Information* 10:105–20.
———. 1971b. "The Politics of American Political Scientists." *PS* 4:135–44.
Lasch, C. 1969. The Agony of the American Left. New York: Knopf.
Lasky, M. J. 1971. "In the Margin: Letter from Berlin." *Encounter* 37 (September): 64–66.
Lazarsfeld, P., and W. Thielens, Jr. 1958. *The Academic Mind*. Glencoe, Ill.: Free Press.
Leuba, J. H. 1921. *The Belief in God and Immortality*. Chicago: Open Court.
———. 1950. *The Reformation of the Churches*. Boston: Beacon.
Lipset, S. M. 1970. *Revolution and Counterrevolution*. Rev. ed. Garden City, N.Y.: Doubleday Anchor.
———. 1972a. "Academia and Politics in America." In *Imagination and Precision in the Social Sciences*, edited by T. J. Nossiter. London: Faber.
———. 1972b. Rebellion in the University. Boston: Little, Brown.
Lipset, S. M., and Richard B. Dobson. 1972. "The Intellectual as Critic and Rebel: With Special Reference to the United States and the Soviet Union." *Daedalus* 101 (Summer): 137–98.
Lipset, S. M., and E. C. Ladd, Jr. 1970. ". . . And What Professors Think". *Psychology Today* 4 (November): 49–51, 106.
———. 1971a. "The Divided Professoriate." *Change* 3 (May–June): 54–60.
———. 1971b. "Jewish Academics in the United States: Achievements, Culture, and Politics." *American Jewish Year Book*. New York: American Jewish Committee.
Lourau, R. 1970. "Sociology and Politics in 1968." In *Reflections on the Revolution in France: 1968*, edited by Charles Posner. Harmondsworth: Penguin.
Martin D. 1969. "The Dissolution of the Monasteries." In *Anarchy and Culture: The Problem of the Contemporary University*, edited by D. Martin. London: Routledge & Kegan Paul.
Merton, R. K. 1939. "Science and the Economy of Seventeenth-Century England." *Science and Society* 3:3–27.
———. 1957. "In Memory of Bernhard J. Stern." *Science and Society* 21.7–9.
———. 1968. *Social Theory and Social Structure*. New York: Free Press.
Nicolaus, M. 1969. "The Professional Organization of Sociology: A View from Below." *Antioch Review* 29:375–88.
Oromaner, M. J. 1969. "The Audience as a Determinant of the Most Important Sociologists." *American Sociologist* 4:332–34.
———. 1970. "Comparison of Influentials in Contemporary American and British Sociology: A Study in the Internationalization of Sociology." *British Journal of Sociology* 21:324–32.
Page, C. H. 1959. "Sociology as a Teaching Enterprise." In *Sociology Today*, edited by L. Broom, L. S. Cottrell, and R. K. Merton. New York: Basic.
Parsons, T. 1928. "'Capitalism' in Recent German Literature: Sombart and Weber." *Journal of Political Economy* 36:641–61.
Popovich, M. 1966. "What American Sociologists Think about Their Science and Its Problems." *American Sociologist* 1:133–35.
Reid, W. 1873. "The Scholar in Politics." *Scribner's Monthly* 6:605–16.
Riesman, D., and G. Harris. 1969. "The Young Are Captives of Each Other: A Conversation with David Riesman and T. George Harris." *Psychology Today* 3 (October): 28–33, 43–67.
Roach, J. L. 1970. "The Radical Sociology Movement: A Short History and Commentary." *American Sociologist* 5:224–33.
Rosenberg, M. 1957. *Occupations and Values*. Glencoe, Ill.: Free Press.
Simpson, R. L. 1971. "System and Humanism in Social Science." *Science* 173 (May): 661–64.
Sjoberg, G. 1967. "Project Camelot: Selected Reactions and Personal Reflections." In

Seymour Martin Lipset and Everett Carll Ladd, Jr.

Ethics, Politics, and Social Research, edited by G. Sjoberg. Cambridge, Mass.: Schenkman.

Spaulding, C. B., and H. A. Turner. 1968. "Political Orientation and Field of Specialization among College Professors." *Sociology of Education* 41:247–62.

Sprehe, J. T. 1967. *The Climate of Opinion in Sociology: A Study of the Professional Value and Belief Systems of Sociologists*. Ph.D. diss., Washington University, Saint Louis.

Steiner, H., and O. I. Schkaratan. 1970. "The Analysis of Society as a System and Its Social Structure." Paper presented at the Research Committee of Social Stratification and Social Mobility, 7th World Congress of Sociology in Varna, Bulgaria.

Suzuki, H. 1970. *The Urban World*. Tokyo: Seishin Shobo.

Sztompka, P. 1971. "The Logic of Functional Analysis in Sociology and Anthropology." *Quality and Quantity* 5:369–87.

Toby, Jackson. 1972. "Gouldner's Misleading Reading of the Theories of Talcott Parson." *Contemporary Sociology* 1 (March): 109–10.

Touraine, A. 1971. *The May Movement, Revolt and Reform*. New York: Random House.

Trilling, L. 1965. *Beyond Culture*. New York: Viking.

Veblen, T. 1934. "The Intellectual Pre-Eminence of Jews in Modern Europe." *Essays in Our Changing Order*. New York: Viking.

Walum, L. R. 1970. "Sociologists as Signers: Some Characteristics of Protestors of the Vietnam War Policy." *American Sociologist* 5:161–64.

Weber, M. 1949. *The Methodology of the Social Sciences*. Glencoe, Ill.: Free Press.

Professionalization of Sociology

Morris Janowitz
University of Chicago

In the years 1965–70, there was a marked increase in writings on the "sociology of sociology" or, more particularly, on the "institutionalization" of sociologists. However, ever since sociology emerged as an academic discipline in the United States, issues of the proper organization and role of sociologists have been central themes for debate. As early as 1894, Ira W. Howerth wrote about the "Present Condition of Sociology in the United States." Edward A. Tiryakian, in *The Phenomenon of Sociology* (1971), offers an extensive bibliography on these topics which indicates that already in the 1920s and 1930s there was an active sociology of knowledge approach to sociology.

These writings reflect the obvious fact that most sociologists in the United States (and throughout most of the world where academic and research freedom exists) pursue their vocation in a university setting. Research into sociology as an institution has been pursued by means of the standard categories of organizational analysis; for example, institutionalization focuses on division of labor, organizational control, internal communication, authority and power, interorganizational relations, and the impact of societal values and norms. Moreover, although the forms and mechanisms of professionalization are relatively undeveloped, sociologists are members of a profession. To speak of sociology as a profession is to focus on a relatively neglected aspect of the organization of the discipline, namely, its clients and the dilemmas of client relations (Hughes 1958).

As an academic profession, students are, of course, the immediate clients of sociologists. It is a professed goal that the academic sociologist will accept the responsibility to teach, although the audience for teaching may be variously defined to include other professional groups or extra-mural assemblies. Ideally, teaching is thought of not only as a professional responsibility per se but as an essential activity for improving one's research.

While the academic sociologist seeks to combine teaching with research, identifying the clients for university research is more difficult. The researcher relates, with his procedures and responsibilities, to his colleagues who help define the standards of performance rather than to clients. As researcher, the sociologist is concerned with the complex issues concerning the treatment, dignity, and privacy of the subjects of his investigations. But strictly speaking, the clients of the sociologist, as researcher, are relatively ambiguous. If one thinks of donors of financial support for research as a kind of client, for instance, the sociologist in a university setting has the minimum responsibility to that client to publish his research findings. However, his primary professional purpose in publishing is to serve other sociologists and all others who are potentially interested in his findings. The ability of the sociologist as researcher to find other clients in various types of nonuniversities settings such as independent research bureaus, voluntary associations, governmental agencies, or business enterprises has been a central theme of analysis and debate (Evan 1962).

Since sociology began as an academic discipline, there has been a continuous effort to create practice roles of sociologists, often called "applied sociology." The objective has been to locate sociologists outside of the university to serve a variety of specific clients in the larger society: in consultation, social planning, the collection of data, and various forms of administration. In fact, sociologists have not created an extensive component that renders specific services to clients—either individual or organizations—in the same sense that medicine, law, or psychology have. Nor have they produced a compelling logic for their practice or an effective system of professional or social control of their activities.

The purpose of this paper is to sketch out the "natural history" of the efforts to create an applied sociology and to try to account for the relative lack of success despite extensive energies invested in efforts to create and develop specific clients for sociology. The underlying assumption is that the theoretical and empirical content of sociology as an intellectual discipline, more than the organization of sociologists, accounts for its inability to develop a practice specialization. As such, sociology needs to be thought of as a staff-type profession based on the fusion of research and teaching roles most effectively institutionalized in a university structure. The teacher-researcher format, rather than that of engineer or clinical psychologist, is the basis for analyzing the performance and social responsibility of sociologists.

In fact, the concentration of sociologists engaged in sociological efforts outside the university is smaller than that of either psychologists or economists. The absence of an effective "applied" element in sociology is not the result of indifference on the part of the profession; the search for an "applied" sociology has had a long tradition. One of the central elements in the natural history of sociology as a profession is the tradition of a liberal and "left of center" personal ideology among sociologists. This personal ideology, more than any other social characteristic, helps account for the persistent effort of many sociologists to "apply" their knowledge directly rather than to be content with the role of teacher-researcher.

The analysis does not discount the impact of sociological thinking on contemporary society and decision making. This impact results, for better or for worse, from its contribution to the general education of generation after generation of undergraduates. Some sociologists would attribute an even greater impact from those books and monographs which have been widely read by informed publics.

The teacher-researcher format has been and will continue to apply to new institutional settings; for instance, sociologists have been appointed to the faculties of medicine, law, and education (Young 1955). Another important professional development for sociologists has been their participation in public commissions of inquiry on crucial and pressing social issues. But, as discussed later, these commissions function most effectively when the sociologists conform to the teacher-researcher format. In addition, even in the absence of a stable and professionalized cadre of applied sociologists, sociological researchers and social statisticians supply the indispensable descriptive social intelligence and data without which decision making in contemporary society could not function (Duncan 1969).

PROFESSIONAL PERSPECTIVES OF SOCIOLOGISTS

That the theoretical and substantive content of sociology inherently limits the development of an applied or practice specialization in sociology is a view not shared by wide segments of the sociological community. Indeed, most sociologists hope for the day when the discipline will develop its theories and research measures to permit the emergence of such a specialization. I have explored this issue elsewhere in terms of the distinction between an "enlightenment" conception of sociological knowledge and an "engineering" conception. The enlightenment conception accepts the above expectation while the engineering conception is oriented toward the ultimately developed nonacademic practice profession in the conventional sense of the term (Janowitz 1970).

The engineering model makes a strong distinction between basic and applied research. The sociological enterprise is defined as a group of highly trained, theoretically oriented specialists supported by methodologists and, as required, field workers (McRae 1970). The actual interaction with clients is not done by theoretical and analytically oriented basic researchers but by the more numerous applied sociologists who are trained in their particular tasks of collating research and in dealing with clients and practitioners.

The enlightenment model sees no strong distinction between basic and applied sociology (Shils 1949). Hauser's formulation is worthy of scrutiny because of the manner in which he reduces the distinction (1949): "In this sense, both pure and applied research are scientific endeavors. The essential difference between pure and applied research is to be found not in the point of view or methods of the investigator, not in the nature of the

Morris Janowitz

phenomena under investigation, but rather in the manner in which the problem is selected, in the auspices of the research and in the immediate, as distinguished from the long run objectives of the research."

The sociologist concerned with testing hypotheses cannot unduly separate any phase of the collection and assessment of data. He must recognize that he is part of the social process and not outside of it. He strives for a high degree of generality but must recognize that sociological knowledge is not to be found in formal propositions alone but in concrete facts and empirical data which give meaning to the search for generalization. Of course, some sociologists are more skilled in logical and formal analysis, while others have stronger skills in quantitative or field work. But an excessive differentiation can only serve to thwart the growth of sociological knowledge.

Sociologists must always be alert to the limitations of their findings and the possibilities of alternative explanations. In fact, many reject the view that sociological knowledge can produce definitive answers on which professional practice can automatically be based. The goal of sociological knowledge is to clarify alternatives and to assist professionals and the public in institution building.

The dissemination and fusion of sociological knowledge cannot simply be devolved to some "secondary" group. Although some division of labor is involved, the researcher himself must be involved in the process. As such, he performs as a teacher in a classroom or seminar, leading the student or the public to understand the processes of the research effort in order to assist them in formulating their own conclusions rather than in the formulation of prescriptions (Znaniecki 1940).

The essential issue is not in the degree of quantification but a much deeper question of the limits and potentials of "scientific" rationality in a democratic society. James Coleman, in the wake of the attention generated by his study on the American school system, articulated the underlying premises of the enlightenment model. "Thus at some point, the researcher must hand over his results to the policy maker and more generally to the public. The more easily interpretable and intellectually digestible he can make them, the better. The task of political digestion itself, however, is not the task of the researcher, but of the whole political process. The research informs that process but it does no more. It cannot, even if its information is perfect, take the place of that process" (Coleman 1970). Students of the history of ideas will note the parallel to the formulations of John Dewey and his pragmatic philosophy, especially in *The Public and Its Problems*. Coleman is indeed bold in formulation since he holds that one criterion in the statistical analysis of his materials is the comprehensibility of the procedures.[1]

[1] The notion of "clinical sociology" as offered by Alvin Gouldner in his earlier writing

108

As of 1970, there exists no adequate statistical information about sociologists' professional commitments to these alternative formulations about the role of sociology in social action. But I venture to estimate that most hold, in one form or another, a hope for a sociology with an engineering component.

SOCIOLOGY AS AN ACADEMIC PROFESSION

By the middle of the 19th century, the intellectual elements of the discipline had been formulated. Only 50 years later—between 1890 and 1900—sociology became an integral part of the academic scene. The first elements were intellectual—the sociological categories for describing society; the constituent components can be traced back to antiquity if one desires, but they were first given a "modern" formulation in the writings of the Scottish Moralists (David Hume, Adam Smith, Adam Ferguson, and Dugald Stewart [Schneider 1967]). In turn, the explicitly "contemporary" formulations can be identified in the writings of August Comte.[2]

Empirical investigations constituted the second element, which sought to describe the social structure and which took many forms on the continent of Europe, in Great Britain, and in the United States. The heritage of social research, for example, can be thought of as emerging in Great Britain in 1834 with the appearance of the Report of the Commission on the Poor Law and the founding of the Statistical Society of London (Philip Abrams 1968). By 1861 Henry Mayhew's noteworthy studies of London were being published. In the United States, long before the Civil War, empirical social surveys, rich in detail, were numerous. However, before 1890 few of these empirical research studies confronted the issues raised by the "theoretical" sociologists. Moreover, the field work was rarely cumulative.

To speak of the institutionalization of sociology as a scientific discipline meant the (a) mutual interpenetration of sociological concepts with empirical research, and the (b) organization of stable groups for the training of new cadres of sociologists who would be aware of past efforts and who could work on the basis of some degree of collegial control and standards of performance. This did not occur until after 1890, when departments of sociology were organized in the universities in the United States and a journal was founded—two hallmarks of the organization of sociology as an academic discipline.

The idea of a systematic sociology with intellectual theory and research

---

appears to be compatible with the enlightenment model (1956, 1957). The import of his later writings is difficult to evaluate since they leave unclear the role of sociological knowledge in social action. See especially Richard A. Peterson (1971).

[2] See R. A. Nisbet, *The Sociological Tradition* (1966), for an analysis of the contributions of Maistre and Bonald to the origins of modern sociology.

came into being at roughly the same time in Europe and the United States. However, it became an academic discipline earlier in the United States—at the University of Chicago, Columbia University, and for a time at Johns Hopkins—than it did in Europe. In his intellectual history of the end of the 19th century, Stuart Hughes (1958) attempts to account for the rise of the sociological enterprise in terms of the societal transformation and the emergence of the notion of individuality. In his view, sociology served as a frame of reference in the intellectual search for a normative order which expresses the idea of individuality and individual conscience. An alternative explanation is to be found in Robert Nisbet, *The Sociological Tradition* (1966), in which he focuses more on the processes of urbanization and industrialization. There are, of course, common elements in these formulations. In addition, Edward Shils's (1970) analysis of the more open structure of the American as compared with European universities helps account for the more rapid institutionalization of sociology in the United States.

The experiences of the Department of Sociology at the University of Chicago, founded in 1892 and by no means atypical, reveal the early institutionalization and professionalization of sociology as an academic discipline. From its origins, the department was intellectually committed to the enlightenment model, although there were recurrent vigorous impulses to develop an engineering component.

Sociology was organized as a research discipline whose findings President William Rainey Harper assumed would have beneficial social consequences. Four professors were authorized, not only to prevent domination by one point of view but in order to assemble the varied skills and interests that were required. The department was oriented toward training new cadres of sociologists, and research was a central aspect of their training. The first sociology journal was founded and department members were active in the affairs of the national association. In short, from its very beginning, sociology had a departmental basis; it was more than the effort of a single professor. Moreover, it could not be thought of as a collection of men who were only part of a learned society. They were academic professionals or, rather, they were striving to be professionals, since professionalization for them meant control over their research and academic freedom.

Indeed, from the very beginning, there was a strong emphasis on teaching. President Harper repeatedly proclaimed that the University of Chicago professors taught because that was the responsibility of a university. Faculty were recruited with the expectation that they would teach, and the norms of the institution meant that the highest prestige was accorded to the men who both engaged in important research and who were effective and stimulating teachers.

This model appealed to the sociologists. Faculty members engaged in extensive teaching both on and off the campus (even on radio later) and placed great importance on the preparation of treatises for teaching, of which the most outstanding example was *Introduction to the Science of Sociology* (1924 [1969]) by Robert E. Park and Ernest W. Burgess. The work agenda of a department member was strikingly similar to that of the 1970s.

In 1910, field studies and participant observations became an integral part not only of graduate training in sociology but also an element in the undergraduate liberal education offered by the sociological faculty. Students were encouraged to "tell it as it was." Cohort after cohort prepared their autobiographies in order to reveal their cultural background, their aspiration and frustration, and these materials became the raw material of class discussions.[3] Training in statistical analysis, as borrowed from economics and psychology, was quickly incorporated.

TRENDS IN ACADEMIC AFFILIATION

Throughout the 75 years of organized departments of sociology, the discipline has remained essentially in its academic base. Until 1920, the graduates with M.A.'s and Ph.D.'s conformed in general to the model of their professors. They aspired to combine a career of teaching and research in a university setting. An important minority went off to church-related colleges and liberal arts schools, but most found employment in the state universities which were developing departments of sociology. Full-time research agencies interested in sociologists were almost nonexistent. However, a minority, mainly with M.A.'s, went into public agencies; some engaged in research, but most did administrative or social work.

Despite repeated exploration of other settings for the employment of sociologists, there has been little change, especially in the period of marked growth since 1945. No evidence indicates that the rapid increase in sociologists has been accompanied by a diminution of academic sociologists. At this point, sociologists are defined as persons who have received training at the graduate level and maintain an active identification with the discipline.

Incomplete data about the employment of sociologists since 1940 underestimate their employment in academic settings. Hollis (1945) reported in 1940 that 79% of Ph.D.'s were employed in educational institutions—nearly all in universities and colleges. Matilda Riley's (1960) comparison of the membership of the American Sociological Association in 1950 and 1959 revealed that the percentage of active members was the same in both

[3] Mountains of biographical and documentary materials accumulated by Ernest W. Burgess remain housed in the archives of the University of Chicago Library and serve as valuable sources of the social history of the period.

111

years, 79%. During this decade, when interest in developing the practice aspects of sociologists was intense, 6% of Ph.D.'s who were members of the ASA shifted from academic to nonacademic positions and 3% or 4% had shifted in the opposite direction.

Based on data collected in 1960, Sibley (1963) found that 78% were in educational settings. Data reported by the National Science Foundation in 1966 reported 75.4% in educational institutions (Hopper 1967) and for 1970, reported an even higher figure of 83%. My evaluation of the sources is that for those who have more than a master's degree (including all but the Ph.D. thesis) more than 90% are employed in education and academic settings. As is well known, most sociologists in nonacademic employment have only a master's degree. For many of them, sociology is only a form of general education, and they lose their sociological affiliation after some years of employment, especially in business, but also in governmental services, although their sociological background may be highly appropriate. However, Sibley did find that over half of the sociologists with a master's degree were employed in academic settings, while only 20% were in health, welfare, religion, or correctional work. Thus, even the M.A. sociologist is oriented toward the academic setting.

Because these surveys of employment are based on membership in the American Sociological Association or the National Science Foundation Register, they underrepresent or even exclude categories of sociologists who are teachers in smaller colleges and who are affiliated with regional association. Other factors explain the fact that the actual concentration in academic settings is higher than that represented in these semi-official surveys.

Many Ph.D.'s in nonacademic posts maintain no effective links with the discipline or its organized associations. While sociology was an important element in their education and career development, such persons cannot be truly designated as practicing sociologists.[4]

Sibley data on Ph.D.'s for the early 1960s presents a useful portrait of the tasks actually performed by sociologists employed outside the university and indicates the small concentration of practice-oriented assignments. Of the 22% employed in nonacademic settings, the largest group (three-fifths) was engaged in full-time research, often in government agencies, while one-quarter were engaged in consulting, planning, or ad-

---

[4] It does appear as if the available data were collected so as to emphasize the extent to which sociologists are employed in nonacademic settings. Thus, for example, the National Science Foundation Register listed 49 sociologists as being employed by the armed forces; however, with the exception of a handful of instructors at the service academies and a few research grant administrators, these sociologists were ROTC officers completing their obligated tour of active duty before returning to civilian educational institutions. An important number of sociologists employed in the government are engaged in serving universities.

ministration. Stated in overall terms, of all Ph.D.'s, 13% were engaged in nonuniversity full-time research, while 7% were in other types of practice-oriented assignments. Sibley found the well-known feeling of "marginality" among nonacademic sociologists; in particular, they reported a strong doubt "about doing it again" if they could have a second chance. Moreover, he found little link between training, preparation, and employment in nonacademic settings; personally generated interests and skills predominated.

Sociologists stand, therefore, in marked contrast to the other social sciences (except anthropologists) which have a much higher proportion of their professionals employed outside the university and with higher salaries. For example, the National Science Register for 1968 reported that 88% of all sociology Ph.D.'s were affiliated with educational institutions compared with 76% for economists and 60% for psychologists.

PERSONAL IDEOLOGY AND PROFESSIONALISM

The long-term concentration on academic affiliation among sociologists has been matched by a parallel and persistent pattern of personal ideology which helps explain their interest in an applied sociology. Lipset and Ladd (pp. 67–104 of this volume) show that American sociologists since the 1930s and even before have been overwhelmingly "liberal," that is, "left of center" (the size of the very small group of radicals is difficult to assess). However, one essential notion of sociologists as professionals—either academically based or practice oriented—is that they are able to separate, in a socially responsible fashion, their personal ideology from their professional roles in dealing with their clients, their publics, and their peers. Clearly, this dimension represents the deepest and most profound issue in the application of the concept of professionalization to sociology and especially in the period of university activism since 1965 (Ben-David 1972). Many sociologists, since the initial organization of sociology as a discipline, have had strong personal ideologies which have pressed them to seek to make their knowledge relevant or effective for social change; yet as academics they have had to face or have been attracted to the norms of the teacher-researcher.

As early as 1913, James Leuba investigated the attitudes of a sample of the members of the American Sociological Society and found that the academic as compared with the nonacademic sociologists were more atheistic and had more "liberal" religious beliefs (1921). Moreover, those who were judged by a panel to be more creative were the least religious. In a repeated series of studies, the "liberal"-left of center and radical orientation of sociologists have been documented, although most of these studies made use of mechanistic and undifferentiated categories of political ideology.

Jerome Davis's (1940) survey of the membership of the Eastern Sociological Association in 1939 is particularly noteworthy because he showed that sociologists of this period were extensively active in their civic roles, particularly in race relations. This characterization appears to be more accurate than the claim of Sibley that after 1945 "the involvement of academically based Ph.D.'s in non-academic activities on a part-time or intermittent basis has been growing greatly" (1963, p. 45). The deep involvement in civic and political activities has characterized the biographies of sociologists such as W. I. Thomas, Robert E. Park, and Robert Lynd from the very inception of the field. No doubt there has been a broadening in scope from local and metropolitan arenas to a national perspective.

Thus, it was not a startling revelation that on the issues of the 1960s—the war in Vietnam, race relations, civil liberties—sociologists were strongly on the "left of center" end of the continuum. Perhaps it was striking that the data collected for the Carnegie Commission on Higher Education documented that, as an academic group, sociology professors had the highest concentration of "left of center" attitudes on these related issues. This and other available sources do not make it possible to identify the fraction of sociologists who could accurately be called political radicals in their personal ideology. Of course, sociology graduate students and young faculty members were conspicuous in their campus activities during the period of student unrest in the late 1960s.

One would not expect, in the American setting, that social origins—father's occupational background or social class—would be a powerful variable in accounting for the pattern of social and political orientations of sociologists (Lipset and Ladd, p. 000 of this issue). While the reported data from the large-scale study sponsored by the Carnegie Foundation, in the absence of additional statistical analysis, does not permit precise estimates of the contribution of particular variables, the social background variable cannot be neglected. Although it throws only very partial light on the differences within the social science disciplines, it does help explain differences between the faculty in the social sciences and in professional schools or the natural sciences. The latter are less "liberal" and are recruited from somewhat higher social backgrounds. Gross categorization of faculty members into Protestant, Catholic, and Jewish background is not very important. There is every reason to expect that a more comprehensive approach based on social structure and personality would be more fruitful since the processes of self-selection into sociology and the system of professional socialization strengthen and refashion attitudes of academics. Sociology tends to recruit those with a "left of center" orientation; their style of life and their work tend to enhance this outlook.

However, the central question at this point in the analysis of the forms of professionalism in sociology is the link between the personal, social, and political ideology of sociologists and their performance as teachers and researchers. To what extent are sociologists able to institutionalize their various roles? Are sociologists able to separate personal ideology from scholarly and teaching performance? It makes very little difference that a small minority of radical sociologists, for example, do not believe that such a distinction can be made. The underlying question which is, of course, in good measure beyond the scope of this paper, is the extent to which sociologists as a corporate group are committed to such professional norms, and the extent to which individual sociologists are actually able to act on the basis of them.

One approach to these issues, although indirect, is to explore the relationship between personal ideology and commitment to either the enlightenment or the engineering model of sociological knowledge. If one separates out sociologists who label themselves as radical sociologists, personal ideology does not seem linked to commitment to either model. Elsewhere I have argued that social background variables such as social class or religion per se would be of secondary importance in accounting for professional orientations (Janowitz 1970). Again we are dealing with a broader pattern of social background, social personality, and professional socialization—in particular, experiences in graduate school—plus the reenforcement that comes from collegial contact and support.

Likewise, Lipset has explored the links between theoretical commitment of sociologists and their own personal ideology. His reanalysis of the survey conducted in the early 1960s by Gouldner presents evidence that there was little relationship between the personal political orientation of sociologists and their acceptance of the importance and relevance of Talcott Parsons's theoretical formulations (Sprehe 1967). Despite its limitations, Lipset's analysis demonstrates one element of professionalism among sociologists. However, the strains within sociology as an academic profession since the 1960s have been enormously increased.

Clearly the links between professional norms and ideology require detailed case-by-case analysis of actual performance. However, from the larger Carnegie Commission sample one can separate out 1,368 sociologists whose teaching appointments were primarily in departments of sociology. They were asked for responses to the statement, "A man's teaching and research inevitably reflects his political values." Although ambiguous, this question indirectly measures one set of professional norms. Clearly the 14.2% who strongly agreed reject or have strong doubts about either the feasibility or validity of separating professional performance from personal ideology. On the other hand, the 10% who strongly disagreed and the 39% who disagreed with reservations are, at least in principle, committed to this norm. It is difficult to evaluate the responses of those 37% who agreed with reservations. Seemingly, after a period of intense politiciza-

Morris Janowitz

tion, there is still widespread acceptance of the professional assumptions that sociological performance is distinct from personal ideology, but there is an important minority who do not have or who have abandoned such a belief. Thus, research into the beliefs of sociologists is relevant, not because of the clarity and richness of explanation of the factors that account for professional and political ideologies, but because the personal ideology of sociologists helps explain their persistent interest in an "applied" sociology.

THE SEARCH FOR AN APPLIED SOCIOLOGY: FIRST PERIOD

Because of their liberalism, many academic sociologists have wished to "apply" their knowledge directly to the larger world or to train "applied sociologists," rather than be satisfied with the teacher role with its indirect and diffuse consequences. Some have seen "applied sociology" as inherent in their philosophy of science. But in each department, such sociologists have had colleagues with a strong skepticism about these efforts.

Thus, it is not strange that the professional issues of sociology have been framed in terms of "basic research" versus "applied research," although the distinction is of limited analytical relevance. In the 1930s and immediately after World War II sociologists drew upon psychoanalysis as a model either for developing a theory of human behavior or for the pursuit of a treatment methodology.[5] Although this interest has declined among sociologists generally, much of the format and practice of the American Psychological Association was adopted by the American Sociological Association.[6]

In fact, the merits of an explicitly organized applied branch of sociology was debated from the establishment of sociology as an academic discipline in the university system. Sociologists almost universally believed that their discipline would have social consequences, if only to sensitize political leaders to the limits of planned intervention. However, no real consensus emerged from these debates. Manifestations of these differences have varied over the years. The earliest period, in the 1890s, to the outbreak of World War II was one of development; the second, the years 1945 to the middle or end of the 1960s, was one of stabilization; and since the latter half of the 1960s, we find counter trends not yet stabilized.

During the initial period, there were sustained efforts to establish an

[5] "It is indeed one of the distinctions of psychoanalysis that research and treatment proceed hand in hand, but still the techniques required for the one begins, at a certain point to diverge from that of the other" (Freud 1949, p. 326).

[6] William Goode (1960) has highlighted the cognitive, normative, and institutional differences between psychology and sociology as organized disciplines, and has argued most strongly against the model of the psychologist for sociology.

116

applied sociology and to develop a set of practice specialties. At the University of Chicago, some members of the faculty were deeply involved in these efforts, as were their graduates in other centers of sociological research and teaching. There is no evidence that a lack of employment opportunities in academic settings was a main cause or even an important factor in these efforts. Certainly, concern about employment was a major preoccupation during the Great Depression of the 1930s, and many sociologists entered government and public service during the New Deal as an immediate alternative, but the expanded role of government offered new opportunities to sociologists. In particular, a group of outstanding sociologists entered the Bureau of Census and related agencies to engage in demographic work and allied social statistics. They served mainly as research specialists and created a model which is directly applicable to the present concern with social indicators and the evaluation of governmental programs of social change.

It seems clear that among university sociologists the interest in applied sociology of particular sociologists represented their intellectual convictions, institutional aspiration, and personal ideology. At Chicago, Ernest W. Burgess and, later, Louis Wirth had the strongest commitment to the "engineering model." Burgess's collaborator, the personally and intellectually powerful Robert E. Park, was his sharpest critic. But he could not sway Burgess from his comprehensive commitments to institutional building for an applied sociology. For Burgess and Wirth, however, advisory or consultative activities had to be grounded in authoritative methodology that would be internally consistent and produce major consequences for action. There was a strong entrepreneurial overtone in these endeavors and, as a result, sociologists began to study a host of social problems and policy issues.

A highlight of the search for an applied sociology can be seen in the contrasting "natural histories" of the relationships between sociologists and two other professional groups, social work and criminology, prior to World War II. In varying degrees, particular sociologists sought to use their discipline as an alternative route into or as alternative bases for professional practice in these two areas. Although they were for a time more successful in criminology than in social work, these efforts essentially failed; new practice specialists within sociology did not emerge as they did in psychology. Instead strong intellectual, conceptual, and research links emerged which, after World War II, became institutionalized.

Professional schools of social work—dedicated to the notion of scientific philanthropy—were established at about the same time that sociology became an academic discipline. From its inception, sociology had therefore to contend with an established and ongoing profession which believed that it could and should make use of various academic disciplines—economics and psychology as well as sociology. While, originally, sociology had intellectual associations with the concerns of social work, professional relations were diffuse and at points antagonistic. This remained the case up through the outbreak of World War II. After all, in popular imagery, sociology and social work were often seen as the same, and sociology may have derived its only relevance from its supposed fusion with social work.

However, the realities were much more complex. Many social workers viewed sociology as a source of information about social welfare problems and a limited number of sociologists taught in schools of social work, but the field of community organization which would have supplied one of the major links between sociology and social work was in effect moribund. There was little systematic effort to incorporate sociological conceptions into this specialization. Because sociologists were developing their concerns with the local community and their ideas about the potentials for community organization, the main intellectual interchange between them and selected social workers focused on the settlement house, although even this brought few changes. Thus, sociologists with an "applied" perspective sought to bypass social workers and directly involve themselves in local community programs. Sociologists and their students had had continuous contact with settlement houses and community organizations. Service in such agencies was conceived as a *rite de passage* for sociologists that would transcend the limitations of social work and develop the appropriate critical attitude—even mild contempt toward social work.

The New Deal only served to heighten sociologists' search for alternative routes to "institutional building" in the urban community (Janowitz 1970). The massive reforms of the New Deal were based on economic and welfare measures that were national in scope and categorical in character. While the importance of these measures was fully recognized, most sociologists were also sensitive to their inherent limitations—they failed to create new forms of social organization required to improve the institutions and character of the local community. They were aware that important experiments in community development, including new forms of administration and citizen participation, were underway in rural areas. Comparable experiments in urban areas were very limited during the New Deal period. Thus, some sociologists sought to apply their notions of social change to the reconstruction of the slum and the social control of delinquency. For example, in the 1930s under the intellectual influence of Burgess, the Chicago Area Project embodied the essential conceptual elements of the community action programs of the 1960s. The goals were to break away from conventional definitions of education and social work in order to develop comprehensive institution building which would permit extensive local participation and generate new elements of social control. These experiments involved Joseph Lohman, Leonard Cottrell, Clifford

Shaw, and Henry McKay, and subsequently the network included a group who have been central in recent theorizing and conceptualization about community organization: Lloyd Ohlin, James Short, and Sol Kobrin.

The Chicago Area Project and comparable endeavors attracted considerable attention but had no impact on social work until these efforts and the concepts were "rediscovered" in the early years of the John F. Kennedy administration. Although a number of sociologists have been associated with the more recent experimental and demonstration community projects, few have devoted their careers to such enterprises. Sociologists have served as idea men and research personnel, while the professional cadres were recruited from social work and related fields.

By contrast, sociology in the 1920s and 1930s did train numerous criminologists, and for a period criminology was thought to be a practice-oriented specialty—largely because schools of criminology were slow to be organized in the United States. Sociology contributed to criminology its holistic approach and its emphasis on the social context. The sociologist's perspective received public attention because it pointed to the limits of existing techniques of social control of crime and delinquency and in particular to the limited effectiveness of the prison. The prison has served as the locus for fundamental and thoroughgoing research, and the literature on the prison is still one of the major accomplishments of the sociological effort in analyzing a social system, although it does not have high prestige in the field.[7]

During the 1920s and 1930s sociologists, including those at first-rank universities, sought to train practicing criminologists by offering both masters and doctoral degrees for this specialty. After 1945 this approach was deemphasized, but sociologists did contribute to the development of a more independent profession of criminology. Graduates with higher degrees tended to accept research and staff posts, while others took operational and administrative posts—perhaps less because of specific training than because of individual skills or desires.

Moreover, professionalism in criminology implied participation in a colleagial group, and those with a sociological background could, by participation in the American Sociological Association, link themselves to their sociological colleagues through their research interests. While many criminologists continued to affiliate with the ASA and in time moved toward academic or quasi-academic careers, those who made a major commit-

---

[7] The traditions included powerful monographic literature from the original work of Donald Clemmer on *The Prison Community* (1940), Gresham Sykes, *The Society of Captives* (1958), to the work of David Street et al., *Organization for Treatment* (1966), plus penetrating theoretical analyses such as Lloyd Ohlin's (1960). This tradition was powerfully enriched and extended by Erving Goffman in his writings on the "total institution" (1962).

ment to criminological practice soon shifted their professional association to groups more closely linked to practice roles.

Sociologists offering training in criminology were aware of the necessity to equip their students with more than a general orientation. They sought to develop an authoritative body of knowledge which could guide practice procedures. In particular, they believed strongly that quantification was essential, partly emulating psychology's development of intelligence testing. As early as the 1920s, sociology developed actuarial prediction studies which assumed that background social factors could be statistically aggregated to predict more accurately a wide range of social behavior for specific individuals. Social background and life experiences could account for success and failure in marriage, in higher education, or on parole.

The decision-making process of parole boards supplied an experimental setting for the utilization of such a technique. Parole boards, typically consisting of lay persons, had to make arbitrary decisions about early release and were willing to accept advice by sociologists as to who would succeed on parole. Although sociologists were trained and appointed to prison systems and did research to update and perfect the statistical techniques and to select the most appropriate variables, the procedures of parole prediction never became as sufficiently institutionalized as did psychological testing or personnel classification procedures. The very limited success of the prediction system, however, was more likely linked to the poor quality of supervision of parolees and the realities of their life chances than to the limitation of the prediction instruments.[8]

THE SEARCH FOR AN APPLIED SOCIOLOGY: SECOND PERIOD

With the close of World War II, the search for an applied sociology centered on the utilization of the sample survey. Of course, social surveys had been in use since the middle of the 19th century in the United States, Great Britain, and France. Some of the early surveys were based on a high degree of intellectual and methodological sophistication. In particular, those sponsored by the Russell Sage Foundation before World War I supplied an important stimulus for local reform.

But the institutionalization of the sample survey after 1930 stemmed from two developments which enhanced the scientific aspects of social research and supplied a new basis for a powerful but again abortive move-

[8] Sociometric technique was another methodological device for research which had a potential for professional practice. Sociologists have displayed a strong interest in "sociometry." Moreno and his disciples offered the procedure not only as a research tool but a device for selection and reorganization of institutional life. Sociometric technique to the extent that it has become institutionalized employs a rating and evaluation procedure of personnel and is associated with the work of a personnel psychologist rather than a sociologist.

ment to develop an applied specialization in sociology. First, a social psychological perspective was incorporated in both the collection and analysis of survey data. Along with concrete "social facts," the social survey included the respondent's attitudes and feelings, and thereby attracted new clients who believed that these motivational findings were important. Samuel Stouffer, one of the major specialists in attitude surveys, had been a student of L. L. Thurstone, who laid the intellectual basis for the social psychological dimension of the sample survey in his classic article (1928), "The Measurement of Opinion." By means of psychophysical techniques, he demonstrated rationale for attitude measurement. The development of the cross-sorter for handling survey data should not be overlooked.

During World War I, psychologists came in contact with government officials and businessmen in connection with the mass intelligence testing undertaken for the War Department. After World War I, psychologists organized corporations to undertake attitude surveys, morale studies, market research, mass media audience studies, and advertising pretesting. Soon specific agencies organized mainly for profit, especially after it was discovered that the results of such opinion polls as the Gallup Poll, could be widely disseminated because newspapers became important consumers of these studies.

In the late 1930s, three social scientists emerge who raised standards and related survey research to academic departments: Rensis Likert, Clyde Hart, and Paul Lazarsfeld. In 1946, with his administrative assistant Angus Campbell, Likert developed a unit at the University of Michigan which emerged as the largest academic related survey research agency; Hart became director of the National Opinion Research Center when it moved to the University of Chicago in 1947; and Lazarsfeld organized the Bureau of Applied Social Research at Columbia University in 1940.

After 1945, Lazarsfeld, with Bernard Berelson and Hans Ziesel, formulated a new type of sociologist, an applied survey research specialist whose generalized techniques could be utilized by a wide variety of clients. They proposed advanced training centers and institutes of applied social research with advanced degrees including the Ph.D. The model was that of the operations research engineer; such graduate professionals would be employed in nonacademic settings After 25 years, survey research units have become integral parts of the American university system, but they have not succeeded in creating a well-defined specialization of applied sociologists, although they do contribute a limited number who are employed outside the university.

While most survey research units were formed on the model of consulting psychology, those that have become attached to an academic setting have pressed to publish the results of their studies and to conform more and more to university research standards. The availability of government and foundation grants enabled selected survey units to move in this direction, and away from specific client relations. However, in part because of the persistent problems of fund raising and in part because of the explicit commitment of key figures to the idea of an applied social research, these units have maintained strong elements for "servicing clients." At a minimum, they have institutionalized feedback sessions and have developed the format of the special client's report which is organized with a view of optimum usage by the clients, but which, in effect, usually guarantees a short intellectual life for the document. The Likert group at the University of Michigan has in fact organized a separate unit designated as the Center for the Utilization of Scientific Knowledge.

Thus, on balance, the academic professors rather than the applied social scientists dominate these survey groups especially with the passage from prominence of the original charismatic leaders. The result is that the second generation of leading figures is concerned with academic tenure and a code of operations which converges with the teacher-researcher. Survey research training has become part of graduate training, and an important fraction of theses are based on their data. But the graduates are in fact oriented toward traditional academic employment rather than "applied settings." In one period, students of the Bureau of Social Research entered commercial and advertising settings in New York City, but the demand for such personnel has been limited and, with new research technologies for market and media research, even this pattern of recruitment and placement declined.

The "natural history" of survey research centers, both the major and the smaller ones, in the United States before 1970 meant that an essential strength of the survey method was neglected—namely, trend studies. Partly because of their funding problems, these survey research centers did not emphasize the long-term collection of sociological and social psychological trend data. In fact, until 1970, the commercial agencies had more and better trend data than did the big three academic based centers.

In the late 1960s and early 1970s, however, there was a rebirth of interest in trends and social indicators deriving from the thinking of William F. Ogburn (1922) and other earlier sociologists (Sheldon and Moore 1968). Aided by federal funds, the major survey units are emerging as national laboratories for the collection and storage of basic social indicator data. Well-grounded data of this sort can overcome the short-time perspective of recent sociological writing and facilitate the emergence of an "applied sociology" that will appeal to various public and private policy makers. Improved data collection is not only indispensable for social research but supplies essential information in the enlightenment model.

Professional organization of survey research specialists, interestingly enough, has not taken place within the sociological fraternity, but instead in the American Association for Public Opinion Research (AAPOR) and its international counterpart, the World Association for Public Opinion Research (WAPOR). These groups, which are loose amalgams of persons with varied backgrounds, the overwhelming bulk of whom are not sociologists, have been preoccupied with professional standards but have not yet had any major effect. The success of nonacademic survey enterprises—commercial or nonprofit—seems to depend on the administrative skill of the organizer. Moreover, while interest in client-sponsored survey research has persisted and even grown during the 1960s, it has encountered competition from other methodologies such as operational research analysis and analysis of organizational records. As a result, survey research is likely to persist as a multidisciplinary effort with an important core located in the university setting and many satellite activities operating as commercial enterprises. In this case also no practice-oriented specialty has emerged.

SOCIOLOGISTS AND THE PUBLIC COMMISSION

The "natural history" of sociology has included participation of sociologists in a series of public commissions of inquiry into basic social issues which may well have had a greater impact on U.S. society than the work of "practice"-oriented sociologists. Before World War II, there were three conspicuous commissions which had essential common features; the Chicago Commission on Race Relations, President Hoover's Research Committee on Recent Social Trends, and the Carnegie Corporation's sponsorship of Gunnar Myrdal's investigation of the American Negro which can be considered a quasi-public commission (1944). After 1945, the scope and frequency of sociologists' participation in public commissions increased and their forms were more varied. Three can serve for comparison: the National Advisory Commission on Civil Disorders (the Kerner Commission), the National Commission on the Causes and Prevention of Violence (the Eisenhower Commission), and the Task Force on Pornography and Obscenity.

The three prewar commissions produced significant research results for the development of sociology and, at the same time, important contributions to public understanding, perhaps largely because they conformed to the enlightenment model. Problems were analyzed in fundamental sociological terms; and the analysis which resulted became standard exemplifications of sociological scholarship. The participating sociologists accepted their dual responsibility of engaging in comprehensive research and at the same time producing a document which served a variety of publics, essentially an extension of the teacher-researcher role. Their findings received widespread attention in the mass media not because of the specific recommendations they made—important though they may have been—but for the deeper public understanding they generated. One can be intrigued by the hypothesis that the high scholarly quality of these early commissions, rather than any special policy orientation, resulted in their significant impact, although there sometimes was prolonged delay in their full impact.

The earliest of these commissions, the Chicago Commission on Race Relations, was established in 1919 by the governor of Illinois at the request of several citizen delegations in the aftermath of the Chicago race riots. The director of research and the person responsible for the collection of the research materials and contents of the published volume was Charles S. Johnson, a Negro and a sociologist, later president of Fisk University. Johnson was a graduate student at Chicago, where he worked with Park who became actively associated with the work of the commission. Three members of Park's seminar on collective behavior were also on the staff of the Commission. The final report, entitled *The Negro in Chicago* (1922), carried the strong imprint of Park's concepts and categories.

The staff of the commission issued a report on the "natural history" of the riot, including an analysis of the underlying causes and the role of the various agencies of social control in dealing with the outbreak, which resulted in an unsurpassed sociological case study using a theoretical framework of collective behavior and social control.

President Herbert Hoover's Research Committee on Recent Social Trends constitutes a similar commitment of sociologists to the enlightenment model. Hoover called for a comprehensive report on social change in the United States which would assist both government agencies and private groups to plan "intelligently." The survey was actively supported by Wesley C. Mitchell, the economist, and Charles E. Merriam, political scientist, who were active in the founding of the Social Science Research Council and who became chairman and vice-chairman of the committee (Karl 1968). William F. Ogburn, of the Chicago department, and Howard Odum, of the North Carolina department, were director of research and assistant director of research. The effort, enormous by the standards of that time, was financed by the Rockefeller Foundation by a grant of $500,000.

The major publication of the commission, *Recent Social Trends* (1933), and the supporting monographs constituted a major landmark in the development of social research in the United States. The intellectual direction of the investigation reflected Ogburn's concern with the development and assembling of statistical indicators of basic social trends. He assumed that the collection of these data were essential both to test basic theories of social organization and social change and of prime importance to groups concerned with planning. The reports of the commission were extensively circulated, and Ogburn's conception of "cultural lag" (1922) entered the rhetoric of public discourse and supplied a stimulus to debates about social planning and institution building. Unfortunately, the depression sidetracked interest in favor of programs that responded to the immediate problems (Karl 1969).

The full consequences of the Research Committee on Recent Social Trends were themselves illustrations of cultural lag. The notion of indicators of social change had been formulated and the extensive research and documentation of the commission temporarily intensified interest in the subject, but after 1945, interest in self-contained and formal theorizing in sociology led to a sharp decline of interest in indicators. In the late 1960s, there was a revival of interest. While the methodology became more sophisticated, social indicators continue to be based on Ogburn's writings; they continue to be both tools for testing theoretical models and data to guide social policy.

Gunnar Myrdal's undertaking which led to the publication of *An American Dilemma* (1944) and the associated monographs also met the common criteria of the first two commissions: a major piece of social research and a report with a broad impact on public affairs. Myrdal was chosen director because the Carnegie officers wished to bring in a foreign scholar from a country without a history of imperialism. The product of Myrdal's large staff, *An American Dilemma*, was widely discussed in the mass media and led to wide debate on the position of the Negro in American society. For more than two decades it was used as a textbook in the social sciences in American universities and colleges. Myrdal was an economist with strong sociological interests, but he included on his staff numerous outstanding sociologists. Much emphasis has been placed on Myrdal's analysis of values and social research, but, important though his analysis may have been, it hardly constituted the central contribution of the effort. As Edward A. Shils points out, Myrdal's study occurred at a time when sociologists were turning away from the study of race and ethnic relations (Shils 1970), and the report undoubtedly stemmed the decline in such investigations that might otherwise have occurred due to the waning influence of the "Chicago School" in the 1950s. The findings served not only as a massive source of documentation but as the basis for conceptual and theoretical formulations such as rank order of discrimination, patterns of interracial marriage, and style of Negro leadership.

In assessing these early commissions, the key sociologists performed with a high degree of professional responsibility, not only as collectors of empirical data, but as writers of clear reports set in a sociological framework which served to enhance the ensuing public debate of policy alternatives.

There were no comparable public commissions in scope and stature involving sociologists in the years 1945–60. While this decline was partly

125

due to the impact of Joseph McCarthy, it was also a period in which sociologists were beginning to operate on their own as individual consultants with governmental agencies and private enterprise. Also in those years, sociologists were engaging in other professional efforts such as those by the "social psychologists" to adjudicate their relations with psychologists. However, these efforts to solve the question of certification availed little to either group.

Again in the 1960s, there was a proliferation of public commissions and national studies, but a full evaluation of the activities after 1945 still requires more historical distance. One is often struck, however, by the absence of the kind of integrated sociological perspective which characterized the early commissions. Perhaps the generous funding which brought with it increased bureaucratization deterred the kind of intellectual leadership which could produce a more unified approach. In any case, sociologists in recent commissions seem to have had more diffuse and less central influence. Thus, the basic report of the Kerner Commission cannot be characterized as a profound or penetrating document which will have an enduring intellectual existence. It lacks both careful documentation and a pervasive perspective for analyzing the position of the black community in the United States. The focal term "institutional racism" appears to be more a label than a basis of analysis, and it has strong elements of a limited tautology. This commission did sponsor the collection of important data which have subsequently entered the literature by the efforts of individual investigators, but pressure of a deadline prevented these materials from being carefully assessed and integrated.

The Milton Eisenhower Commission (the National Commission of the Causes and Prevention of Violence) represented a very different approach. From the outset, it was decided that there would be a strong scholarly component and its research was codirected by two outstanding and vigorous sociologists, James F. Short, Jr., and Marvin Wolfgang. They organized a strong interdisciplinary effort and in fact organized one part of their staff as a "Task Force on Historical Perspectives." The scope and objective of this commission plus the talent that was assembled resembled the three earlier commissions. Especially important is the fact that the two-volume collection of monographic studies entitled *Violence in America: Historical and Comparative Perspectives*, which contains considerable material of lasting scholarly worth (Graham and Gurr 1969) resembled the publications of the earlier commissions.

In the 1930s, Quincy Wright and Harold Lasswell attempted to introduce the naturalistic study of violence into the curriculum and research agenda of political science departments. To their credit, the efforts of Short and Wolfgang on the Eisenhower Commission helped achieve this early objective. From an intellectual point of view, however, the final report failed either to integrate effectively the massive findings or to demonstrate effectively the links between the research and policy recommendations.

Otto Larsen, a specialist on mass communications, and Marvin Wolfgang represented the sociological component on the Task Force on Pornography and Obscenity. They undoubtedly represented the majority viewpoint among sociologists—that all censorship should be removed. While the work of this task force was a historical milestone in the formulation of perspectives toward public policy, it is problematic whether its content and research will command lasting attention for its sociological contribution.

Of the variety of national studies conducted during the 1960s, the Coleman report commissioned by the United States Office of Education was the most conspicuous and influential. While basically a research document, it had many overtones of a public commission of inquiry. The effort achieved a new threshold in sociological research because of the massive collection of data and the imposition of systematic modes of analysis. One consequence of the "inquiry" was to intensify the question of privacy in the collection of data. The findings—that a heterogeneous student body optimizes classroom learning—may have been less significant than the stimulus the report provided to new forms of educational experimentation. As a research document, this report focused on specific findings and on a search for statistically meaningful relations. However, as a commission of public inquiry some of its shortcomings became rapidly apparent. It could not and did not probe the alternative arrangements for handling the policy problems it encountered. The document became the major argument for school busing in order to achieve racial and social balance, but it did not examine either the full range of approaches to school busing or alternative systems for achieving greater student heterogeneity or a wider range of social and class contacts. Moreover, it failed to identify teaching procedures, formats of school organization, or patterns of educational leadership which, although statistically infrequent, were markedly more productive and could therefore result in more effective mass education (Janowitz 1971). In the end, its public commission characteristics were submerged, and it remains one of the outstanding pieces of contemporary social research.

No doubt there is an economy of public commissions; the relatively high frequency of such bodies during the 1960s probably implies a much lower number for the decade of the 1970s. Moreover, the accumulation of massive amounts of data and monograph research may call for a changing pattern for public commissions. The task is now to assess and integrate the available documentation. The Surgeon-General's Scientific Advisory Committee on Television and Social Behavior is a step in this direction (U.S.

Morris Janowitz

Public Health Service 1972). A panel of experts was appointed to review the existing research on the impact of television, and especially of violent contact, on young people.

Despite the fact that the final report of this group produced immediate controversy, its contribution cannot be brushed aside. Certainly the selection of panel members is open to question; those research specialists who were concerned with broad systematic consequences rather than specific and micro effects, were eliminated from the original list of nominations. Also, the report did not present majority-minority positions which would have sharpened the issues. Moreover, it failed to identify sufficiently those aspects of the problem which must be dealt with on the basis of political or moral principle. Nevertheless, this commission did produce a public document which, for the first time, acknowledged with some degree of scholarly authoritativeness the negative impact of commercial television.

THE REDEFINITION OF PROFESSIONAL BOUNDARIES

The search for an applied sociology reasserted itself with renewed energy in 1971. First, the theme of "relevance" which had been so prominent during the years of student activism left its impact of university faculties. In the absence of disruptive student pressures, many sociologists felt obliged to judge their work in terms of this criterion, and, for them, the term "applied sociology" had renewed meaning. Others advocated that relevance could be found for students in the format of fewer years of academic work, easier entrance and exit procedures from college life, or a mixture of work-study programs. They argued that in-service training could better be administrated in occupational, professional, and administrative settings off campus.

Second, pressure for a redefinition of the boundaries of the profession was the result of the reduction of federal support for graduate training plus the projected decline in the demand for Ph.D.'s in sociology. Concern about employment prospects in teaching led to renewed discussion of careers in applied sociology.

Estimating the supply and demand for sociologists is a hazardous task, although it is clear that the demands in the 1970s will be markedly lower than in the 1960s. The trends in the growth in the number of sociologists in the years 1967–71 are most revealing in that they demonstrate a heavy decline in the rate of growth even before the reduction in support for graduate students. The rate of growth of the total membership in the ASA for the years 1966–67 reached over 13% and since has steadily and sharply declined until it was below 5% for 1971.[9]

_____
[9] Closer examination indicates that the greatest growth was in foreign members; for

However, the contemporary concern for an applied sociology rests mainly on factors internal to sociology. It reflects an old and persisting intellectual commitment. It expresses ideological interests and professional concerns about the social role of the man of knowledge which repeatedly come to the forefront. Three self-study reports on the organization of social science and sociology launched in the mid-1960s supply the background for the contemporary debate.

These three reports need to be assessed in terms of the widespread feeling among sociologists that they do not have the prestige, influence, and impact that their knowledge warrants. These self-study groups addressed themselves to this underlying issue as much as to an evaluation of the quality and scholarly character of contemporary sociology—perhaps a more important and antecedent question.

The most comprehensive of these efforts was the so-called BASS report—the Behavioral and Social Sciences Survey Committee—appointed in 1966 by the National Academy's Committee on Science and Public Policy (Social Science Research Council (1969). Beyond a sweeping overview of recent and projected substantive and methodological developments, the committee recommended the recruitment and training of applied behavioral scientists explicitly within the engineering model. The limited intellectual impact of this undertaking can be measured from the almost complete absence of the report from the bibliographies of graduate school instruction and from its failure to generate extensive debate in the professional journals.[10]

The other two reports with a narrower but sharper focus on the utilization of social science research were organized by two officials of the Russell Sage Foundation, which has been deeply concerned with the role of sociology in professional practice. A committee, under Donald Young, was appointed in 1965 by the National Academy of Sciences National Research Council to "review the organization and operation of behavioral sciences programs in the federal government" (1968). Orville Brim, Jr., was chairman of the Special Commission on the Social Sciences of the National Sciences Foundation Board (1969). The pluralism and affluence of the United States is reflected in the organization of three distinct but related study groups. However, these two groups displayed greater recognition than the BASS report to the differences between the social role of

---

1971 almost one-third of the net increase of 657 was foreign. Thus the rate of increase dropped to about 3% for 1971 among Americans; and, in the future, increases among foreign members can be expected to drop as well. While a growing number of sociologists are not members of the ASA, these data indicate a discounting of future demand even before steps were taken to reduce the supply. However, it is, of course, very difficult to judge whether the steps taken in 1970 and 1971 to reduce student enrollment will be effective for any length of time.

[10] For an exception, see Albert Biderman's review, "Self Portrayal" (1970).

the natural and the social sciences and did not espouse simplified programs for training an "applied" behavioral science profession.

On the basis of the inherent logic of sociological inquiry and knowledge, plus the results of past efforts and experiences, there is little reason to assume that sociology will soon develop a strong practice-oriented specialization. A great deal of valuable energy can be lost in such an enterprise which would weaken the intellectual vitality of the profession. On the contrary, there is every reason to assume that sociology will remain basically a staff-oriented profession rooted in academic and education settings. Even more pointed, the bulk of new cohorts of sociologists will remain oriented toward a career in the academic setting. In fact, the key question in the training of new cadres is their appropriate involvement and exposure in nonteaching experiences as part of their training.

Such assumptions do not rule out marked changes and redefinitions in the boundaries of the sociologist as a professional group. Nor does it rule out the likelihood of new roles compatible with a staff orientation or the clarification of old ones. Four problematic areas can be identified.

First, the most probable area of innovation will focus on the central clients—the students of sociology. The underlying question remains: who shall be the students of teaching sociologists. The American Sociological Association has invested considerable effort and government funds in the preparation of teaching materials for high school students, on the belief that these young people should be exposed to sociological materials. There is little evidence to project a marked growth enrolled for sociological instruction at the high school level. In this connection, it is noteworthy that a variety of sociologists of different theoretical and methodological persuasions—James Coleman, Albert J. Reiss, Jr., and David Riesman, for example—have expressed strong reservations about sociology in the high schools. New directions will likely extend sociological instruction to more mature students, students in professional schools, adults in the midst of their occupational careers, and students entering or reentering post high school institutions after work and community experience. Old directions will continue to mean that sociology will provide one form of liberal or general education for students entering a variety of occupations, especially those in the public sector.

Second, it appears likely that there will be some growth in nonacademic research centers which may have a limited number of new posts for sociologists. In particular, a major development in the sociological enterprise both for the needs of the discipline and for public and social policy will be the expansion of large-scale data collection centers and laboratories concerned with trend analysis or social indicators as the term is currently being used (Horowitz 1968). The period ahead parallels the introduction of sociologically trained demographers into the Bureau of the Census and other governmental agencies in the 1930s. For data collection and analysis of social indicators, the sociologist will share responsibilities with the social statistician.

Third, sociologists will continue to be drawn into various consultative services. However, the role of either full-time or permanent consultant for a sociologist remains unstable and difficult to institutionalize (Wilensky 1956). Instead, sociologists are likely to serve as consultants for short-term and specific assignments. Sociologists from academic and educational settings will be the main source of such personnel; therefore, their services require an ethic which will not distort their teacher-researcher role. Interestingly enough, discontinuous and limited consultation can insure higher standards, and the responsible sociologist must publish the findings he accumulates from such experiences, with due regard to the rights of the individuals involved. The role of the sociological consultant in the enlightenment model can be seen as an extension of the teacher-researcher.

Roland L. Warren in *Social Research Consultation* (1963) has incisively explicated the professional responsibility of the sociologist both to his clients and to social science, and has underlined the central implication of the enlightenment model that consultation is not "hackwork" by lesser minds, but involves conceptual analysis and the creative role analogous to the outstanding teacher. "For if the research consultant is to honor his obligation to the client organization, as well as to behavior science and research methodology, he must not only be aware of the need for conceptual analysis of the social process in which he and the client system are involved, but must develop the social interaction skills which this dynamic conception of the research consultation demands" (Warren 1963, p. 141).

In the consultative role, the sociological equivalent of the public defender has not developed; a central issue is to make available consultative services to groups not familiar with such resources or unable to engage such talents. Minority organizations, labor unions, cooperative and community agencies do not have adequate access to existing social research facilities. New independent agencies, and essentially nonprofit ones, have been gradually developing to meet such needs. Thus, for example, under the leadership of Kenneth Clark and Hylan Lewis, a Center for Applied Metropolitan Research has been established in New York City to focus on social issues for the black community.[11]

---

[11] One is struck by the fact that various community leaders are aware of the need for professional standards. At a 1971 conference on community organization, a militant black community leader requested a well-known white sociologist to undertake a piece of research which would evaluate the effectiveness of an experimental education program in which he was deeply involved. When the sociologist raised the question of research access, the black community leader indicated that he felt that such problems could be overcome by *tact* and patience, but he insisted that the result of the study

Fourth, it remains to be seen whether the professional associations of sociologists will develop and modernize the contributions made by earlier public commissions. The American Sociological Association in 1968 established a Committee on Social Policy which was charged with this type of objective but failed to formulate effective procedures. However, there is real promise in the format of a professional equivalent of the British Royal Commission, which would seek to assess the policy implications of social research. The objective—majority and minority reports where agreement cannot be readily achieved—is not to collect new data but to synthesize existing findings and draw attention to alternative policy implications. Such a mechanism would in effect be implementing the enlightenment "model" since it would not be limited to a particular client but would be related to a series of broad publics and would not seek to displace the role of elected officials or institutional leaders.

Albert Biderman has argued that "as they [the social sciences] have become larger and more consequential, they have increasingly become objects of public attention: the social sciences themselves have become social issues" (Biderman 1970, p. 1064). Such a formulation tends to underemphasize the extent to which, in the past, sociology as an academic and staff profession has been subject to internal and external controversy.

Contemporary controversy about the social and professional roles of sociologists reflect the social and political tensions of the larger society. No doubt, new elements in the debate include the sheer growth and increased visibility of sociologists. Before World War II, most sociologists felt that the maintenance of academic freedom was their crucial and essential professional problem. Of this period, Everett Hughes has written, sociologists realized that their sociological theories were critical of the existing mores (Hughes 1970). Sociology and the teaching of sociology have supplied life space for students who were from particularistic subcultures and who were seeking entrance into the larger cosmopolitan world. He spoke of teaching as a kind of field work; the intellectual endeavor and the intellectual experiences were liberating for teacher and student.

In the contemporary scene, conflicting notions of the consequences of social knowledge and extra-university obligations have emerged as of equal or greater importance. Social and political movements have arisen within the university which called into question the traditional format of the sociologist as teacher-researcher. In the well-known extreme version, the

---

would have to be submitted to a professional journal for publication. As an explanation, he indicated that "if I go out and hire a commercial research organization—white or black—to work on a black community problem, they will very likely give me the answers they think I want to hear. Only if I get your professional self-interest involved will I know that the results are worthwhile; and if you are going to publish them, I know that they will be good and that you will not run out when the heat gets turned off."

intellectual effort of the university is seen in opposition to revolutionary change. While such an outlook commands very little support, it is the view held by campus activists—both faculty and student—that if it is to survive, the university must be a direct and immediate agency of social and political change. It is not enough, they say, for the university to be an indirect source of change through teaching and research. Such a viewpoint draws on the traditions of the land grant universities and their orientation toward public service. The specific recommendations are numerous and any assessment of their implications is a complex task, but for the purposes at hand it needs to be emphasized that there is often a persistent element of mistrust of reason in such formulations and recommendations.

Reinhard Bendix has argued that the form and content of modern sociology, because it has engendered a mistrust of reason, has contributed to the undermining of its own enterprise and of the university in general. No doubt, sociology and the university can be faulted for many major errors, one being the endless pressure for expansion. Sociology may also have neglected to place sufficient emphasis on key topics such as the social and psychological preconditions for a democratic society. But I believe that the reverse of Bendix's argument may be even more correct. The impact of sociology, it can be argued, has been to contain and reduce the mistrust and revolt against reason. Without a vigorous sociological inquiry in the enlightenment model, the essentials for a free society are weakened. If sociologists perfect their discipline, and understand that they are part of a staff-oriented profession—academic and nonacademic—and if they assume their responsibilities to their various publics, they will make their maximum impact and contribution. We are not dealing with a Hegelian dialectic in which rational inquiry produces its own seeds of self-destruction but a pragmatic thrust in which human motives and voluntaristic commitments fashion and are fashioned by rational pursuits.

REFERENCES

Abrams, Philip. 1968. *The Origins of British Sociology, 1834–1914.* University of Chicago Press Heritage Series. Chicago: University of Chicago Press.

Ben-David, Joseph. 1972. *American Higher Education: Directions Old and New.* New York: McGraw-Hill.

Biderman, Albert. 1970. "Self Portrayal." *Science* 169 (September): 1064–67.

Chicago Commission on Race Relations. 1922. *The Negro in Chicago: A Study of Race Relations and a Race Riot.* Chicago: University of Chicago.

Clemmer, Donald. 1940. *The Prison Community.* Boston: Christopher.

Coleman, James. 1970. "Reply to Cain and Watts." *American Sociological Review* 35, no. 2 (April): 242–49.

Davis, Jerome. 1940. "The Sociologist and Social Action." *American Sociological Review* 5 (April): 171–76.

Duncan, Otis Dudley. 1969. "Social Forecasting: The State of the Art." *Public Interest*, no. 17 (Fall), pp. 88–119.

Evan, William M. 1962. "Role Strain and the Norm of Reciprocity in Research Organizations." *American Journal of Sociology* 68, no. 3 (November): 346–54.

Freud, Sigmund. 1949. *Collected Papers.* Vol. 2. London: Hogarth.

Goffman, Erving. 1962. *Asylums.* Chicago: Aldine.

Goode, William J. 1960. "Encroachment, Charlatanism, and the Emerging Profession: Psychology, Sociology, and Medicine." *American Sociological Review* 25 (December): 902–14.

Gouldner, Alvin. 1956. "Explorations in Applied Social Science." *Social Problems* 3 (January): 169–81.

———. 1957. "Theoretical Requirements of the Applied Social Sciences." *American Sociological Review* 22, no. 1 (February): 92–102.

Graham, Hugh Davis, and Ted Robert Gurr. 1969. *Violence in America: Historical and Comparative Perspectives.* Washington, D.C.: Government Printing Office.

Hauser, Philip. 1949. "Social Science and Social Engineering." *Philosophy of Science* 16, no. 3:161–81.

Hollis, Ernest V. 1945. *Toward Improving Ph.D. Programs.* Washington, D.C.: American Council in Education.

Hopper, Janice. 1967. "Preliminary Report on Salaries and Selected Characteristics of Sociologists in the 1966 National Science Foundation Register of Scientific and Technical Personnel." *American Sociologist* 2, no. 3 (August): 152–55.

Horowitz, Irving Louis. 1968. *Professing Sociology: Studies in the Life Cycle of Social Science.* Chicago: Aldine.

Howerth, Ira W. 1894. "Present Condition of Sociology in the United States." *Annals of the American Academy of Political and Social Sciences* 5 (September): 260–69.

Hughes, Everett Cherrington. 1958. *Men and Their Work.* Glencoe, Ill.: Free Press.

———. 1970. "Teaching as Fieldwork." *American Sociologist* 5, no. 1 (February): 13–19.

Hughes, Stuart. 1958. *Consciousness and Society.* New York: Vintage Books, Random House.

Janowitz, Morris. 1970. *Political Conflict.* Chicago: Quadrangle.

———. 1971. *Institution Building in Urban Education.* Chicago: University of Chicago Press.

Karl, Barry D. 1968. "The Power of Intellect and the Politics of Ideas." *Daedalus* 97 (Summer): 1002–35.

———. 1969. "Presidential Planning and Social Science Research: Mr. Hoover's Experts." In *Perspectives in American History III,* edited by Donald Fleming and Bernard Bailyn. Cambridge, Mass.: Harvard University Press.

Leuba, James H. 1921. *The Belief in God and Immortality.* Chicago: Open Court.

McRae, Duncan. 1970. "Social Science and the Source of Policy: 1951–1970." *Political Scientist* 3, no. 3 (Summer): 294–310.

Myrdal, Gunnar. 1944. *An American Dilemma.* Vols. 1 and 2. New York: Harper.

National Academy of Sciences. 1968. *The Behavioral Sciences and the Federal Government.* NAS Publication 1680. Washington, D.C.: Government Printing Office.

National Science Foundation, Special Commission on the Social Sciences of the National Foundation Board. 1969. *Knowledge into Action: Improving the Nation's Use of the Social Sciences.* Washington, D.C.: National Science Foundation.

Nisbet, Robert A. 1966. *The Sociological Tradition.* New York: Basic.

Ogburn, William F. 1922. *Social Change.* New York: Huebsch.

Ohlin, Lloyd. 1960. "Conflicting Interests in Correctional Objectives." In Richard A. Cloward et al., *Theoretical Studies in Social Organizations of the Prison.* New York: Social Science Research Council.

Park, Robert E., and Ernest W. Burgess. 1924 [1969]. *Introduction to the Science of Sociology.* 3d ed., rev. University of Chicago Press Heritage Series. Chicago: University of Chicago Press.

Peterson, Richard A. 1971. "Review Symposium." *American Sociological Review* 36, No. 2 (April): 326–28.

President's Research Committee on Social Trends. 1933. *Recent Social Trends in the United States.* New York: McGraw-Hill.

Riley, Matilda White. 1960. "Membership of the American Sociological Association, 1950–1959." *American Sociological Review* 25 (December): 914–26.

Schneider, Louis, ed. 1967. *The Scottish Moralists on Human Nature.* University of Chicago Heritage Series. Chicago: University of Chicago Press.

Sheldon, Eleanor Bernert, and Wilbert E. Moore. 1968. *Indicators of Social Change.* New York: Russell Sage Foundation.

Shils, Edward A. 1949. "Social Science and Social Policy." *Philosophy of Science* 16, no. 3:219–42.

———. 1970. "Tradition, Ecology and Institution in the History of Sociology." *Daedalus* 99, no. 4 (Fall): 760–826.

Sibley, Elbridge. 1963. *The Education of Sociologists in the United States.* New York: Russell Sage Foundation.

Social Science Research Council. 1969. *The Behavioral and Social Sciences: Outlook and Needs.* A Report by the Behavioral and Social Sciences Survey Committee under the auspices of the Committee on Science and Public Policy, National Academy of Sciences, and the Committee on Problems and Policy. Englewood Cliffs, N.J.: Prentice-Hall.

Sprehe, J. T. 1967. *The Climate of Opinion in Sociology: A Study of the Professional Values and Belief Systems of Sociologists.* Ph.D. diss., Washington University. Ann Arbor, Mich.: University Microfilms.

Street, David, Robert D. Vinter, and Charles Perrow. 1966. *Organization for Treatment.* New York: Free Press.

Sykes, Gresham. 1958. *The Society of Captives; a Study of a Maximum Security Prison.* Princeton, N.J.: Princeton University Press.

Thurstone, L. L. 1928. "The Measurement of Opinion." *Journal of Abnormal and Social Psychology* 22:415–30.

Tiryakian, Edward A., ed. 1971. *The Phenomenon of Sociology.* New York: Appleton-Century-Crofts.

U.S. Public Health Service, The Surgeon-General's Scientific Advisory Committee on Television and Social Behavior. 1972. *Television and Growing Up: The Impact of Televised Violence.* Washington, D.C.: Government Printing Office.

Warren, Roland L. 1963. *Social Research Consultation.* New York: Russell Sage Foundation.

Wilensky, Harold L. 1956. *Intellectuals in Labor Unions.* Glencoe, Ill.: Free Press.

Young, Donald. 1955. "Sociology and the Practicing Professions." *American Sociological Review* 20, no. 6 (December) 642–48.

Znaniecki, Florian. 1940. *The Social Role of the Man of Knowledge.* Julius Beer Foundation Lecture. New York: Columbia University Press.

On Gouldner's *Crisis of Western Sociology*[1]

John K. Rhoads
Northern Illinois University

The Coming Crisis of Western Sociology (1970), by Alvin W. Gouldner, is a highly provocative and stimulating work about the development of sociological theory and may prove to have an influence on the future development of that subject. After analyzing a few of the dominant social theories from the beginning of the 19th century to the present, Gouldner concludes that sociology is presently in the early stages of crisis.

He contends that every social theory has an "infrastructure" consisting of a number of "domain assumptions" learned by the person before he became a sociologist, which, although not a part of the theory, leave an indelible imprint upon it (p. 46). These domain assumptions concern conceptions of the nature of man and society, such as that men are rational or that social problems will correct themselves without planned intervention. They may reflect value judgments as well as purely testable assertions. The infrastructure affects not only the way a theorist constructs a theory and what it states but also its chances for acceptance by some audience, whose own domain assumptions it may or may not "resonate" (pp. 39–40). Gouldner goes on to contend that when dissonance occurs between the infrastructure of a hitherto accepted theory and a rising structure of antithetical assumptions, the science in question is ripe for crisis (p. 34). And, according to Gouldner, this is what is now happening to sociology.

Since *The Coming Crisis* treats of ideas central to the discipline, sociologists need to take the work seriously, scrutinize it closely, and evaluate it carefully. Despite its importance for sociology and the provocativeness of its conclusions, however, the work contains serious errors about the development of social theory that can leave misleading impressions about social theory and its future direction. To correct these impressions, I hope, with the use of documentation drawn largely from the original works of the theorists Gouldner discusses, to disclose some of these errors. Second, I want to dispute Gouldner's conclusions about an impending crisis in sociology. The second of these objectives is related to the first insofar as Gouldner bases his conclusions about the crisis on his analysis of the development of social theory.

[1] I am grateful to Professor Eleanor Godfrey for her helpful review of the style and substance of this manuscript.

SOCIOLOGICAL POSITIVISM AS A COUNTERBALANCE
TO UTILITARIANISM

In his model[2] of the development of western sociology, Gouldner contends
that the social theory of the first period, the period of the sociological
positivism of Saint-Simon and Auguste Comte, was constructed to a large
extent as a counterbalance to the cultural utilitarianism of the middle
class. Gouldner distinguishes cultural utilitarianism as a technical philosophy, and concludes that it was cultural utilitarianism that stimulated the
theories of Saint-Simon and Comte rather than the philosophical utilitarianism of Jeremy Bentham and John Stuart Mill. The prinicipal characteristic of cultural utilitarianism was the importance of utility as a
standard of evaluation, according to which men were to judge others by
what they achieved rather than who they were. With the rise of the
bourgeoisie, achievement supplanted ascription as a dominant value, for
the middle class successfully opposed the value of utility to the ascribed
values of the aristocrats (pp. 61–65).

The rise of utilitarianism, however, brought forth some dire consequences. The evaluation of actions according to how effectively they
achieved certain goals introduced relativity into men's thinking, weakening
traditional standards (p. 66). If one action failed to achieve a goal, no
matter how much it conformed to tradition, the thing to do was to substitute another action that would achieve the objective. Thus, moral judgments were subordinated to cognitive ones; the focus of action shifted to
the achievement of useful objectives, and purely technical requirements
became uppermost (pp. 66–67). As an efficacious means to attain ends,
power became divorced from morality, for the attainment of an end was
what mattered and not the morality of the end or the means by which
it was attained (pp. 84–85). In sum, in its preoccupation with success and
failure the utilitarian thinking of that period possessed an inbuilt disposition toward anomie, Gouldner says.

He goes on to say, moreover, that the unique historical context of this
utilitarian-produced anomie was Restorationist France. The collapse of
the Old Regime after the French Revolution and the decay of the
church's moral authority both contributed to the need for new beliefs.
Men had to know what kind of society France should be, but the Restorationist elites and the middle class held divergent ideas. Thus, the need
to remake France and the need to counteract the anomic pathology of the
cultural utilitarianism of the middle class presented social theory with the

---

[2] The discussion of Gouldner's work must be selective, for it is not possible to deal
with all of even his major arguments. Of his major points I have chosen those that
are debatable and particularly those that are most crucial to his case for a crisis in
sociology.

John K. Rhoads

task of remapping the social world and, through reducing ambiguity and anxiety, making it whole once again (pp. 83–84).

Saint-Simon and Comte heartily responded to this twofold challenge with their theories of sociological positivism. Positivistic sociology, particularly in Comte's version, presented the middle class with a mapmaking technique based on scientific method, on the one hand, and a religion of humanity, on the other. The religion of humanity congenially resonated with individuals' needs for new moral beliefs, and the mapmaking system resonated with their commitment to the scientific method that was winning allegiance. Thus, the origin of social theory was informed by certain domain assumptions and unfulfilled sentiments of the middle class.[3]

Utilitarianism and the problems it posed reappeared in the future development of social theory. As Gouldner sees it, the importance of utility was reaffirmed in the functionalist theory of classical sociology (pp. 124, 133), and the attempt to remap the social world in order to unify it was later evident in the social theory of Talcott Parsons (pp. 199–209). Thus, the domain assumptions of the theory of the first period of Western sociology continued to influence sociology as it evolved.

Since the middle-class orientation of social theory in the founding period is a central point made by Gouldner, a closer look at Comte's intentions and his audience may prove revealing. In a letter to the czar of Russia, Comte stated: "In France my attitude as a philosopher is necessarily anomalous, *because the unfitness of the upper class obliges me habitually to appeal to the lower*; a course which gives a revolutionary colour to the best counsels [italics mine]. In Eastern Europe alone can enlightened theories now find chiefs disposed to appreciate and able to utilize them. This contrast is a natural result of Western anarchy" (Comte 1876, p. xxiv). That Comte was concerned with appealing as much to the working class as to the middle is also the opinion of W. M. Simon,[4] who contends that in Comte's view the workingmen and women were ripe for a new philosophical appeal because their minds had not been contaminated by metaphysics (1963, p. 11).[5] In the preface to *The Catechism of Positive*

[3] Gouldner admits that Saint-Simon and Comte wrote within a political context that also included the aristocrats, but on balance their principal target was the middle class (pp. 91, 106, 111): "After the sprawling genius of Saint Simon, Western Sociology underwent a kind of 'binary fission' into two sociologies. . . . One was Comte's program for a 'pure' sociology . . . the university sociology of the middle class, that achieved its fullest institutional development in the United States. The other was the sociology of Karl Marx, the party sociology of intellectuals oriented toward the proletariat" (p. 111).

[4] Simon, an intellectual historian, has researched the history of positivism subsequent to Comte's death.

[5] Simon compiled an occupational breakdown of a positivist group of about 200 in

138

Religion, Comte designated as positivism's "true social audience" women and "proletaries," who were the only groups able to appreciate the need for a new philosophy. Hence, it was necessary to acquaint the public with philosophical terms (1883, pp. 9–10).

The fact is that Comte did press his case for a reconstructed society to a wider audience than the middle class. His writings reveal his trust in the working class's ability to play a crucial role in the new society—a role that could not be fulfilled by the more privileged members of society, who, contaminated by false philosophies, had already demonstrated their incompetence in official positions. There is little doubt that Comte intended to "resonate" his theories in the minds of middle-class individuals, but this was not his only audience; to argue for the middle class as a selective focus of his work is to mistake the part for the whole of his orientation.[6]

We must also be dubious of Gouldner's attempt to connect sociological positivism with the unique historical context of Restorationist France alone. According to Gouldner's formulations, the construction of a theory is affected not only by its infrastructure but also by its chances for acceptance; the theorist and his receptive audience share domain assumptions (pp. 39–40). In the light of these formulations it is instructive to note positivism's diffusion to England. There Richard Congreve became the founder of a formally organized Positivist Church in 1870. It was precisely the religious element of Comte's philosophy that fascinated Congreve. Simon quotes Congreve as saying, "It is a new religion I am engaged in putting forward and . . . I claim as much as the ministers of the existing faiths" (1963, p. 49).

Although there was a school of orthodox positivists in France after Comte's death, a brand of positivism that rejected the organized religion of humanity also appeared there around the leadership of Émile Littré. Congreve's church in England and Littré's positivism in France are cases which argue against Gouldner's explanation of sociological positivism. Although the social structure of England was *not* shattered by a revolution as occurred in France, Comte's religion diffused to England through Congreve's church. On the other hand, the purely secular elements of Comte's philosophy persisted in France under Littré despite the presumed need for a new religion after the destruction of the old order by the French Revolution.

Another of Gouldner's conjectures about sociological positivism deserves comment. He conjectures that society's failure to accept and institutionalize

---

France and found that 25% were manual workers. Although certainly not definitive, these figures indicate that workers were receptive to Comte's positivism (Simon 1963, pp. 69–70).

[6] A distinction must be made between the class position of the theorist and the class whose domain assumptions the theory resonates. Gouldner is concerned with the latter.

John K. Rhoads

Comte's religion of humanity was one of the factors that led to the adoption of value neutrality by social theory. According to Gouldner, value neutrality was the "anomic adaptation" by the positivists to their own political failure and their political impotence (p. 102). Frustrated in the political arena, the Comtean faction of positivism relinquished the grand design of the religion of humanity to become exclusively preoccupied with the methodology of map making instead of the map itself. As a result, value neutrality and the idea of sociology as a science became institutionalized in the academic sociology of the classical period.

This conclusion is questionable. It is not true that positivism relinquished the map-making function of religion when it failed to win the latter's acceptance, for the religion of humanity was retained by some positivists in France down to World War I (Simon 1963, pp. 68–69). In addition, the notion of value neutrality was not institutionalized in the sociology of the classical period insofar as Emile Durkheim subscribed to a science of ethics (Durkheim 1964a, chap. 3). Durkheim's well-known attempt to establish scientific rules to distinguish normal from pathological elements in society was inconsistent with value neutrality and consistent with Comte's philosophy.

THE CLASSICAL PERIOD

The reaction of social theory to middle-class utilitarianism continues into the classical period, according to Gouldner's reconstruction. Although the two theorists of this period were Emile Durkheim and Max Weber, Gouldner's analysis is directed primarily to the former. The centrality of utility continues into classical sociology and lays the foundation of Durkheim's theory of functionalism.

Functional theory required that the sociologist explain a social fact with reference to its contributions to the maintenance of other institutions—in other words, with reference to its utility. It asserted that if an institution survives, the latter must be contributing to social welfare in some way. One obvious set of social facts contributing to society's maintenance is moral values that restrain men's appetites, regulate occupational roles, and urge the poor to be content. In Durkheim's version of functional theory moral values reduce anomie. The search for functions replaced traditional legitimations of institutions with the legitimation of usefulness. The domain assumption that for an institution to be legitimate it had to be useful resonated congenially with the sentiments of the bourgeoisie (pp. 119–24). At the same time, the assumption joined utility with morality within the theory itself.[7]

[7] Gouldner recognizes that Weber, the other major classical sociologist, took a different view of the role of moral values and of functionalism from the views of Durkheim.

140

Furthermore, functional sociology of this period was absent in Britain, but the theory appeared in British anthropology instead. The explanation of functionalism's absence in British sociology, states Gouldner, is to be found in the peculiar development of the class struggle in Britain. Because the middle class feared the French Revolution and the working-class movement, it accommodated itself to the aristocracy rather than opposing it as in France (p. 125). With the middle class and the aristocracy fused into one composite ruling elite, middle-class utilitarianism did not come to dominate British culture; hence, a functional sociology of industrial systems did not find a congenial structure of sentiments with which to resonate. However, a functional anthropology, developed by Malinowski and Radcliffe-Brown, was attuned to Great Britain's colonial concerns (Gouldner 1970, pp. 131–34).

There is little doubt of the functionalist perspective in Durkheim's social theory (1964a, pp. 95–97), nor is there any doubt of the centrality of moral values (1964b, pp. 129–30; 1951, pp. 209–16, 321–25). Gouldner is correct. Nevertheless, there is another side to Durkheim's treatment of values, which Gouldner, in his enthusiasm to relate the stress on moral values to cultural utilitarianism, fails to consider. In *Suicide* Durkheim observed that too great a consensus on moral values leads to negative consequences, one of which is high rates of altruistic suicide (1951, pp. 220–21). An overintegrated society has a stultifying effect on the personality, and there is "feeble individuation itself"—an observation that softens somewhat his stress on moral consensus.[8] In short, Durkheim chose a middle ground between the extremes of moral laxity and moral overregulation.

Furthermore, Gouldner's interpretation of the role of utility in functional theory becomes questionable when we consider Durkheim's analysis of religion. In this classic study, Durkheim defined religion as those beliefs and rites relative to sacred things which unite into a moral community those who adhere to them (1961, p. 62). He drew a sharp distinction between sacred and profane things, the latter distinguishable from the former not by degree but by kind. Sacred things inspire the kind of respect that precludes considerations of utility: "We say that an object . . . inspires respect when the representation expressing it in the mind is gifted with such a force that it automatically causes or inhibits actions, *without regard for any considerations relative to their useful or injurious effects.* When we obey somebody because of the moral authority . . . we are not determined by the advantages or inconveniences of the attitude which is prescribed or

---

[8] Durkheim wrote: "In the order of existence, no good is measureless. . . . So with social phenomena. If, as we have seen, excessive individuation leads to suicide, insufficient individuation has the same effects. When man has become detached from society, he encounters less resistance to suicide in himself, and he does so likewise when social integration is too strong" (1951, p. 217).

recommended to us" (Durkheim 1961, pp. 237–38). Sacred things are also symbols of society and its rules of morality (1961, pp. 236, 244–45).

This religious focus of Durkheim's functional theory contrasts dramatically with Gouldner's interpretation of functionalism as legitimating social arrangements strictly in terms of their usefulness. The purely nonutilitarian aspect of Durkheim's theory is further revealed in the importance he attached to religious ritual. By failing to call attention to these aspects, Gouldner exaggerates the utilitarian emphasis in Durkheim's work.

Although it is true, as Gouldner observes, that classical sociology was weakly developed in Great Britain, the contention that a functional sociology was absent is not true. Herbert Spencer not only designated as a task of sociology to interpret the development, structure, and functions of social aggregates as produced by individuals' actions (Rumney 1965, p. 24), but he also put this methodological precept into practice. He noted the similarities between an organism and a society and proceeded to show how the differentiations of various structures fulfill functions in evolving societies and how such differentiations are paralleled in organisms. In line with his functional focus, Spencer explained the origin of institutions not by men's intentions but by society's structural and functional exigencies (Spencer 1967, pp. 135–42).

Once again a cross-cultural comparison makes one hessitate to accept Gouldner's explanation of social theory as a reaction to utilitarianism. Strong anti-utilitarian elements appear in Durkheim's classical sociology, and strong functional elements appear in social theory in Great Britain, whose class structure, according to Gouldner, militated against utilitarianism.

However, Gouldner points out that there was another ingredient in the context of classical sociology besides utilitarianism-Marxism. After Saint-Simon's death, sociology bifurcated into the Comtean positivism and classical sociology of the West and the Marxist sociology of Eastern Europe. Marxism became a prime target of the classical theorists because it threatened the middle class, Gouldner states (p. 116).

Classical sociology's anti-Marxist polemic was evident in Durkheim's approach to the problem of solidarity in industrial societies. Gouldner contends (pp. 248–51) that Durkheim recognized a defect in the institution of private property. The trouble was that this institution frequently mismatches the talents of individuals with the requirements of occupations,[9] and this "forced" division of labor undermines solidarity. Nevertheless, Durkheim retreated from a more extended analysis of property and turned his attention instead to the lack of consensus on moral beliefs as the cause of industrial societies' troubles. This direction of his thought

[9] An example of such a mismatch is an individual who inherits a factory but who lacks the capability to run it (Durkheim 1962, pp. 15–16).

eventuated in his celebrated notion of anomie. Gouldner attributes great importance to Durkheim's retreat from his initial critique of private property. The reason for the turnabout, Gouldner argues, was that to continue this critique would have placed Durkheim in the uncomfortable position of being on the side of the socialists from whom he was striving to differentiate academic sociology.[10]

Durkheim's *Socialism* reveals the dubiousness of this explanation. In his discussion of Saint-Simon's proposals for a reorganized society, it becomes clear that what distressed him about the latter's proposals was not Saint-Simon's policies on property[11] but rather his vision of a society devoted solely to the encouragement of economic appetites. Durkheim believed that strivings to fulfill such appetites completely are futile, since appetites can easily be multiplied more rapidly than an economy can provide for them. What was lacking in Saint-Simon's vision was a mechanism to restrain men's appetites and adjust them to the possibility of fulfillment (Durkheim 1962, pp. 235–47).

THE ATTACK ON MARXISM AND THE DEFENSE OF CAPITALISM

Gouldner's title for the contemporary period of historical reconstruction is Parsonsian Structural-Functionalism. The title makes it obvious that, in his view, Talcott Parsons is its dominant theorist. The principal elements in the sociohistorical context to which Parsonsian theory responded were World War I, the Soviet Revolution, the rise of fascist movements, and the world depression (p. 144). These events made the international middle class anxious, and Gouldner argues that it became Parsons's task to create a theory that would restore their confidence in the traditional social order and, more specifically, in capitalism (pp. 145–48). If this explanation of Parsonsian structural-functionalism proves correct, Gouldner will have gone a long way in demonstrating the conservative infrastructure of the contemporary period's most influential theory.

Parsons's attempt to defend capitalism and provide an alternative to the Marxian challenge to capitalism assumed the form of his voluntaristic theory of action, which he later elaborated into his comprehensive systems theory. Gouldner singles out two facets of the voluntaristic and systems theories as contributing to the defense of capitalism and the subversion of

---

[10] Gouldner puts the matter as follows: "If Durkheim had followed up his own lead on the forced division of labor . . . it would have been difficult to tell the difference between Durkheim and Jaurès. If modern Functionalism had pursued Durkheim's critique of the forced division of labor, it too would have to move toward *some* form of socialism" (p. 250).

[11] Saint-Simon did not propose to disposess wealthy "idlers" of their property but merely to exclude them from the exercise of political power (Durkheim 1962, p. 175).

Marxism's appeal. They are the antideterministic tendency of the voluntaristic theory and the emphasis on interdependence of his systems theory.

Gouldner infers (pp. 180–83) that the early Parsons was disturbed that both Werner Sombart and Max Weber agreed with Marx that capitalism is a deterministic system—one that coerced businessmen into seeking profit by exploiting others. This determinism placed capitalism in a bad light; Parsons created an antideterministic theory to restore capitalism's vitality, Gouldner says. The antideterminism of the voluntaristic theory is manifest in the assumption "that men's efforts always make a difference in what happens"; men's actions are shaped by their desires, volitions, choices, and strivings. Furthermore, the choices and strivings of men are oriented to moral values. In the final analysis it is conformity to value systems that makes a difference in society; capitalistic man, therefore, can once again control his destiny (Gouldner 1970, pp. 185–86).

However, Parsons imposed an important qualification on the idea that men's strivings enable them to control their fates. As Gouldner interprets Parsons, men's actions make a difference in what happens, but seldom do their actions actually achieve their goals (pp. 189–90), for there are always unintended consequences of actions. Men are free to strive but not necessarily free to achieve what they strive for. This conclusion, states Gouldner, provided an apt lesson for men in a depression, for it encouraged them to strive to make the capitalist system work. At the same time it admonished New Deal reformers not to go too far because outcomes are not predictable (p. 194). The system was not to be disrupted, for ameliorating changes may be fraught with unpredictable and perilous consequences.

Before proceeding further with Gouldner's analysis of the infrastructure of Parsons's theory, let me reply to his observations about this antideterminism. The only proof he offers for his interpretation is a simple quotation from Parsons: "An end, then, in the analytical sense must be defined as the difference between the anticipated future state of affairs and that which it could have been predicted would ensue from the initial situation *without the agency of the actor having intervened*" (p. 197, n. 17). Gouldner's inference that Parsons implied from this that men rarely achieve their goal is a mistake. In *The Structure of Social Action* Parsons defines an end as the difference between what would have occurred had the actor failed to act and what would occur as a result of his having acted.[12] The difference in outcome may be both foreseen and desired by the actor, and the formulation is consistent with the possibility of an actor's having achieved his

---

[12] "An end, for these purposes, is a future state of affairs to which action is oriented by virtue of the fact that it is deemed desirable by the actor(s) but which differs in important respects from the state which they would expect to supervene by merely allowing the predictable trends of the situation to take their course without active intervention" (Parsons 1949, p. 75).

end. A footnote on the same page clarified why Parsons defined an end this way: "to include the maintenance of an existing state of affairs as an end, as well as the bringing into being of a state differing from the initial situation" (1949, p. 75, n. 1). Thus, if an actor predicts that a given state of affairs will be maintained without his acting to intervene, and if this state is his end, by refusing to act he will attain his goal. Parsons's definition here does not imply that men seldom achieve their goals but just the opposite.

Furthermore, in the same work, Parsons set forth an "analytical law," which states: "In any concrete system of action a process of change so far as it is at all explicable in terms . . . of the intrinsic means-ends relationship can proceed only . . . toward the realization of the rational norms conceived as binding on the actors in the system. That is, more briefly, such a process of action can proceed only in the direction of . . . rationality" (1949, p. 751). Parsons means by this, following Weber, that there is a trend toward the realization of men's ends in those action systems where there is a conscious attempt to be rational (1949, p. 752). These formulations render questionable Gouldner's interpretation that men do not often achieve their goals.

Gouldner advances another reason for his conclusion of an anti-Marxian infrastructure. Whereas the Marxian model is a single-factor one in which the economy generates a diversity of effects, the Parsonsian systems theory is a multifactor one in which every variable affects every other. This is the familiar notion of interdependence (Gouldner 1970, pp. 228–29, 346–47). Conceiving of society as an interdependence of parts avoids the difficult problem of causal priority and the weighting of the factors. Change is made difficult because the reformer has no direction as to what powerful "levers" of the society he may grasp to change it (pp. 226–29, 346–47).[13] Here again, Gouldner states, the theory discourages a restructuring of capitalism.

In replying to Gouldner, I note that Parsons posits a hierarchical order of control. At the highest level is the cultural system, which controls the social system, which in turn controls the personality system, which finally controls the behavioral organism (Parsons 1961, p. 38). Paralleling this hierarchy of cybernetic control among these systems is the hierarchy of control of functions *within* the social system. The hierarchy of functions from highest to lowest in accordance with their relevance to the problems confronted by the system is: pattern maintenance, integration, goal attainment, and adaptation (Parsons 1961, p. 38). It is therefore not true that Parsons's model consists of an unqualified interdependence without causal

---

[13] It should be noted, however, that Gouldner qualifies his observation that Parsons's theory fails to state causes, for shared moral values are central (p. 230).

priority, for these are parallel hierarchies which rank the controlling elements. Nor is this ranking peripheral to the theory, for Parsons advances it as the third of three "essential axes of theoretical analysis," the others being the structural-functional and the dynamic axes. The theory, therefore, *does* yield clues to the levers of change, namely, the values and norms of the pattern-maintenance function. In addition, Parsons takes the position that a multideterminism is compatible with planned change (1960, pp. 156–57).

There is little doubt that causal determinism is built into Parsons's theory. The voluntaristic theory was created as a synthesis of the causal-functional elements of the positivistic theory of action, on the one hand, and the symbolic-meaningful elements of the idealistic theory on the other (Parsons 1949, pp. 81–82, 486, 698–719). The causal elements from positivism are the conditions of action and the technically adequate means to attain the end of the action. If one knows the conditions, means, ends, and norms, he can understand the action and predict its course. In this sense the action is determined.

Insofar as Gouldner's case for a conservative infrastructure underlying Parsonsian structural-functionalism rests on the pillars of antideterminism and system interdependence with causal priority, the preceding arguments undermine his case. There is little evidence that the voluntaristic and systems theories were developed as an anti-Marxist, pro-capitalist attempt, and Gouldner's evidence cannot withstand criticism.

THE SACRIFICE OF INDIVIDUAL AUTONOMY TO THE SOCIAL ORDER

Gouldner continues his analysis of Parsonsian theory by observing that the latter creates an image of society as a unity by relating every part of the system to the whole (pp. 211–12). With a focus on the whole rather than the parts, Gouldner interprets Parsons as saying that individuals pursue ends originating not within themselves but within the system. Men are hollowed-out shells into which the substance of society is poured, with a consequent reduction of friction between the individual and society. Society is a delicately balanced, self-regulating mechanism. Adaptive mechanisms that maintain its boundaries come into play spontaneously and automatically, seemingly apart from the intentions of individuals (pp. 346, 231–32). As problems arise, adjustive mechanisms restore equilibrium spontaneously. One such mechanism is socialization, which "fills" the individual with the experiences of the social system, Gouldner tells us Parsons says (pp. 218–19). Through the socialization process the individual is carefully trained to exercise restraint over his desires for material gratifications because the system's stability depends upon the curbing of appetites by moral values (pp. 237–41, 430–32). Material gratifications are replaced by the gratification of conformity to moral values. The latter are grounded in religion, which plays a central role in Parsons's theory.[14]

This description of system interdependence implies a deterministic cast to Parsons's theory, which contradicts Gouldner's previous attempt to reveal an antideterminism within it. Apart from the inconsistency, however, his interpretation of the relationship between the individual and the social system does violence to Parsons's formulations.

In *The Social System*, Parsons distinguishes three systemic foci of any system of action. Three systems, the social, personality, and cultural, are always interacting. He describes the interrelationships among the three as interdependence, interpenetration, and irreducibility. This means that each system affects the way in which the other two function; all three share some elements in common; yet no one system can be fully understood simply from a knowledge of the other two. The mutual irreducibility of the systems in their relations to one another most strongly belies Gouldner's analysis, for it accords a sphere of autonomy to each of the three. It follows that an individual's actions are influenced, but not totally determined, by the social system, despite the fact that Parsons has not developed the systematics of personality as fully as one might like. Thus, he has avoided the pitfalls of a cultural, a social, and a psychological determinism (Parsons 1951, p. 6).

In addition to the partial autonomy of each system, each must meet its own functional imperatives. The personality, for example, optimizes gratification and utilizes the mechanisms of allocation and integration to achieve gratification (Parsons and Shils 1951, pp. 120–23). It would be a mistake to equate these functional prerequisites, states Parsons, with those of the social system (1951, p. 18). To be sure, mechanisms of socialization are accorded an important place in Parsons's theory, but it is also true that persons are by no means uniform products, for the socializing processes are quite diverse.

In his attempt to reinterpret Parsons's view of the social system as a whole and therefore to conclude that personalities lack autonomy, Gouldner has failed to take account of the total theory of action. By calling attention to only one of action's foci, namely, the social system, he has created a misleading impression of a purely social determinism.

Gouldner emphasizes, in addition to the holism of Parsonsian theory, the centrality of moral values within it. As he interprets Parsons, compliance with morality guarantees order and supplies the conformist with gratification (pp. 249–50, 428–29). Individuals are taught to conform and to enjoy their conforming acts. The theory stresses morality so much that it

---

[14] Here Gouldner again detects a continuity in social theory. The preoccupation with religion appeared in Comte's and Saint Simon's positivism and in Durkheim's and Weber's classical sociology.

John K. Rhoads

neglects the gratifications from material things and the technology that produces the latter, Gouldner says. Durkheim's view that values *limit* material desires prevails in Parsons. Moreover, Parsons is said to be generally unaware that action occurs within contexts of scarcity. "Parsons' Ego and Alter do not seem to live in a world of scarcity; scarcity seems to have no effect on their behavior or on their relationship" (p. 237). In short, Parsons's theory supposedly lacks concern with men's material desires—a lack consistent with its subordination of the individual to the system.

Once again a closer scrutiny of the theory urges qualification of Gouldner's interpretation. Although there is little doubt of the central contribution of values to order, Parsons continually calls attention to the costs of conformity to some values. An outstanding example is the universalistic achievement value of the occupational sector. Also difficult to adhere to is affective neutrality, which requires an actor to renounce the immediate pleasure that might be forthcoming from his situation (Parsons 1951, pp. 267–68, 225–26). The costs that some values inflict on the individual are a source of deviance. Moreover, Parsons is skeptical about how any degree of conformity to a value can by itself yield gratification: "There is a sense in which as we have seen, all normative patterning involves an element of affective neutrality, in that as was noted, conformity with a normative pattern cannot in itself be a source of direct and immediate gratification" (1951, p. 267).

Furthermore, his theory does allow room for strictly material gratifications. There is a tendency, he says, for the personality to optimize its gratifications and minimize deprivations, and undoubtedly some needs are genetic (1951, pp. 7, 9, 27). It is obvious that genetically determined needs are satisfied not by moral conformity but by material objects and processes. The theory also takes account of technology. In outlining the principal characteristics of industrial societies, Parsons delineates the sociological counterparts to the economic factors of production. The parallels to land are technological knowledge and commitment to cultural values (1960, p. 134), and in his discussion of the factors of production, Parsons considers technology as equal in importance to such values as achievement.

Finally, the charge that Parsons's actors interact in a situation where there is no scarcity overlooks his well-known critique of the "Hobbesian problem of order" in *The Structure of Social Action*. According to Hobbes, men in a state of nature utilize their reason in the service of their passions. Because men's passions are basically similar, they want the same things. But because these things are scarce, men inevitably conflict. Since each has the right of self-preservation, each is justified in using force and fraud to attain his ends against others, and the outcome is incessant warfare (Parsons 1949, pp. 89–90). Parsons was dissatisfied with Hobbes's solution to scarcity-produced warfare, namely, a powerful government enforcing peace by its superior power.

THE POVERTY OF THE PARSONSIAN THEORY OF SOCIAL CHANGE

One of Gouldner's major theses is that system wholeness, the individual's lack of autonomy, the system's self-regulation, and the centrality of values preclude an adequate explanation of change within a structural-functional framework. Gouldner quotes Parsons himself as deeply pessimistic over the prospect of an adequate theory of change. His pessimism, says Gouldner, stems from the substance and structure of his theory, which distinguishes mechanisms that maintain equilibrium. Conformity to values works towards stability; factors such as conflict that upset stability are considered to be not quite as "real" as the equilibrating mechanisms. Although the theory does take conflicts, tensions, and strains into account, Gouldner goes on to say, they are relegated to the status of "fortuitous illnesses" rather than necessary conditions. The system is endowed with immortality (p. 354).

This conclusion that the theory accords greater reality to stability than to conflict is incorrect. Parsons's formulation of "the institutional integration of action elements," which depicts absolute harmony among interacting individuals and a mutually gratifying conformity to the normative order, is an ideal type from which empirical departures are the rule. The continuation of stability is a theoretical assumption, not an empirical generalization, and harmony is only a point of reference for the analysis of empirical events. Furthermore, in existing systems the normative patterns need *not* be maintained; their boundaries may dissolve into their environments or their patterns be transmuted into others (Parsons 1951, pp. 43, 481, 482). The equilibrium of normative patterns can also be a moving one. It follows that theory must provide explanations of change as well as stability.

Gouldner is correct when he reports Parsons as pessimistic about the prospects for a general, well-integrated theory of change. But this pessimism is traceable not to his preoccupation with an ideologically dictated stability, but rather to his recognition that no theory yields a set of laws describing the system's operations. Laws connecting the values of one variable with those of other variables of the system is the aim of theory. With such knowledge, the theorist could predict one change from another. In the absence of such laws, the closest approximation is a theory that outlines the structural categories of a system. Parsons's pessimism, therefore, stems from the absence of a knowledge of laws of process.[15]

[15] In documenting Parsons's pessimism Gouldner refers to the following quotation

Another criticism Gouldner levels at Parsons's discussion of change is his failure to accord technology the place it truly deserves. Once again Gouldner comes down hard on Parsons's work for its neglect of material gratifications in favor of moral rewards. In an article about evolutionary universals in human history, Gouldner says, Parsons lists cultural legitimation, money, and democratic associations but omits science and technology. The latter are relegated to the status of "prerequisites" of evolution rather than accorded the rank of evolutionary universals. Gouldner attributes this glaring omission to Parsons's objective of proving the superiority of America over the Soviet bloc of nations. The United States institutionalizes some evolutionary universals such as money and markets, universalistic legal codes, and democratic associations, which are not fully developed within totalitarian systems. On the other hand, totalitarian societies do possess science and technology and in these areas would compare favorably with the United States. By choosing the first factors as evolutionary universals, Parsons can demonstrate the greater adaptiveness and superiority of the United States over these other systems (Gouldner 1970, pp. 366–67). Thus, Gouldner states, the pro-capitalist, anti-Marxist infrastructure of the voluntaristic theory of the early Parsons continues to underlie his recent work.

This conjecture by Gouldner that Parsons is here attempting to demonstrate American superiority is simply out of place. The following quotation proves that Parsons *does* include technology as a universal: "These four features of even the simplest system—"religion," communication with language, social organization through kinship, and technology—may be regarded as an integrated set of evolutionary universals at even the earliest human level. No known human society has existed without *all* four in relatively definite relations to each other" (1964, p. 342).

In sum, a look at various aspects of Parsons's functional theory casts a different perspective on its orientation to change than the one Gouldner sets forth. Systemic interdependence and equilibrating mechanisms do not preclude processes of change. The theory is not dualistic in its treatment of stability and change. Material factors and technology are factors of importance within its framework.

---

from *The Social System:* "We do not have a complete theory of the processes of change in social systems, *we do have a canon of approach to the problems of constructing such a theory.* When such a theory is available the millennium for social science will have arrived. This will not come in our time and most probably never. *But progress toward it is much more likely to be assured and rapid if we know what we want and need"* (1951, pp. 534–35; italics mine). However, Gouldner (p. 354) conveniently omits the italicized parts in this quote, which soften Parsons's pessimism about the prospects of a theory of change.

IS THERE A CRISIS?

The preceding account of social theory and its deficiencies lays the foundation for Gouldner's principal conclusion that academic sociology is now in the early stages of a crisis.[16] By crisis he means a rapid change with much upheaval occasioned by the fundamental character of the change. "A crisis implies that taxing changes are proceeding at a relatively rapid rate; that they entail relatively sharp conflict, great tensions, and heightened costs for the system undergoing them; and, finally, . . . the system may soon find itself in a significantly different state than it had recently been" (pp. 341–42). What is causing this crisis?

The most important source of this crisis is the inability of functional sociology in its current state of theoretical development to fulfill the demands made upon it by the welfare state.[17] The welfare state demands solutions to current social problems. Hence, academic sociology is caught in a contradiction between its structure and infrastructure, on the one hand, and the expectations laid upon it, on the other. The proofs Gouldner offers for this conclusion are found in his discussions of social theory's historical development. Since the acceptance or rejection of the idea of the imminence of a crisis depends upon his interpretations of the development of social theory, a brief recapitulation of these is in order. Reduced to a few statements, Gouldner's principal points are as follows:

First, the sociological positivists and the functionalists created theories of society as a system with spontaneous rather than planned regulatory mechanisms. These spontaneous mechanisms automatically alleviate social problems and restore order, so planned intervention is superfluous. Second, positivist, classical, and functional theories attribute little importance to the state. This tendency was presumably related to the value-neutrality posture, itself an outcome of the political failure to reorganize society in the early periods. Third, functionalists fail to weight the variables of the social system, making it impossible to exert leverage to change society in planned directions. Fourth, functionalists, with their emphasis on moral values, falsely attribute problems to the collapse of morality and suggest

---

[16] Actually Western sociology which includes Marxism as well as academic sociology, is in crisis. My critique omits Gouldner's analysis of Marxism, which commands but a fraction of his attention.

[17] There is another cluster of conditions contributing to the crisis, namely, the sentiments of the New Left, which are not resonated by functional sociology. The New Left has not yet formulated an opposing theory, but Gouldner contends that young sociologists are not accepting Parsonian structural-functionalism (pp. 5, 399–402). I shall not comment extensively on these aspects of the crisis, mainly because their contribution to the crisis does not grow out of Gouldner's reconstruction of the history of social theory. Furthermore, there is no way of knowing what proportion of young sociologists will not accept functionalism in the future.

the inadequate solution of education rather than the mobilization of populations. Fifth, this same emphasis causes sociologists to neglect the redistribution of material gratifications and the contribution of technology to solving social problems. Indeed, Durkheim positively distrusted such gratifications. Sixth, the voluntaristic theory extols individual striving rather than social planning. Finally, the functional theory of change, which depicts problems as "aberrations," is inadequate to suggest needed changes (pp. 352–68).[18]

My critique of Gouldner's reconstruction is at obvious variance with these statements. At the risk of being repetitive, let me briefly restate some opposing contentions. Both Saint-Simon and Comte, far from being content with society's spontaneous adjustive mechanisms, devoted their lives to achieving a conscious, deliberate social reconstruction. The action theory of Parsons does not describe men as hollowed-out vessels for social forces, but rather as personality systems with their own partially autonomous system requirements. Functional theory does not preclude technology and material gratifications, substituting moral gratifications for them. The voluntaristic theory is not an antideterministic theory that urges men to strive but not to expect to achieve, but rather one that offers the possibility of a rational analysis of the means-ends relationship. System interdependence is not inconsistent with causal priorities. Functional theory does not depict conflicts and changes as unreal; the works of both Durkheim and Parsons show an authentic interest in social change.

Most of these contentions are adequately documented in the preceding commentary on Gouldner's reconstruction. Insofar as his predictions about a forthcoming crisis, now in its beginning stages, rest upon questionable interpretations and explanations of the history of social theory, it is prudent to assume a skeptical stance with respect to such predictions. He has not proved that contemporary social theory is deficient to meet the welfare state's demands; contrary to his view, it does allow for such factors as technology, autonomy, and change. It is also not obvious that the welfare state, if indeed it is the wave of the future, will be dependent on academic sociology. Neither has he marshalled sufficient evidence to substantiate the existence of a crisis. He can also be criticized for not spelling out more detailed criteria of crises.

The significance of Gouldner's study, however, transcends the problem of whether there is a crisis in sociology, for it focuses our attention on the approach that has come to be identified as the sociology of knowledge.

[18] Gouldner notes that the later Parsons *has* accepted the principle of governmental intervention, and Gouldner even detects a convergence of Parsons's theory with Marxism. Nevertheless, academic sociology's main thrust is still out of harmony with the welfare state.

His concepts of domain assumption and infrastructure are ingenious ones that link the substance and form of theories with events and structures in the sociohistorical contexts of the theorist and his readers. They mediate the impact of life situations on thinking, even scientific thinking, and thereby help to clarify and account for the products of thinking. The concept of infrastructure generates Gouldner's basic hypothesis that social theories rest on extrascientific as well as purely scientific notions; for anyone to understand a social theory fully, he must therefore take extrascientific considerations into account (Gouldner 1970, pp. 29–35).[19]

To those sympathetic to the sociology of knowledge, these notions are appealing, for they are consistent with this approach and plausible. Nevertheless, a problem arises, as it does in Gouldner's study, when the notion of a theory's infrastructure is built into specific hypotheses. For if a theorist's domain assumptions are not known to him insofar as they are outcomes of his prescientific thinking, the task of verifying their existence in his theory becomes empirically difficult. What is the empirical status of the domain assumptions that a sociologist of knowledge detects in a social theory if the theorist himself denies their existence as part of his thinking? The next link in the sequences of scientific analysis is even more dubious. The analyst must now draw a causal connection between the domain assumptions of a theory's infrastructure and some condition within the theorist's sociohistorical context that presumably stimulated those assumptions. Usually the number of plausible events within the theorist's context is so legion that the selection of those presumed to bear a causal relationship to his theory is vulnerable to the threat of arbitrariness.

These general questions concerning the sociology of knowledge are not answered here, but they must be faced when any theorist undertakes the exacting task of bringing this perspective to bear on specific items of knowledge. Formulating the sociology of knowledge in abstract terms is one thing, but utilizing propositions derived from it as explanations of identifiable thought products is another. Apart from Gouldner's ambitious attempt to reconstruct the evolution of social theory, another merit of his work is his attempt to relate the sociology of knowledge to sociology.

---

[19] Gouldner makes it clear, however, that domain assumptions are neither necessarily required in theory construction nor inevitable, but that sociologists have not been able to escape them. Neither does Gouldner deny that a theory should be judged according to its cognitive validity. He states: "The ideological implications and social consequences of an intellectual system do not determine its validity, for theory does indeed have a measure of autonomy" (p. 13). While recognizing the need to judge a theory with respect to its cognitive validity, Gouldner directs his principal efforts in this work toward understanding the infrastructure of social theories.

John K. Rhoads

REFERENCES

Comte, A. 1876. *System of Positive Polity.* Vol. 3. New York: Franklin.
————. 1883. *The Catechism of Positive Religion.* 2d ed. London: Trübner.
Durkheim, E. 1951. *Suicide.* Glencoe, Ill.: Free Press.
————. 1961. *The Elementary Forms of the Religious Life.* New York: Collier.
————. 1962. *Socialism.* New York: Collier.
————. 1964a. *The Rules of Sociological Method.* 8th ed. New York: Free Press.
————. 1964b. *The Division of Labor in Society.* New York: Free Press.
Gouldner, A. 1970. *The Coming Crisis of Western Sociology.* New York: Basic.
Parsons, T. 1949. *The Structure of Social Action.* 2d ed. Glencoe, Ill.: Free Press.
————. 1951. *The Social System.* Glencoe, Ill.: Free Press.
————. 1960. *Structure and Process in Modern Societies.* New York: Free Press.
————. 1961. "An Outline of the Social System." In *Theories of Society,* edited by T. Parsons et al. Vol. 1. Glencoe, Ill.: Free Press.
————. 1964. "Evolutionary Universals in Society." *American Sociological Review* 29 (June): 339–57.
————. 1966. *Societies: Evolutionary and Comparative Perspectives.* Englewood Cliffs, N.J.: Prentice-Hall.
Parsons, T., and E. A. Shils. 1951. "Values, Motives, and Systems of Action." In *Toward a General Theory of Action,* edited by T. Parsons and E. A. Shils. Cambridge, Mass.: Harvard University Press.
Rumney, J. 1965. *Herbert Spencer's Sociology.* New York: Atherton.
Simon, W. M. 1963. *European Positivism in the Nineteenth Century.* Ithaca, N.Y.: Cornell University Press.
Spencer, H. 1967. *The Evolution of Society.* Chicago: University of Chicago Press.

Political Judgments and the Perception of Social Relationships: An Analysis of Some Applied Social Research in Late 19th-Century Germany[1]

Vernon K. Dibble
Wesleyan University

INTRODUCTION

This paper is about two interrelated questions in the history of sociology and of social thought, and about a more general issue concerning the nature of certain concepts which sociologists of knowledge and intellectual historians often use.

First, how could the perception of social relationships, a prerequisite to the development of sociology, arise in market capitalist societies among people who were neither classical conservatives nor Marxists? There is a strong tendency in capitalist societies, and in the liberal ideologies which have been associated historically with their formation and growth (as compared with other societies and other ideologies), to see social systems as aggregates of individual persons instead of seeing systems of social relationships.[2] For example, in the vocabulary of feudal hierarchies, every word—such as "lord," "liege," "vassal," "villein," and "serf"—denotes a position in a system of social relationships. But in the vocabulary of industrial hierarchies—with terms such as "worker," "foreman," "superintendent," "chairman of the board," "industrialist," and "manufacturer" —some denote positions in social systems while others do not.[3] It is

---

[1] This paper is a revision of a paper presented at the annual meeting of the American Sociological Association, Denver, September 1, 1971. I am grateful to many colleagues, including John Brewer, Jeffrey Butler, William Martin, J. Ronald Milavsky, Louis Mink, Hubert O'Gorman, Ellen Kay Trimberger, and Harrison White for comments on earlier drafts. I regret that I have not been able to use many of the valuable suggestions, or to meet all of the objections, which these readers have offered.

[2] This dichotomy, perception of aggregates versus perception of social relationships, is, of course, somewhat forced. Perhaps there is a continuum, with the perception of social categories somewhere in the middle, between aggregates on one side and social structures on the other. What is more, the identification in this paper of the perception of social relationship with the central subject matter of sociology is discussable, at least, if not arguable, although it seems that no classical theorist in sociology limited his thought to social categories and that all (in various ways) dealt with social relationships. Though further refinements in these points seem desirable, this paper does not deal with them.

[3] This point, as concerns the vocabulary of industrial hierarchies, was suggested by

Vernon K. Dibble

possible to think of a worker as a person who works, independently of his relationship to a foreman. It is not possible to think of a vassal independently of his relationship to a lord.

Or compare the estate (*staendisch*) images of society in feudal thought —"There be in this world thre maner of men, clerkes, knythis, and commonyalte" (in the words of an English medieval sermon)[4]—with the individualist, aggregative images in liberal doctrine and in liberal social science. In Adam Smith's hypothetical tribe, for example, one person "makes bows and arrows . . . with more readiness and dexterity than any other." That person, because there is a "propensity in human nature . . . to truck, barter, and exchange one thing for another," and for certain other reasons inherent in human nature, exchanges bows and arrows for cattle or venison. He finds that he obtains more cattle and venison in this way "than if he himself went to the field to catch them." Hence, "from a regard to his own interest . . . the making of bows and arrows grows to be his chief business." That is, social structures—in this case, the division of labor in a system of market transactions—emerge out of the bumping together of individual persons, each of whom is pursuing individual goals and acting upon individual motivations or "propensities." The basic building blocks of a society are its individual members, not clerics, knights, and commoners, or proletariat and bourgeoisie, or even families. They are individual persons (Smith 1910, bk. 1, chap. 1, pp. 12–14).[5]

Now, the development of sociology in the 19th century depended upon (among other things) the existence of people who could resist, or who did

---

various passages in Gouldner (1955). For example (p. 24): "The workers defined their main role obligation to be that of 'working' or 'producing.' Their 'obedience' obligations, however were not equally stressed. . . . [and] . . . workers would have been amazed if, instead of being awakened in the morning with the call, 'Time to go to work, dear,' their wives called out, 'Get up, dear, it's time to go to *obey*.' "

[4] Quoted in Thrupp (1962, p. 288). As quoted here, the spelling has been slightly simplified and modernized.

[5] For another example see Hobhouse (1964, pp. 67–68). He espoused what he called (p. 67) "the organic view of society." But the units in the organism are individual persons, not hereditary estates, social classes, families, or social groupings of any sort. The organic view "means that, while the life of society is nothing but the life of individuals as they act one upon another, the life of the individual in turn would be something utterly different if he could be separated from society." Or again (p. 68), "Society consists wholly of persons. . . . The British nation is a unity with a life of its own. But the unity is constituted by certain ties which bind all British subjects, which ties are in the last resort feelings and ideas, sentiments of patriotism, of kinship, a common pride, and a thousand more subtle sentiments that bind together men who speak a common language, have behind them a common history, and understand one another as they can understand no one else." This book was first published in 1911 and illustrates both the transition from laissez faire liberalism to social welfare liberalism and the absence, in this transition, of any fundamental change in the liberal, aggregative images of society, in which the basic units are individual persons who have subjective "propensities," or motives, or (in Hobhouse) feelings, ideas, and sentiments.

not share, the strong individualist bent—individualist in cognitive orientation—of classical liberalism, and of market capitalism. Such people included, of course, both Marxists and classical conservatives.[6] But, with a few exceptions, most sociologists during the second half of the 19th century (and ever since) were neither Marxists nor classical conservatives. They were centrist reformists of one or another type.[7] How did such people come to see—to the extent they did—social relationships instead of aggregates of individual persons?

Content analyses of 102 research reports (using that term loosely) published in Germany during the 1880s and early 1890s by the Verein fuer Sozialpolitik (Association for Social Policy) suggest who such people might have been. Briefly, and subject to qualifications which appear below, the more involved authors—those who made explicit evaluations, who took sides in social conflicts, and who made policy recommendations—and those who looked to the German state to implement their policy recommendations, were relatively more likely to perceive social relationships. The more detached authors, writing on identical topics, for the same audience, and following the same observation protocols, were more likely to see aggregates of people instead.

These findings are consistent with our analysis of another series of

---

[6] On the extent to which sociology has roots in European conservative thought of the early 19th century, see Nisbet (1952, pp. 167–75). On one Marxian contribution to the development of sociology, consider this cryptic, suggestive remark by J. D. Y. Peel in *Herbert Spencer: The Evolution of a Sociologist* (1971, p. 58). Peel writes: "Spencer, like Marx, predicted on the basis of current developments, a withering away of the state. This premiss of the radical view of society (which was an absolute prerequisite for the emergence of sociology) was put succinctly by Thomas Paine: 'Society and government are different in themselves and have different origins. Society is produced by our wants and government by our wickedness. Society is in every state a blessing; government even in its best state a necessary evil.'" (Peel's quote is from Paine's *Common Sense*.) On Marx's distinction between "state" and "civil society," see Arthur (1970, esp. pp. 5–14); and McGovern (1970, pp. 430–66). It was probably more difficult, and more significant intellectually and ideologically, to arrive at this distinction in the German language than in English. For *Staat*, in German, often means not "state," in the more narrow English sense, but rather "politically organized society," as for example in the terms *Staendestaat* and *Klassenstaat*.

[7] To cite only American examples, see the following. On Cooley, see the various passages (such as pp. 50–52, 199–212) on his political views in Jandy (1942). Jandy sums up these views (p. 201) by stating: "To classify Cooley as an intellectual liberal is to state an evident fact." On Ross, see chap. 4, entitled "Edward Alsworth Ross: The Natural Man And The Community of Constraint," in Wilson (1968). See esp. pp. 104 ff. and, on Ross's support for Theodore Roosevelt and opposition to Bolshevism, pp. 111–12. On Albion W. Small, see, among many other writings, his novel, *Between Eras: From Capitalism to Democracy* (1912). On Giddings, see chaps. 24 and 25, entitled "Progress" and "Democracy," respectively, of Giddings (1906)—for example, pp. 298–99 on "The Policies of Liberalism" ("World Intercourse," "Free Thought," and "Legality") and pp. 312–34 on "False Notions of Democracy" (democracy is not class rule by the poor or by wage earners but is government of, by, and for all of "the people").

reports which the Verein sponsored and published, not included in the data reported here. In the early 1890s, Max Weber and five other authors participated in a series of studies of agricultural laborers in the various regions of Germany (*Schriften des Vereins fuer Sozialpolitik* 1892*b*).[8] Weber, as much as or more than the five others, made explicit evaluations, took sides in social conflicts, and made policy recommendations. And he had a much stronger perception of social structure than any of the other five authors did.[9]

Such findings, however, pose the second of our two historical questions. Most early sociologists, like the young Max Weber, did not conceive of sociology as a value-free science. Durkheim, for example, distinguished clearly between studying moral phenomena to understand them and studying them in order to make moral judgments (1926).[10] But he went on to assert not only that knowledge must precede judgment but that knowledge is the basis for judgment. "The science of moral opinion provides us with the means for judging moral opinion and, if need be, for correcting it" (1951, p. 86).[11] And Albion Small argued at length not only that ethics presupposes sociology and that a generally accepted sociology is a precondition of ethical consensus, but also that "the ultimate problem on the side of pure science is: What is worth doing?" (1903, p. 119; emphasis in original omitted). These examples are consistent with the data reported here. Among our authors, evaluative involvement was associated with the perception of social relationships: most sociologists who worked at the same time did not conceive of sociology as a value-free science.

How did it happen, then, that in the 20th century the notion of "value-free science," in a variety of meanings which this paper does not go into, became associated with sociology more than it did with any of the other social sciences, with economics, say, or with history or political science?

[8] The other five authors were Karl Kaerger, H. Losch, Kuno Frankenstein, Friedrich Grossman, and Otto Auhagen. For a summary of Weber's contribution to these studies, see Bendix (1960, pp. 14–23).

[9] For a comparison of Weber's work on agricultural laborers with the work of the five other authors, see Dibble (1968).

[10] For example (Durkheim 1926, pp. xxxvii–xxviii), "Ce livre est avant tout un effort pour traiter les faits de la vie morale d'après la méthode des sciences positives. . . . Les faits moraux sont des phénomènes commes les autres; ils consistent en des règles d'action qui se reconnaissant à certains caractères distinctifs: il doit donc être possible de les observer, de les décrire, de les classer et de chercher les lois qui les expliquent. C'est ce que nous allons faire pour certains d'entre eux. . . . Ainsi entendue, cette science n'est en opposition avec aucune espèce de philosophie, car elle se place sur un tout autre terrain."

[11] Détermination du Fait Moral" was first presented to the Société française de philosophie in 1906 and first published in the *Bulletin* of the society. The point made in the quotation is developed and argued at some length (1951, pp. 85–89). Durkheim had asserted the same point years before, in the preface to the first edition of *The Division of Labor* (see 1926, pp. xxxix-xl).

The data reported below suggest what part of the answer might be. Briefly, the association between a "high" tendency to make explicit evaluations and a "high" tendency to perceive social relations holds only among the authors who were not professional officials. Among the officials, a different dynamic prevailed. Officials were more likely than nonofficials to look to the state for the implementation of their policy recommendations; and those who looked to the state were more likely to perceive social relationships. Evaluative involvement, then, made for the perception of social relationships; being in power, or being oriented to power, was the functional equivalent, in this respect, of evaluative involvement.

Third, a more general, nonhistorical point: some of the findings reported here suggest the necessity to be wary of certain rather global concepts—concepts such as "style of thought" or "climate of opinion"—which sociologists of knowledge and intellectual historians sometimes use. They suggest the necessity to break down such concepts into their component parts.

One of the central variables in the analysis presented here is the implicitness or explicitness of the evaluations in the 102 research reports in question—the extent to which the authors are explicitly evaluative, as against the extent to which they make evaluations as if they were making descriptive statements. As seen here, explicitness of evaluations is associated with the perception of social relations: implicit or pseudoneutral evaluations are associated with the perception of aggregates. But these two variables have, in part, different determinants or correlates. They have to be understood on somewhat different terms, suggesting, more generally, that (a) the evaluative style component and (b) the purely cognitive component in concepts such as "style of thought" may refer to quite different phenomena which have different determinants.[12]

METHODS AND SOURCES OF DATA

Turning to the methods of investigation and to the sources of the data presented below, it is necessary to note that the Verein fuer Sozialpolitik was a combination intellectual forum, research organization, and pressure group for social legislation. It was dominated largely by "academic socialists" (*Kathedersozialisten*) who had founded the organization in 1872.[13] Economists of the historical school who opposed laissez faire, who supported social legislation—in part because they viewed social legislation as a means of reconciling conflicting classes and resolving class struggles—and who

[12] Talcott Parsons makes this same point, not with respect to particular concepts, but with respect to the global concept of "knowledge," as commonly used in the term "sociology of knowledge" (Parsons 1970, p. 282–306).

[13] For a history of the Verein, see Boese (1939).

supported state action for social welfare were prominent among the founders. In their view, detailed quantitative studies of social conditions would show the need for social reform and catch the real richness of social reality, as against the abstractions of laissez faire theory.[14]

Hence, the Verein organized and published numerous studies on such topics as housing conditions of urban workers, sources of credit for peasants, emigration, local government, and the condition of agricultural laborers. They sometimes sponsored survey research, as in the mammoth survey of the conditions of agricultural workers—based on questionnaires sent to landlords all over Germany—in which Weber participated. More commonly, however, the Verein used informants, people who were presumably knowledgeable about their own localities.

For a given project on a given topic, the Verein sent questionnaires, or observation protocols, to clergymen, landowners, professional bureaucrats in the state administration, private officials such as officers of peasant associations, and local notables of various sorts. These people wrote about the housing conditions, or the state of the peasantry, or whatever, in their own localities, following (more or less) the observation protocols which the Verein had provided. These reports were then published in the proceedings (*Schriften*) of the Verein. Hence, it is possible to compare the ways in which different people, writing for the same audience and following the same observation protocol or list of questions, wrote about the same topic.

The data of this paper are from five projects—on "Peasant Conditions," "Usury in the Countryside," "The Housing Crisis," "Local Government," and "Emigration," which included a total of 102 reports by almost as many different authors (*Schriften des Vereins fuer Sozialpolitik* 1883, 1886*a*, 1886*b*, 1890, 1892*a*). These five were chosen after other projects were excluded for various reasons. Given the purposes of the study, it was not possible to use projects in which there was only one author or only a small number of authors, or projects in which all or most of the participants were of a single social type—all professional bureaucrats or all professors. And it was not possible to use projects in which the authors could not follow the observation protocols without making value judgments and policy recommendations. The purpose of the study was to compare different social types in a number of respects, including their tendencies to make unsolicited evaluations and unsolicited policy recommendations. I also excluded the occasional non-German authors, writing about conditions outside Germany, and all studies published after 1920. However, the protocols for one of these five, the one on local government, did end with a request for policy recommendation. Therefore, when that variable, making or not

[14] On the German historical school of economics in the 19th century, see Eisermann (1956).

making policy recommendations, appears below, the fourteen reports in this series are excluded, and the number of cases drops from 102 to 88.

I coded the 102 reports in the five projects for a number of variables, including the seven variables which are used in this paper.[15] It is necessary to explain in some detail the coding of three of these variables: (1) the tendency to perceive social relationships, (2) the tendency to make evaluations, and (3) the making of explicit as against implicit evaluations.

I read each report as a series of topics. Most of the topics were defined by questions in the observation protocols, and the majority of authors in a given series dealt with most of the topics which appeared in any one report in that series. For example, some of the topics in the series on "Peasant Conditions" were "size of land holdings and distribution of ownership" (in all 39 reports), "indebtedness" (in 35 out of 39 reports), "inheritance law and practices" (in 37 out of 39 reports), "sources of credit" (33 out of 39), "trade in land" (31 out of 39), and so forth. For each topic, I asked whether the author addressed himself to social relationships. That is, in connection with a given topic, did the author write as if he were making some observation of individual persons which he could not make in principle, unless he were also observing others with whom the object of his observation interacted. For example, if an author says that large landowners use more advanced agricultural techniques than small landowners, then he is not addressing himself to social relationships. He is writing only of social categories, of occupants of different statuses, and not about the interaction between them. If however, he goes on to say that the small landowners in his district have begun to emulate the large landowners, and that the large owners encouraged this emulation and are thus exerting a wholesome influence on the small landowners, then he is coded as having discussed social relationships in connection with the topic "agricultural techniques." For each topic, there is a score of zero or one. The score for the entire report is the number of topics in connection with

[15] I did all of the coding myself. Hence, there are no checks on intercoder reliability. I devised the coding procedure after first reading a number of reports and ranking them, judgmentally and impressionistically, relative to one another, with respect to three variables for which there are quantitative scores. The impressionistic rankings and the rankings by numerical scores came out the same. The less precise and the more precise procedures gave the same results. I, of course, did not look at the name or titles of any author until I had completed the coding of his report. But this check was not always effective, since the authors sometimes identified themselves by the nature of their work, for example, in the text of their reports. In my view, perhaps the most solid basis for believing that the coding did not consist primarily of the projection of previously formulated hypotheses onto the raw data is the number of unexpected contingent associations between variables in these data, of which some are reported here. It is easy to distort coding so as to make it conform to simple, two-variable hypotheses. It is more difficult to distort coding so as to make it conform to more complex hypotheses, and such distortion seems most unlikely when, as in this case, the complexities were not anticipated.

which the author mentioned social relations, divided by the total number of topics. Observations of purely legal relations or of purely economic transactions were not coded as being observations of social relationships. If an author speaks simply of buyer and seller or of debtor and creditor, he was not coded as having looked at social relations. But if he goes on to say that the relationship is marked by friendship, trust, and mutual aid, or by hostility and suspicion, between debtor and creditor, then he was classified as having looked at social relationships.

Similarly, for each topic, I asked if an author made evaluations. Now, when an author makes an evaluation as if he were making a descriptive statement, as if he were describing some attribute of objective reality, and if he does so without stating any criteria of evaluation, then he was classified as having made an implicit evaluation. For example, when an author writes that the distribution of landownership in his district is "satisfactory," or when he says that existing sources of credit are "insufficient," or when he writes that the labor supply is "adequate," then he is making an implicit evaluation. Such statements purport to be objective descriptions of phenomena but are made on the basis of unstated criteria of evaluation.

In contrast, (a) when an author erects explicit criteria of evaluation, or (b) when he uses evaluative words with denotations or connotations which are so clearly subjective that he is not purporting to describe objective phenomena, or (c) when he uses evaluative words which are strongly emotive, then he is regarded as making an explicit evaluation. Some examples are: (a) a prosperous middle-class peasantry is the strongest support for throne and altar, which all right-thinking people want to defend, and the existing distribution of landownership is clearly inadequate since it prevents the growth of such a class; (b) the lot of the slum dwellers is a sorrowful spectacle, and the author personally approves of measures to improve their lot; or (c)—a very infrequent type—usurers are bloodsuckers and are cancers on the body politic.

Numerical scores for an entire article on the variable, tendency to make evaluations (of either type), were calculated as they were for the variable tendency to perceive social relations. For the third variable, tendency to make explicit evaluations, a somewhat different procedure was used. Instead of the ratio of all topics explicitly evaluated to all topics in the article, we used the ratio of all topics explicitly evaluated to all topics evaluated in one way or the other. This measure is, in effect, a measure of the propensities of the various authors to be explicit or implicit in their evaluations, controlling for their propensities to be evaluative in the first place.

The raw scores on these three variables had quite different distributions in different projects. For example, the overall tendency to perceive social relations in the reports on workers' housing was weaker, quite naturally, than the overall perception of social relations in the reports on usury in the countryside. Hence, it was necessary to standardize the scores across projects. I used two different procedures. I classified raw scores as "high," "medium," or "low" relative to other raw scores in the same project by trichotomizing the range of scores (resulting in highly skewed distributions of standardized scores), and by trichotomizing the distribution of raw scores, such that the number of reports falling into any one of the standardized categories was equal to or almost equal to the number of reports falling into each of the other two. In the data presented below, standardized scores are based on trichotomizations of ranges, but the same substantive results appear when the other procedure is used.

The other four variables which appear in this paper do not require such extensive discussion. They are: (4) whether an author is a professional official,[16] with information from a wide variety of biographical sources;[17] (5) whether an author expressly takes sides with some social class or other social grouping, and against some other class or grouping—workers against landlords, say, or peasants against merchants; (6) whether an author makes policy recommendations; and (7) if an author does make policy recommendations, whether he looks to private means (such as cooperatives, for example) or to state action, or to a combination of private means and state action, for the implementation of his recommendations.

These, then, are the seven variables which appear in this paper—perceiving social relationships; making evaluations; making explicit evaluations, official or nonofficial; taking sides in social conflict; making or not making policy recommendations; and calling for private or for state action to implement recommendations.

The sections which follow deal, first, with certain differences between the professional state officials and the other authors; second, with the correlates of explicitness of evaluations; and, third, with the correlates of the perception of social relations. On this third point, however, it will be necessary to go simultaneously into a fourth matter—that is, into some of the ways in which the differences between officials and others, the correlates of explicitness, and the correlates of the perception of social relations all tie together.

---

[16] Some of their titles, either at the time they wrote reports for the Verein's projects or at some other point in their careers, were *Regierungsassessor, Regierungsrat, Oberregierungsrat, Landrat,* and *Ministerialrat.*

[17] A few of the more than 50 sources consulted were *Allgemeine deutsche Biographie, Badische Biographien, Biographiches Jahrbuch und deutscher Nekrolog, Familiengeschichtliche Bibliographie, Parlamentarisches Handbuch fuer den deutschen Reichstag und den preussischen Landtag, Deutscher Gelehrtenkalendar, Wer ist's, Wuerttembergischer Nekrolog,* and *Das akademische Deutschland.* I am grateful to Ruth Heydebrandt for taking on the onerous job of tracking down the biographical information.

Vernon K. Dibble

TABLE 1

OFFICIALS TENDED TO MAKE LESS EXPLICIT EVALUATIONS
THAN NONOFFICIALS

Explicitness of Evaluations	Officials	Nonofficials
High	12%	25%
Medium	35%	34%
Low	53%	41%
Total	100%	100%
	(34)	(68)

SOME DIFFERENCES BETWEEN OFFICIALS AND OTHERS

Turning first to some of the differences between officials and others, the professional officials were somewhat less likely than the other authors to be explicit in their evaluations. As seen in table 1, they were somewhat more likely than the nonofficials to make evaluations as if they were making descriptive statements, to use words such as "favorable" or "unfavorable," without specifying favorable for what. Professors, clergymen, attorneys, or landowners were somewhat more likely to regard the same phenomena in the light of their own feelings, or in terms of explicit criteria of evaluation.

This difference between bureaucrats and the other authors is, of course, consistent with our received images of what bureaucrats are like. Max Weber decried the bureaucratization of the political system of Bismarckian Germany, and the absence of genuine parliamentary government, because (among other grounds) bureaucrats, in his view, are not trained to set political goals as parliamentary politicians are. Bureaucrats know how to pursue political goals which others establish but not how to define them (1958, pp. 294–431). If professional officials tend to take goals for granted and to regard them as unproblematic, then they should be less likely than the nonofficials to make value criteria explicit, and more likely to use a pseudo-neutral language. Or perhaps the bureaucrats tend (slightly) to be more implicit in their evaluations than the nonbureaucrats for reasons which have nothing to do with bureaucracy. Perhaps we have here a difference between people who are in and people who are out of power. People who are in power can assimilate more things in a cognitive orientation, while people who are out of power may be more constrained to make explicit value challenges.

As seen in table 2, the professional officials were also somewhat more likely than the other authors to look to the state, instead of looking to private means such as cooperatives or self-help movements, for the im-

TABLE 2

Officials Were Neither More Likely nor Less Likely than
Nonofficials to Make Policy Recommendations, and Were
More Likely than Others to Look to the State*

Means Chosen to Implement Policy Recommendations	Officials	Nonofficials
State action	30%	12%
Mixed state and private action	10%	21%
Private action	35%	43%
No policy recommendations	25%	25%
Total	100%	101%
	(20)	(68)

* Excluding the series on local government, in which policy recommendations were solicited.

plementation of their policy recommendations. In this respect, also, the results seem consistent with the received images of bureaucrats.

In two other respects, however, the results are not consistent with the received images. According to data not reported here, the percentage of officials who took sides in social conflicts did not differ from the percentage among the other authors. If anything, the officials were slightly more likely to take sides. And as seen in table 2, the officials were neither more nor less likely than the other authors to make unsolicited policy recommendations. Such results seem inconsistent with the image of bureaucrats who go about their assigned tasks, as defined by higher authority, impersonally and without fear or favor.

These results may be an artifact of our "sample." Perhaps officials who felt strongly about the topics under investigation were more likely to agree to participate in the Verein's projects, while no such selective factor operated among the clergymen, landowners, and other nonofficials. But the entire history of officialdom in Bismarckian Germany, not simply our findings on 102 research reports, was inconsistent with our received images of bureaucracy.

To a rather large extent, the state bureaucracy in Bismarckian Germany (including the military) was an institutional base for *Junker* power, to which the *Junkers* turned after capitalist economic development had severely weakened their traditional economic base in agriculture. For their former positions in the social relations of production, distribution and exchange, they substituted positions in the institutions of political administration and rule. The civil service was not, and did not claim to be, politically neutral. For example, professional civil servants held elected office under party labels. And political tests insured their political reliability. The oath of Prussian civil servants included the provision that they represent the interests of the government at the polls. And, beginning in the 1880s, only those officials who were also reserve officers were eligible for the highest offices in the civilian administration.[18]

This was the kind of civil service which Max Weber knew and which he deplored in some of his political writings. But in his more scholarly writings he presented a very different image—just as he decried the German bourgeoisie's aping of the aristocracy (Bendix 1960, pp. 36–48)—and then presented a very different, ideal image of the bourgeois in *The Protestant Ethic*. And it is this very different image of bureaucracy, in Weber's scholarly writings, which we American sociologists have inherited. But Weber knew that this image was not historically real.

Given this kind of civil service, then, it seems quite possible that the absence of any difference between bureaucrats and other authors with respect to taking sides in social conflicts and making policy recommendations is not an artifact of our "sample," and that similar results would obtain if it were possible to use more representative sampling procedures. State officials, in short, were somewhat less explicit in their evaluations than nonbureaucrats, were neither more nor less likely to make policy recommendations, were more likely to look to the state for remedial action, and were, if anything, a bit more likely to take sides in social conflicts.

SOME CORRELATES OF EXPLICIT EVALUATIONS

Turning to some other correlates of explicitness of evaluations, taking sides in social conflicts is associated with explicit evaluations—as seems to make sense, intuitively. Those who commit themselves to peasants against merchants, say, or to urban workers against landlords, are less likely to use a pseudo-neutral language and more likely to make explicit evaluations. And as seen in table 3, taking sides and being a nonofficial are associated additively with explicitness. Further, taking sides is associated with making policy recommendations; and these two variables, in turn, are associated additively with explicitness.

As seen in table 4, explicit evaluations, in turn, go along with a relatively greater tendency to perceive social relations instead of aggregates of persons. In fact, according to data not reported here, the greater the tendency to make evaluations of any kind, explicit or implicit, the greater the tendency to perceive social relationships. In contrast with the later asso-

---

[18] To state that the military and the civilian administration were a substitute base for *Junker* power is only part of the story. For a view which emphasizes the extent to which aristocrats in and out of the bureaucracy coalesced with nonaristocrats in the bureaucracy, in agriculture, and in commerce and industry to form a new upper class, see Gillis (1971, esp. chap. 9, "Bureaucracy and Society"). This paragraph is based also on the following sources: Dibble (1971); Kehr (1929, pp. 253–72); and Muncy (1944).

TABLE 3

BEING A NONOFFICIAL AND TAKING SIDES IN SOCIAL CONFLICTS ARE ADDITIVELY
RELATED TO EXPLICITNESS OF EVALUATIONS

Explicitness of Evaluations	Officials Who Took Sides in Social Conflicts	Officials Who Did Not Take Sides in Social Conflicts	Nonofficials Who Took Sides in Social Conflicts	Nonofficials Who Did Not Take Sides in Social Conflicts
High	20%	5%	44%	12%
Medium	47%	26%	37%	32%
Low	33%	68%	19%	56%
Total	100%	99%	100%	100%
	(15)	(19)	(27)	(41)

ciation of sociology with the notion of value-free science, among our authors, making evaluations and making them explicit went along with the perception of the central subject matter of sociology— the perception of social relations instead of aggregates.

It is possible to interpret this association in various ways. One possibility is that a greater tendency to make evaluations, and a greater tendency to make explicit evaluations, goes along with a heightened awareness of social structural obstacles to the realization of one's goals. That is, perhaps those authors who were less evaluative or more pseudo-neutral were more likely to think in technical, nonsocial terms. But whatever the explanation, the association between explicit evaluations and the perception of social relations holds up under various controls (not reported here) and is one of the clearest findings in these data.

THE PERCEPTION OF SOCIAL RELATIONSHIPS

Now, if officials were less likely to make explicit evaluations, and if a weaker tendency to make explicit evaluations went along with a weaker

TABLE 4

AUTHORS WHO MADE EXPLICIT EVALUATIONS WERE MORE LIKELY THAN THOSE
WHO MADE IMPLICIT EVALUATIONS TO PERCEIVE SOCIAL RELATIONSHIPS

PERCEPTION OF SOCIAL RELATIONS	EXPLICITNESS OF EVALUATIONS		
	High	Medium	Low
High	43%	9%	4%
Medium	33%	40%	24%
Low	24%	51%	72%
Total	100%	100%	100%
	(21)	(35)	(46)

tendency to perceive social relations, then it ought to follow, logically, that officials were less likely to perceive social relations. But this result does not occur in our data. For there are certain complications in the data which vitiate such a simple conclusion.

First, officials did not differ from nonofficials in their propensity to make policy recommendations. But they were more likely than the nonofficials to look to the state for implementing their recommendations. And, judging from data based on very small totals, those authors (especially those officials) who looked to the state were more likely to perceive social relations instead of aggregates.[19] An author who counted on the automatic operation of the market, or on technical improvements in the mechanisms of credit for peasant landholders, or in agricultural methods, did not necessarily concern himself with social relationships. He might or might not. But an author who looked to the state did, necessarily and by definition, concern himself with certain kinds of social relationships, with relationships of power and authority. And perhaps this orientation carried over into the way he looked at the housing of the urban working class or at the condition of the peasants down on the farm. That is, a statist orientation is likely to be holistic, and to lead people to ask how everybody fits in with everybody else, into the fabric of society underneath the state. In contrast, perhaps those who looked to cooperatives or to self-help movements were closer to the individualistic, aggregative outlook of classical liberalism.

Whatever the reason, the expectation that officials were relatively less likely to perceive social relations because they were more likely to make implicit or pseudo-neutral evaluations is undercut by their greater tendency to look to the state, which goes along with a greater tendency to perceive social relationships. The expectation for bureaucrats to be less likely to perceive social relations holds only among those authors who did

[19] When we compare authors who made no policy recommendations or who made recommendations but called for implementation by private means with authors who made recommendations and called for a combination of private and state action, or for state action alone, to implement them, 83% of 12 officials who did not look to the state, as against half of the eight officials who did, had a "low" perception of social relationships. None of the 12 officials who did not look to the state and one of the eight who did, had a "high" perception of social relationships. The corresponding percentages among the nonofficials were 61% (of 46) and 50% (of 22) for "low" perception and 11% and 18% for "high" perception of social relationships. The difference is clearer among the officials, despite the very small totals, than among the other authors. The totals are small because it was necessary to exclude from these data the fourteen reports in the series on local government in the rural areas of Prussia. The protocols sent to participants in this series called for policy recommendations concerning agencies and methods of local government. Hence, all authors in this series made recommendations; and, by the very nature of the subject matter, they all looked to the state for implementation. It was therefore not possible to include them in the results on the point in question here.

not call for any state action. Among this group, officials do seem somewhat less likely than nonofficials to perceive social relations.[20]

In brief, making explicit evaluations went along with the perception of social relationships. Although officials were somewhat less likely to make explicit evaluations, they were no less likely than the others to perceive social relationships. Regarding the ability to perceive social relationships, their statist orientation was the functional equivalent of evaluative involvement.

This contention is borne out in two ways. First, among those authors who do not look to the state, the officials seem less likely to perceive social relationships, as we would expect, given their tendency to make fewer explicit evaluations than the other authors did. Second, as noted above, the association between explicit evaluations and the perception of social relationships (table 4) remains strong under various controls. But, as seen in table 5, there is one control which considerably alters this association.

TABLE 5

Explicit Evaluations Are Associated with a "High" Perception of Social Relationships Only among Nonofficials

PERCEPTION OF SOCIAL RELATIONS	OFFICIALS: EXPLICITNESS OF EVALUATIONS		NONOFFICIALS: EXPLICITNESS OF EVALUATIONS	
	High or Medium	Low	High or Medium	Low
High	6%	11%	28%	0
Medium	56%	11%	30%	32%
Low	37%	77%	42%	68%
Total	99%	99%	100%	100%
	(16)	(18)	(40)	(28)

Explicitness of evaluation went along with a greater likelihood of a "high" perception of social relationships only among those authors who were not professional officials. Among the officials, the finding does not hold.[21] Among them, a different dynamic is at work.

If "official" here really means "in power," or "viewing society from the perspective of those in power," and not the particular historical character-

[20] Restating some of the data in n. 19 somewhat differently, in order to bring this point out, among authors who did not call for any state action, 83% of the 12 officials and 61% of the 46 nonofficials had a "low" perception of social relationships. Among those who did call for state action, the corresponding percentage is 50% for both categories of authors.

[21] Note, however, that in table 5 "low" explicitness of evaluations is associated with "low" perception of social relationships both among officials and among nonofficials.

Vernon K. Dibble

istics of German bureaucrats in the 1880s and 1890s, then these findings suggest one approach toward an answer to our second historical question. As sociology in the 20th century became more professionalized, more established in the academy, and (through applied research, for example) more closely associated with centers of power, evaluative involvement was no longer necessary for maintaining the perception of social structure, and it was possible to adopt a supposedly value-free stance instead.

CONCEPTUALIZATION IN THE SOCIOLOGY OF KNOWLEDGE

Turning to our third, more general point, note that in our data on the perception of social relationships there are a number of contingent associations. For example, taking sides is associated positively with perceiving social relations only among the bureaucrats.[22] And being a nonbureaucrat goes along with the perception of social relations only among those authors who do not take sides.[23] In contrast, among the correlates of explicitness of evaluation there are many simple, additive associations. For example (table 3), taking sides and not being an official are additively related to explicitness, as are taking sides and making policy recommendations.[24] What is more, the number of correlates or determinants of the perception of social relations is greater than the number of correlates of explicitness of evaluations. For example, looking to the state is related to the perception of social relations but is not related to explicitness.

Perhaps the various components of evaluative styles—in this instance, taking sides, making policy recommendations, and making explicit evaluations—hang together by their own internal logic, or their own internal psychology to a greater extent than is the case with purely cognitive orientations. And perhaps the connections between peoples' social positions and their cognitive orientations are more numerous, and more complex,

[22] Among the 15 officials who took sides in social conflicts, 40% had a "low" perception and 20% had a "high" perception of social relations. Among the 19 officials who did not take sides, 74% (as against 40%) had a "low" perception and none (as against 20%) had a "high" perception of social relationships. Among the nonofficials 52% (out of 27) of those who took sides and 54% (out of 41) of those who did not take sides had a "low" perception, while 26% and 10%, respectively, had a "high" perception of social relations.

[23] Restating some of the data in n. 22 to bring out this point, among authors who did not take sides, 74% of the 19 officials and 54% of the 41 nonofficials had a "low" perception of social relations. Among those who did take sides, the corresponding percentages are 40% (out of 15) and 52% (out of 27).

[24] Excluding four authors who took sides but made no policy recommendations, 32% of the 31 authors who both took sides and made recommendations were "high" in explicitness, as against 11% of the 35 authors who did not take sides but did make recommendations, and none of the 18 authors who neither took sides nor made recommendations.

170

than the connections between social positions and evaluative styles. For example, and just impressionistically, it seems that professors in different disciplines, or in different schools within a university, or with different relationships to students, who face a campus crisis, differ much more widely in what they see going on around them than they do in their styles of evaluating what they see. Fine differences in social position seem to make for more differences in cognition than they do in evaluative style.

One line of speculation about this issue proceeds as follows. As regards cognitions: first, the greater the inherent ambiguity of an objective stimulus, the greater the impact of social determinants upon the way people respond to it. Second, the greater the number and variety of culturally given, alternative ways of viewing that stimulus, the greater the impact of social determinants. And, third, differences in social positions are associated with different styles of thought—legal, clinical, ideological, scientific, applied-technological, or commonsensical—which vary in the ways in which and in the extent to which cognitions and evaluations are experienced as different, separate, incommensurable activities. The greater the institutionalized fusion of cognitions and evaluations in a style of thought, the smaller the extent to which cognitions are simple reflections of objective stimuli. Social determinants, then, would have the greatest impact on people who are responding to objectively ambiguous stimuli, for whom a variety of culturally given modes of response is available, and who are thinking within a style of thought which fuses cognitions and evaluations. Such specifications of the conditions under which social determinants have varying degrees of impact would not apply to evaluations, however. For evaluations do not have objective stimuli in the same sense in which cognitions do. Hence, we should expect, as seen in the data of this paper, that the social determinants of cognitions are more numerous and more complex than the social determinants of evaluations. Whatever the validity of this line of speculation, these data do suggest that sociologists of knowledge need very different approaches to understanding the cognitive and the evaluative sides of any given ideology, doctrine, or system of beliefs.

REFERENCES

Arthur, C. J. 1970. "Editor's Introduction." In *The German Ideology,* by Karl Marx and Frederick Engels, pt. 1. New York: International.

Bendix, Reinhard. 1960. *Max Weber: An Intellectual Portrait.* New York: Doubleday.

Boese, Franz. 1939. *Geschichte des Vereins fuer Sozialpolitik. Schriften des Vereins fuer Sozialpolitik,* vol. 188. Berlin: Duncker & Humblot.

Dibble, Ursula. 1971. "The Relationship between Institutions of Property and Bureaucracy in 18th-Century Prussia, in Imperial Germany, and in the German Federal Republic." Manuscript, University of Connecticut.

Dibble, Vernon K. 1968. "Social Science and Political Commitments in the Young Max Weber." *European Journal of Sociology* 9:92–110.

Durkheim, Émile. 1926. *De la division du travail social.* Paris: Félix Alcan.

———. 1951 (1906). "Détermination du fait moral." In *Sociologie et philosophie*. Presses Universitaires de France.

Eisermann, Gottfried. 1956. *Die Grundlagen des Historismus in der deutschen Nationaloekonomie*. Stuttgart: Enke.

Giddings, Franklin Henry. 1906. *The Elements of Sociology: A Text-Book for Colleges and Schools*. New York: Macmillan.

Gillis, John R. 1971. *The Prussian Bureaucracy in Crisis, 1840–1860: Origins of an Administrative Ethos*. Stanford, Calif.: Stanford University Press.

Gouldner, Alvin. 1955. *Wildcat Strike: A Study of an Unofficial Strike*. London: Routledge & Kegan Paul.

Hobhouse, L. T. 1964 (1911). *Liberalism*. New York: Oxford University Press.

Jandy, Edward C. 1942. *Charles Horton Cooley: His Life and Social Theory*. New York: Dryden.

Kehr, Eckart. 1929. "Das soziale System der Reaktion in Preussen unter dem Ministerium Puttkamer." *Die Gesellschaft: internationale Revue fuer Sozialismus und Politik*, vol. 6. Reprinted in Kehr, Eckart, 1965. *Der Primat der Innenpolitik*. Berlin: Walter de Gruyter.

McGovern, Arthur F., S.J. 1970. "The Young Marx on the State." *Science and Society*, vol. 34 (Winter).

Muncy, Lysbeth Walker. 1944. *The Junker in the Prussian Administration under William II, 1888–1914*. Providence, R.I.: Brown University Press.

Nisbet, Robert A. 1952. "Conservatism and Sociology." *American Journal of Sociology*, vol. 58 (September).

Parsons, Talcott. 1970. "An Approach to the Sociology of Knowledge." In *The Sociology of Knowledge: A Reader*, edited by James E. Curtis and John W. Petras. New York: Praeger.

Peel, J. D. Y. 1971. *Herbert Spencer: The Evolution of a Sociologist*. New York: Basic.

Schriften des Vereins fuer Sozialpolitik, vols. 21–23. 1883. *Bauerliche Zustaende in Deutschland*. Berlin: Duncker & Humblot.

———, vols. 30–31. 1886a. *Die Wohnungsnot der armeren Klassen in deutschen Grosstaedten und Vorschlaege zu deren Hilfe*. Berlin: Duncker & Humblot.

———, vol. 35. 1886b. *Der Wucher auf dem Lande*. Berlin: Duncker & Humblot.

———, vol. 44. 1890. *Berichte ueber die Zustaende und die Reform des laendlichen Gemeindewesens in Preussen*. Berlin: Duncker & Humblot.

———, vol. 52. 1892a. *Auswanderung und Auswanderungspolitik in Deutschland*. Berlin: Duncker & Humblot.

———, vols. 53–55. 1892b. *Die Verhaeltnisse der Landarbeiter in Deutschland*. Berlin: Duncker & Humblot.

Small, Albion W. 1903. "The Significance of Sociology for Ethics." In *Investigations Representing the Departments: Political Economy, Political Science, History, Sociology and Anthropology*. Decennial Publications of the University of Chicago, 1st ser., vol. 4. Chicago: University of Chicago Press.

———. 1912. *Between Eras: From Capitalism to Democracy*. Kansas City, Mo.: Inter-Collegiate.

Smith, Adam. 1910 (1776). *An Inquiry into the Nature and Causes of the Wealth of Nations*. New York: Dutton.

Thrupp, Sylvia L. 1962. *The Merchant Class of Medieval London*. Ann Arbor: University of Michigan Press.

Weber, Max. 1958 (1918). "Parlament und Regierung im neugeordneten Deutschland." In Weber, *Gesammelte politische Schriften*, edited by Johannes Winckelmann. 2d ed. Tuebingen: Mohr.

Wilson, R. Jackson. 1968. *In Quest of Community: Social Philosophy in the United States, 1860–1920*. New York: Wiley.

Marxist Thought in the First Quarter of the 20th Century

Lewis A. Coser

State University of New York at Stony Brook

Marxist theorists have contended that Marxism is exempted from the claims of the sociology of knowledge that all thought structures and ideas need to be investigated in relation to the existential conditions and social structures in which they originate and find reception. I reject this claim and make an attempt in terms of the methods of the sociology of knowledge to investigate a variety of Marxian doctrines that emerged in the first quarter of the 20th century.

This paper investigates Kautskyan Marxism, Bernsteinian revisionism, the teachings of Rosa Luxemburg and her co-thinkers, Russian Menshevism and Bolshevism, the political writings of Georg Lukacs, and those of Antonio Gramsci in terms of the societal milieu in which they originated, the social location of their authors, and the audiences and publics to which they addressed themselves.

It is found that ideas that originated in the industrial heartland of Europe and found mass reception there transformed Marxism into a largely evolutionary and positivistic doctrine, whereas the activistic and voluntaristic interpretation of Marxism was mainly developed by intellectuals in the industrially undeveloped rimland of Europe. Attempts to transfer voluntaristic Marxism to the heartland of Europe failed since they lacked a basis in the social structure.

"It is not the consciousness of men that determines their existence," says Marx (1912, pp. 11–12), "but, on the contrary, their social existence which determines their consciousness." While this statement, which is at the very root of Marxian doctrine, would seem to have enjoined Marxists to inquire into the existential roots of their own ideas, this has emphatically not been the case. In fact, as Mannheim (1936, p. 249) pointed out long ago, "this relationship [between existence and consciousness] was perceived only in the thought of the opponent." Marxists used ideological analysis to undermine the thought of their adversaries but claimed that their own doctrine had a privileged status exempting it from such analysis.

It is logically indefensible to select Marxism, of all sets of ideas and winds of doctrine, for exemption from the type of inquiry into existential roots that is being applied to all others. I agree with Mannheim (1936, p. 111) that "as sociologists there is no reason why we should not apply to Marxism the perceptions which it itself has produced."

Lewis A. Coser

This paper will attempt to apply the method of inquiry of the sociology of knowledge to Marxist thought in the first quarter of this century. I shall review various trends in Marxian doctrine, from Kautskyan and Austro-Marxist orthodoxy to the revisionism of Bernstein, from Leninism to the various heterodox doctrines of Luxemburg, Gramsci, and Lukacs, in terms of their social location and in relation to their audiences and publics. Although not all varieties of Marxian thought can be considered, all those that presented a certain theoretical distinctiveness and enjoyed a measure of success will be discussed. What is intended here is a broad outline of what Mannheim used to call a "structural analysis" of the main Marxist trends from the beginning of the century until, roughly, the death of Lenin (1924). I shall attempt to show that the variants of Marxist ideas that emerged in the developed and industrialized parts of Europe differed significantly from those that had their origin in the nonindustrialized rimland of Europe, and that attempts to transfer Marxian ideas originating in that rimland failed to gain acceptance in Europe's industrial heartland.

KARL KAUTSKY AND MARXIST ORTHODOXY

The German Social Democratic movement was the exemplar and beacon of all other European socialist movements, not only because of its wide appeal to the working class, but because it based its politics and actions on well-developed political and economic theories. This movement pioneered in providing leadership to large masses of people, not only politically, but intellectually as well. In spite of being persecuted and outlawed by Bismarck for many years, it had gained an impressive stature on the social and political scene around the turn of the century.

In the elections of 1890, the Social Democrats returned 35 deputies to the Reichstag; this number increased to 110 seats just before World War I, when their 4.5 million voters were about one-third of the total. Even though the party was hampered in Prussia, where under the prevailing electoral system working-class votes counted for far less than those of the middle class, social democracy was solidly entrenched in the German parliamentary system on state and national levels. It was even more powerful on lower political levels. The party had become a mass movement, strongly supported by the trade unions which it led and based on a well-organized party apparatus. It employed impressive numbers of functionaries, most of whom were of working-class origin. The daily socialist press, for example, had a circulation of 1 million in 1909. Its editorial and distribution staff numbered 330 (Michels 1949, p. 276). Already by 1904, the union movement had nearly 700 permanent officials (Michels 1949, p. 276). The social composition of the party was solidly working class, and it offered means of upward social mobility for a significant number of self-educated workers who made their career in the party and union hierarchy. While 65 percent of the members of the Social Democratic group in the Reichstag of 1903–6 were skilled workers by origin, 43 percent listed their current occupation as employees in the labor movement (Michels 1949, pp. 271–72).

This attraction of workers to Social Democratic politics expressed the realities of German social and political conditions. The rapid expansion of industry had strengthened the working class economically, and it had led to an improvement in working-class conditions, accompanied as it was by an increase in the social security benefits which earlier had been granted by Bismarck. Yet, the political structure of German industrial society did not match its economic development. Political power was not held by the rising middle class or by the workers but by the Prussian Junkers and their hangers-on. Ample middle-class and working-class representation in parliament was not translated into real political power.

The contradiction between the socioeconomic and the political structure of German society helped determine the ambivalent character of German social democracy as well as its political theory. The party attempted to combine a politically revolutionary stance with a pragmatic commitment to gradual social and economic evolution.

The major theorist and codifier of the doctrines of German social democracy was Karl Kautsky. Born in Prague in 1854 of a Czech Jewish stage painter and a German Jewish mother, he studied history and the natural sciences at Vienna University and first dreamed of becoming a painter or an actor. Soon after, he was converted to a Darwinian-evolutionist interpretation of history as well as to Marxism. After moving first to Zurich and then to London, he soon came to the forefront among the intellectual leaders of the Social Democratic movement. A close intellectual companion to the aging Engels, he became the foremost theorist of official German social democracy. The theoretical organ of the Party, the *Neue Zeit*, which he founded and edited from 1883 on, was considered in Germany as well as abroad to be the recognized fountainhead of orthodox Marxist doctrine (Osterroth 1960).

Practically the entire career of Kautsky was within the Social Democratic party. Moreover, it was a career within a party that grew and developed impressively during the whole period before World War I. The Marxism that he and his associates developed bore the imprint of these circumstances. Kautsky's Marxism was no longer the revolutionary credo which Marx and Engels had developed in the late 1840s. Benign optimism replaced apocalyptic vision. Marx himself, and Engels more decisively after Marx's death, already had considerably softened the early revolutionary creed. Marx had admitted the possibility that in a number of nations the working class might attain power through parliamentary means rather than through revolution, and Engels had further bent the doctrine in the direction of an evolutionary and deterministic positivism. Hence, when Kautsky began to transform Marxism into an essentially positivist doctrine predicting the inevitable victory of socialism as following from the deterministic laws of historical development, he was not aware that he departed in any way from authentic Marxist tradition.

The fact is that Marxism under Kautsky's guidance became the official doctrine as well as the expression of a mass movement which had lost its revolutionary impulse. Kautsky's determinism was well-suited to a movement that was essentially tuned to passive acceptance of the benign course of history. It was the doctrine of a movement that had been shorn in fact, though not in rhetoric, of the activism and tense expectations of imminent revolution that had once characterized Marx and Engels (cf. Lichtheim 1961).

The German Social Democratic movement led by Wilhelm Liebknecht and August Bebel had little desire to transcend the social framework within which it operated with such impressive success. As Lichtheim has put it, "Marxism functioned as an integrative ideology, not as a theory of action" (Lichtheim 1970a, p. 234). This ideology helped differentiate and separate the working class from the middle class and instilled in it a sense of its peculiar mission. It helped to immunize the workers to liberal ideas and to articulate their corporate political and social awareness. It created a socialist subculture within the surrounding official culture, but it did not energize the workers into the preparation for large-scale revolutionary action. To be sure, it was programmatically committed to revolution, but by this was meant, in fact, a purely political upheaval which would do away with Germany's autocratic political structure and replace it with fully democratic institutions. Once democracy would be attained, so reasoned its major theoretical spokesmen, the replacement of capitalism by a socialist society would inevitably follow from the laws of social and economic evolution.

The Social Democratic movement and its official Kautskyan orthodoxy could not, given the political situation in autocratic Germany, commit itself officially to a policy of "the inevitability of gradualness" in a Fabian vein. The political structure of the Kaiser's Germany was antidemocratic and was designed to keep not only the workers but also the middle classes from effective political power. The Social Democrats, therefore, fought against a political regime that denied them political and citizen rights. Hence, the party kept talking of revolution and looked to its many non-German admirers, among whom was Lenin, as the incarnation of Marxist orthodoxy. But, in fact, it became the ideological expression of a social movement that had grown rapidly within the economic framework of expanding German industry and expressed its confident optimism in a historical process that was conceived as essentially benevolent. Kautsky, the prototypical party insider, fashioned a doctrine that appealed to the mass of party leaders and militants who had in their own lives experienced the forces of beneficent evolution (cf. Roth 1963; and Rose L. Coser 1951).

Two incidents help highlight the ambiguities of Kautskyan social democracy. Soon after Eduard Bernstein had raised the banner of revisionist reformism and urged the party to throw off its revolutionary ballast, a young Russian revolutionary who had recently moved to Germany, Alexander Helphand-Parvus, asked his Dresden comrades to propose that the coming party congress at Stuttgart in 1898 pass a resolution that would state that reform could not eliminate the class character of the state; this could only be done through revolution. Such a statement apparently seemed to him to be fully in line with official party policy. Yet Babel wrote to Kautsky, "His resolution has not the slightest understanding of our condition. The last thing we need is the congress solemnly to resolve that it strive for a social revolution" (quoted in Zeman and Scharlau 1965, p. 40).

A few years later, when the party orthodoxy was fully mobilized in the struggle against Bersteinian revisionist reformism, when congress debates and newspaper polemics resounded with attacks against Bernstein's backsliding, Ignaz Auer, a defender of Kautskyan orthodoxy, wrote privately to Bernstein, "My dear Ede, you *don't* pass such resolutions. You don't *talk* about it, you just *do* it" (quoted in Gay 1962, p. 270).

Official Social Democratic Marxist ideology was attuned to the needs of the movement in which it grew. Shorn of the dialectical, action-oriented elements of classical Marxism, it stressed inevitable and benign evolution, shunning any apocalyptic vision of catastrophic breakdown or violent final struggle. It was the doctrine of a movement that felt that it could trust in the course of history, even while it aggressively defended the interests of its working-class constituency and helped organize it as a powerful counter-culture willing to challenge the official culture which denied it full democratic participation.

BERNSTEIN AND REVISIONISM

Eduard Bernstein, the father of revisionism, was even more a Party insider than his close friend Kautsky. He was born in a lower-middle-class section of Berlin in 1850, the son of a plumber who later became a railway engineer. The family lived in genteel poverty. He never finished Gymnasium. His formal education ended at age 16 when he began an apprenticeship in a Berlin bank. Bernstein worked as a bank clerk until 1878. He became a convert to Marxist socialism in 1872. Six years later, he accepted the offer of a wealthy well-wisher to move to Switzerland, and soon thereafter he became associated with the *Sozialdemokrat,* the official organ of the German Party, which had by then been outlawed by Bismarck. During the rest of his long career, Bernstein worked wholly within the party. Moving to London after his Swiss apprenticeship, he collaborated intimately with Engels. In fact, he and Kautsky came to be seen as the chief exponents of Engels's version of Marxist orthodoxy (cf. Gay 1962).

Yet, in 1886, only about a year after Engels's death, Bernstein broke with orthodox Marxism. First in a series of articles in the *Neue Zeit* from 1896 to 1898, and then in the famous book *Die Voraussetzungen des Sozialismus und die Aufgaben der Sozialdemokratie* (Bernstein 1961) of 1899, Bernstein urged the party to discard its revolutionary baggage, to recognize the inevitability of gradualness, and to travel the Fabian road. The Erfurt party program of 1891, which had been written by Kautsky, foresaw an increase in the bitterness of class struggles, increasing exploitation of the workers, and the gradual disappearance of the middle class in an increasingly polarized society. None of these prognoses had been fulfilled, argued Bernstein. Class contradictions had become attenuated, not exacerbated, and the middle classes were thriving. The whole catastrophic outlook of original Marxism, which was due in part to the snares of the Hegelian dialectic with its stress on contradictions, had to be given up. The socialist movements should no longer be beholden to metaphysical doctrines; it should build on positive and empirical investigations which had disproved Marxist catastrophism. Not revolution but evolution was the order of the day. Arguing that "in all advanced countries we see the privileges of the capitalist bourgeoise yielding step by step to democratic organization" (Bernstein 1961, p. xiii), Bernstein urged his party to put aside all hopes in a great economic crash and "to organize the working classes politically, . . . develop them as a democracy, and to fight for all reforms in the state designed to raise the working classes and to transform the State in the direction of democracy" (Bernstein 1961, p. xv).

Bernstein's writings created an enormous sensation in the party and led to a frantic movement of defense on the part of the orthodox. This may seem surprising, since Bernstein clearly "represented," as Peter Gay has said, "no startling novelty but the rational recognition of an already existing state of affairs" (Gay 1962, p. 110). Yet, upon reflection, it seems fairly obvious that by revealing that state of affairs, Bernstein threatened the elaborate Marxian superstructure which Kautsky and his colleagues had so patiently erected. Much like an overeager psychoanalyst who brutally brings hidden springs of motives to the attention of his patients and destroys their defenses, Bernstein exposed the gap between theory and actual practice in his party and threatened to undermine the Kautskyan ideological defense. Such things, as Auer had said, can be done, but they must not be said.

Revisionism was condemned and defeated at several party congresses; yet, when Bernstein returned to Germany from England in 1901, he had become the leader of a significant group within the party. Originally, most of the leading revisionists were intellectuals, but soon many leaders who were only minimally concerned with the fine points of doctrine rallied to revisionism. Its main support came from two sources, the South German party and the trade unions.

South Germany had no three-class electoral system like Prussia. It allowed full participation of Social Democrats in the parliaments of Bavaria and other southern states. Here, as distinct from the North, collaboration between liberals and Social Democrats in pursuit of progressive social legislation was a live option (Gay 1962, p. 258). While, in the North, a political revolution still seemed required to institute democratic process, in the South the political arena was wide open to all entrants. Hence, reformism in Bernsteinian or other dress appealed to Social Democratic militants and leaders in the South.

In addition to the leaders in the South, revisionism found its strongest supporters among the trade-union officials. These men were hardly sensitive to the details of Bernsteinian theory, but they found its stress on the day-to-day struggle much more to their liking than the hopes for the "final collapse of capitalism." Solid and stolid functionaries, pragmatic strategists of bread-and-butter struggles for more, they found in revisionism a convenient ideological defense against the claims of Social Democratic political leaders who attempted to mobilize the unions for their wider political aims. Finally, many of the party functionaries, Reichstag members, municipal councillors, or local deputies who were engaged daily in a politics of compromise were attracted to a simplified version of Bernsteinian doctrine.

Bernstein's career was as completely tied to the Social Democratic party as was that of Kautsky. While his doctrine was officially rejected by the party, it still grew deep roots within it. It found an audience especially among those strata and sections that were engaged in the daily struggle and were less concerned with maintaining the distinctiveness of a working-class subculture to be kept in readiness for the coming democratic revolution. Kautskyism thrived in Prussia, where the working class was effectively excluded from the political arena. Revisionism developed where the socialists already could participate in the political game. Kautsky's doctrine remained victorious in the party as a whole for which the political struggle still loomed largest. Revisionism or pseudorevisionism predominated among the trade-union pragmatists.[1]

---

[1] Austro-Marxism, although it differed in certain respects from Kautskyan orthodoxy, will not be discussed here. Victor Adler, the founder of Austrian Marxism, was a close political and personal friend of Kautsky and differed from him only marginally.

Lewis A. Coser

ROSA LUXEMBURG, PARVUS, AND RADEK: THE LEFTIST REVOLT AGAINST KAUTSKY AND BERNSTEIN

In contrast to the revisionists who developed within the core of the party and who were faithful party stalwarts, the chief exponents of leftist heterodoxy in the German movement were outsiders. Its three most brilliant theorists, Rosa Luxemburg, Parvus, and Radek, had come from Eastern Europe.

Mannheim has remarked that "to the extent that Marxian proletarian groups rise to power, they shake off the dialectical elements of their theory and begin to think in the generalizing methods of liberalism and democracy . . . whilst those who, because of their position, still have to resort to revolution, cling to the dialectical element" (Mannheim 1936, p. 118). This remark is exceedingly perceptive of the trends we analyze. Those who represented Marxian groups on the road to (democratic) power, be they Kautskyans or Bernsteinians, in fact abandoned dialectical or voluntaristic thinking in favor of positivistic evolutionism, while those whose experience had been formed in the revolutionary struggles against Czardom clung to an action-oriented revolutionary Marxism even when they transferred the seat of their activity from the East to Germany.

"The contrast between *postulating* revolution and *being* revolutionary," Luxemburg's biographer, Nettl (1966, p. 5), has written, was the central issue that separated her from Kautsky. She never produced a comprehensive or even logically cohesive system, casting her ideas almost invariably in the form of criticism and polemics (Nettl 1966, p. 9), but what unity there was to her thought came from her revolutionary conviction, from her total identification with the idea of revolution. This idea, in turn, was nourished in an environment that was far removed from that in which Kautsky and Bernstein had grown up. Although she spent her most productive years in the German Social Democratic movement, Rosa Luxemburg had her roots in the Polish revolutionary tradition.

Rosa Luxemburg was born in 1871 in the Polish provincial town of Zamosc. Her father was a timber merchant, and the family was comfortably well off. Her parents were Jews who spoke and thought in Polish and rejected any identification with the traditional Jewish community. As a consequence, they were largely thrown back on their own resources. Neither in Zamosc nor in Warsaw, where they moved when Luxemburg

---

The later generation of Austrian Marxists, men like Max Adler, Otto Bauer, and Rudolf Hilferding, tended to stand somewhat to the left of Kautsky, even though some of them rejected both dialectical thought and positivism in favor of a Kantian ethical doctrine akin to that of Bernstein. Their "leftism" is explained in terms of their realization of the extreme frailty of the structure of the Austro-Hungarian empire and their sense of its impending breakup. It was much harder to believe in peaceful progress in an environment like that of Austria which was racked by exacerbated national struggles than in ethnically homogeneous Germany.

was a small child, did they seem to have formed wider attachment. Luxemberg's father had been educated in Germany, and German was read and spoken in his house, where German culture was much admired. Shunned by the traditional Jewish community, without ties to Polish friends, and admiring things German from a distance, the family seems to have lived in a condition of triple marginality.

During her last few years at the girls' high school in Warsaw, Luxemburg was already in contact with groups of illegal revolutionaries. When she was 15, four leading revolutionaries of the group Proletariat were hanged on the gallows. Soon after graduation, she became a member of a cell of the Revolutionary Party Proletariat. From that time on, the revolutionary socialist movement came to be for Luxemburg the only "home" she was ever to know, the only environment that allowed her to come to terms with her thrice-compounded cultural marginality. The movement allowed her to transcend her alienation through allegiance to socialist internationalism.

In 1889, warned of the imminence of her arrest, Luxemburg was smuggled out of the country and went to Switzerland to study economics and to deepen her knowledge of Marxism. In Zurich she established close political and personal contacts with the leaders of the Polish Social Democratic movement in exile. Here she met Leo Jogiches, her close companion for many years. She soon moved to the forefront of a revolutionary group which split from the main Polish socialist party because of its uncompromising rejection of the idea of Polish nationalism and national independence. From then on, until the war, Luxemburg was a leading member of a small band of brilliant Marxists who directed from abroad the underground *Social Democracy of the Kingdom of Poland*. Throughout these years she was intimately involved in the debates and factional quarrels of the organization, and she wrote major parts of its political statements and programmatic announcements. Even though she was to become an active participant in the German Social Democratic movement, she remained all the while deeply immersed in the revolutionary underground struggle of Poland.

When Luxemburg left Switzerland for Germany in 1898, it was not because she had special admiration for things German. In fact, she personally never liked Germany or Germans. She went because, says Nettl, "the political quality of German Socialism dominated her thinking" (Nettl 1966, p. 31). "Throughout her life in Germany she remained a self-conscious Easterner" (Nettl 1966, p. 32). Germany simply happened to be the country where the action was, the country with the strongest and, as she then thought, the most orthodox Marxist movement in the world. Her allegiance was not to Germany but to the German Social Democratic party (SPD).

What Luxemburg and her associates, such as Parvus, brought into German politics, was a quality hardly known there before. It was what Trotsky had called "the Russian method" —"the idea that action was of a superior order to any other facet of political life" (Nettl 1966, p. 34).

When Luxemburg arrived in Germany, the great Bernstein controversy had just broken out. The elders of the party had been slow to pick up the gauntlet Bernstein had thrown them. In fact, Parvus, another Easterner, wrote the first series of sustained attacks against "Bernstein's Overthrow of Socialism." Kautsky initially disassociated himself from Parvus's fiery attacks and only gradually came to realize the challenge revisionism posed to his position. In the meantime, Luxemburg joined Parvus in violent and often quite personal attacks against Bernsteinian heresy. At last Kautsky came to appreciate their polemical onslaughts, even though he continued to agree with many party leaders that their violent personal tone was "tasteless."

Although Luxemburg eventually became an ally of Kautsky during the Bernstein controversy, these allies in fact were operating on a different wavelength. For Kautsky this was a family quarrel to be carried out with all the personal tact and consideration owed to old party comrades. For Luxemburg it was a passionate fight against a heresy that threatened her very revolutionary identity. To her, Bernstein was not just in error but in sin. The German party spokesmen who complained of Luxemburg's tactlessness or who deplored the "unpleasant tone in the party press produced by the male and female immigration from the East" (Nettl 1966, p. 187) failed to realize that what was at issue was, not only a matter of manners and morals, but a profound difference in overall vision. Luxemburg felt that by questioning the final aim of revolution Bernstein was destroying the need for any proletarian class consciousness. "The entire difference [between revisionism and orthodox Marxism]," she wrote, "becomes this: according to the traditional conception, the Socialist purpose of trade-union and political struggle consists in preparing the proletariat for social upheaval, i.e., *emphasis on the subjective factor.* . . . In the traditional conception the trade-union and political struggle brings the proletariat to realize that it is impossible to alter its situation through such a struggle . . . and convinces it of the inevitability of its final seizure of political power" (Nettl 1966, p. 224; italics mine).

To the Polish revolutionary, emphasis on the subjective factor meant the rejection of any passive trust in evolution. It meant the need for the Social Democratic movement to energize the class consciousness of the working class. The concrete improvements in the immediate conditions of the workers which were in the forefront of Bernstein's concerns, and which in the last analysis also informed Kautsky's orientation, were to Luxemburg and her co-workers only important to the extent that they helped prepare the workers for the revolution to come. For the Eastern revolutionaries, who were only inorganically appended to the German Social Democratic movement, what counted was, not the party as such or its multiple affiliated organizations, but only its role as an instrumentality for heightening the class consciousness of the German workers.

This fundamental divergence of views helps explain Luxemburg's break with Kautsky in 1910. Kautsky had welcomed her support against Bernstein, and he found her useful in many other respects, but when she embarked on a defense of the mass strike as the privileged instrumentality for the radicalization of the movement, he felt that the parting of the ways had come. Luxemburg's advocacy of the mass-strike strategy was especially galling to the party leadership because it was based on the experiences of the revolutionary movement during the first Russian revolution in 1905. When Luxemburg argued for a "leapfrog" effect by which the achievements of the Russian working class would serve as a model for the German workers, she attacked the ingrained sense of German superiority that was so strong an element in Kautskyan orthodoxy and in the SPD, and, in addition, challenged their evolutionary world view.

Most of Luxemburg's writings before 1905 were in defense of the SPD. After her return from Poland, where she took an active part in the revolutionary events, Luxemburg changed her general attitude. She now saw in the organization of the party, and especially in the trade unions, a potential hindrance to the development of class consciousness and revolutionary activity. "Where previously discipline and tradition had served to eradicate errors, now only mass action could sweep them away" (Nettl 1966, p. 513). From now on, Luxemburg trusted only in the revolutionary potential of the masses. She prodded them, appealed to them, idealized them, and believed until her last day that only they would bring salvation to suffering mankind. When, during the war, practically the entire party betrayed the cause of socialist internationalism, Rosa Luxemburg was saved from utter despair by her belief that the masses had been betrayed by their leaders but that they would, in due time, rise from the ashes to realize the vision the party had abandoned.

After Luxemburg's assassination in 1919, Kautsky wrote in his tribute to her, "I take my conception of theory from the French, German and Anglo-Saxon experiences, rather than the Russian; with Rosa Luxemburg it was the other way around" (quoted in Nettl 1966, p. 512). Kautsky here touched upon the crux of the matter. Despite her many years in Western Europe, Luxemburg's conception was basically shaped by her Eastern background and experience. She failed to realize that the German working class, settled, disciplined, solid, and on the way to *embourgeoisement*, had but little in common with the disinherited proletarians who had demonstrated in the streets of Saint Petersburg and Warsaw in 1905.

She endeavored to infuse into the German working class that revolutionary spirit and ardor which she had absorbed in her Polish milieu, and she never understood the extreme structural differences between a highly industrialized society in which the working class had a stake and conditions in which it was an outcast underclass.

Even after her break with Kautsky, Luxemburg seems not to have fully realized how far her alliance with the official SPD leadership had been based on mutual misunderstanding. Kautsky opposed Bernstein because the latter's outspoken revisionist realism threatened to upset the cozy equilibrium of revolutionary programmatic statements and reformist practice through which the party officials had established their intellectual dominance in the party. Luxemburg fought Bernstein because he opposed the messianic vision of a coming cataclysmic proletarian revolution on which her whole world view was premised.

In the last analysis, and this makes for her profound appeal as a person as well as for her ineffectiveness as a theoretician, she was moved by moral revulsion against capitalist society and by deeply ingrained humanitarian ideals. She represented one of the last offshoots of the great tradition of the enlightenment. This tradition was already dying in the West at a time when it still energized the Russian-Polish intellectual circles in which Rosa Luxemburg had spent her formative years. It was her tragedy that she approached German and Western European society with sets of ideas and ideals which had already become obsolescent there. She thought that she represented the vanguard of the European proletariat, while, in fact, the alleged renegade Bernstein had a better grasp of the shape of things to come.

When the war broke out, and international socialism collapsed, Luxemburg's world came to an end. The world of the Second International was her world even though for many years she had riddled most of its leaders with her well-aimed arrows. As the intellectual leader of the Spartakus League, that little band of self-sacrificing socialists who opposed the war, her activities were morally admirable but politically largely ineffective. The league had little political influence during the war, and it remained a marginal force thereafter. Even the disastrous uprising of January 1919, which led to the assassination of Luxemburg, Jogiches, and Karl Liebknecht, had not been planned by the league's leaders. They followed it out of the morally estimable and politically suicidal impulse "not to abandon the masses."

I take it to be of considerable sociological significance that the two most consequential exponents of the revolutionary Left in the prewar SPD besides Luxemburg, Parvus and Radek, stemmed like her from the Eastern revolutionary movement and never gained secure roots in German soil. Alexander Helphand-Parvus was born a Russian Jew in the province of Minsk in 1867. His father was a locksmith or a blacksmith who moved to Odessa when Parvus was a small child. Already involved in socialist circles in his homeland, Parvus was fully converted to revolutionary Marxism when he moved to Switzerland in 1887. After the conclusion of his academic studies in Basle, Parvus left Switzerland in 1891 for Germany. Like Rosa Luxemburg, he wanted to join the ranks of the SPD to serve it as a revolutionary activist. "Whether Russian or German," he wrote, "the struggle of the proletariat always remains the same, and it knows neither national nor religious differences. . . . When I became unfaithful to my native Russia, I also became unfaithful to that class from which I originated: the *bourgeoisie*. My parting of company with the Russian intelligentsia dates from that time" (quoted in Zeman and Scharlau 1965, p. 21). Yet, although Parvus disengaged himself from his Russian homeland, he never fitted into his new home, the German SPD. Just as in the case of Luxemburg, its powers-to-be made use of his dazzling intelligence when it suited their needs, even when they deplored his polemical manners; but they rejected what they judged to be his revolutionary romanticism. As a result, Parvus was, as his biographers put it, "a strategist without an army." Having few of Luxemburg's endearing human qualities and living the life of a bohemian, Parvus never managed to establish the close personal relations with men like Kautsky that had stood Luxemburg in good stead in her years of German apprenticeship. As a result, he remained an outsider whose revolutionary ardor and analytical rigor served the cause of anti-Bernsteinism but whose subsequent theories, anticipating Trotsky's notion of a permanent revolution which would be initiated by the Russian proletariat and would spread over the whole of the globe, failed even to ruffle the doctrinaire feathers of Marxist orthodoxy.

What characterized Parvus's Marxism, as it characterized that of Luxemburg, was its emphasis on revolutionary activity. "Only a revision to the left of our party principles is now possible," he wrote in 1900, "in the sense of the extension of political activity, . . . of the intensification of social-revolutionary energy . of a bold endeavor and will, and not of fearful, reserved softness" (quoted in Zeman and Scharlau 1965, p. 45). It was precisely that revolutionary activism which went against the grain of the party orthodoxy and led to Parvus's isolation.

As with Parvus, so with the third major figure on the revolutionary Left, Karl Radek. The son of "modernist" Galician Jews of the lower middle class, the father a minor post-office employee, Radek grew up in a milieu in which traditional Jewishness was rejected and German culture was extolled. His father having died when Radek was a small child, he was taught by his mother and his uncles to consider himself a child of the German Enlightenment and to shun contact with the despised Poles or with "retrograde" Jews. In reaction against this constricting and petty-bourgeois milieu of Austrian Poland, the young Radek turned to the tradition of the Poles and immersed himself in the Polish revolutionary heritage. By 1902, he had become a convert to Marxism, and in 1903 he emigrated to Zurich, the traditional haven for uprooted Eastern socialists. After a few years, like Luxemburg and Parvus, he went to Germany to become a militant in the SPD. And, as in their case, his revolutionary activism failed to make more than a minor dent in the armor of party orthodoxy (cf. Lerner 1970). Perhaps the most talented of all of Luxemburg's younger followers—although Luxemburg herself disliked him intensely and eventually had him expelled from her Polish oganization—Radek, even more of a bohemian than Parvus, failed to find many supporters in the German party. This became obvious after he attacked Kautsky's relatively benign theory of imperialism in 1912, shortly before the upheaval of the war. (Soon thereafter, Luxemburg published her *The Accumulation of Capital,* a more consequential attack against Kautskyan optimism, in which she argued that imperialism was doomed to end in revolutionary breakdown.) Kautsky had argued that pacifist elements in capitalist society were opposed to such aspects of imperialism as the arms race and that socialists should cooperate with them to help tame imperialism from within. Radek bridled at such heresies. He summed up his lengthy refutation with a rhetorical flourish: "Out of fantasy one can create poetry; out of speculation, inferior philosophy; but the struggle demands a sword" quoted in Lerner 1970, p. 27). Soon after, Radek was expelled from the Germany party under the pretext that he was no longer a member of its Polish sister organization. Men who brandished revolutionary swords apparently had no place among the orthodox defenders of benign evolutionary necessity.

Emphasis on three Easterners as major representatives of the Left revolutionary tradition in prewar Germany does not imply, of course, that the Left did not have German members. As a whole, however, these men were not of the same intellectual stature, and they did not play major roles in the theoretical battles. Karl Liebknecht, the son of one of the founders of the Social Democratic party, was mainly an organizer and agitator; Clara Zetkin, Luxemburg's intimate friend, had considerable moral authority but little intellectual distinction. The only Left leader who was a native German and ranked high as an intellectual was Franz Mehring. He was a most atypical figure. Babel once called him "a psychological riddle" (quoted in Osterroth 1960, p. 220). Having started his career as a liberal and antisocialist writer, he was converted to socialism in the early nineties, when he was already 45 years old. As the author of a multivolume *History of the German Social Democratic Party,* of the classical biography of Karl Marx, and of a series of important historical studies, he was highly respected in the party but carried relatively little weight in current debates. Long a defender of Kautskyan orthodoxy, he moved into the Luxemburgist camp only shortly before the war, when he was already an old man and his main energies were spent.

The Left attracted to its banner a number of younger intellectuals impatient with the staid ways of the party. Luxemburg's fiery oratory, her impassioned writings, as well as her teaching at the Berlin party school made her a beloved figure in militant and activist circles. The Left at times managed to take over party newspapers in Saxony, Bremen, and in the South and used them as springboards for its revolutionary agitation. But it never managed to touch the inner core of the party or its ordinary followers. The trade-union leadership, in particular, seems to have agreed with the pithy saying of one of its leaders, "General strike is general nonsense." When the war came, the two most consistent supporters of Luxemburg among socialist journalists and editors, Paul Lensch and Konrad Haenisch, became German superpatriots. Surely, the revolutionary message had sunk no deep roots in German soil. We shall now turn to examine it on its Eastern home ground.

RUSSIAN MARXISM

Kautsky and the main stream of Marxist orthodoxy in Germany expressed in their political theories the need for Germany to catch up with the achievements of the French Revolution which the German middle class had not managed to emulate. The early Russian Marxists aimed in a similar way at making their country catch up with enlightened Western Europe and replace "Asiatic" and autocratic czardom by liberal democracy. Since the middle class was exceedingly weak, they reasoned that the working class would have to accomplish the major share in the democratic transformation of Russia even as it prepared itself for the task of socialist transformation that was to follow a democratic revolution. But while the German working class was powerful and organized and had a heavy specific weight in society and economy, the Russian working class was still numerically weak, unorganized, and largely shaped in its attitudes and orientations by its recent rural origins. These circumstances helped determine the character of the Russian Marxist movement and created the dilemmas with which it was faced.

The first major theorist of the Russian Marxist movement, Georgi Plekhanov, followed closely in Kautsky's footsteps. His Marxism was rigorously deterministic and evolutionary. Yet the idea of evolution did not, to him, exclude the idea of revolution. "There can be no sudden change," he wrote, "without a sufficient cause, and this cause is to be found in the previous march of social evolution. But, inasmuch as this evolution never ceases in societies that are in the course of development, we may say that history is continually preparing for sudden changes and revolutions. . . . These political catastrophes are absolutely inevitable" (quoted in Baron 1963, p. 293).

Plekhanov had been converted to Marxism from his earlier Populist allegiances when he became convinced that Russia could not skip the stage of capitalism on its road to socialism. Henceforward, he kept rigorously to the idea that the growth of proletarian consciousness, on which the achievement of socialism rested, depended on the continued growth and development of capitalism in Russia. Without large-scale capitalism, no powerful working class movement was possible.

Practically all Russian Social Democrats, whether Menshevists or Bolshevists, were originally disciples of Plekhanov. But, in their attempt to apply his teachings in the political and economic struggles of Czarist Russia, they soon faced difficulties that Plekhanov had but imperfectly foreseen. In particular, they began to realize that Russian workers, although they welcomed the radical intelligentsia when it aided them in their economic struggles, tended to remain cool to the larger revolutionary aims of the Marxist radicals. Through propaganda and agitation, socialist intellectuals hoped to energize a politically indifferent working class. Yet, most of the time, the proletarian masses, when they acted spontaneously, restricted their vision to purely pragmatic economic issues. Since the masses seemed unable spontaneously to embrace wider political aims, the partisans of spontaneity among the Social Democrats gathered in one camp; and the advocates of political consciousness, in another (cf. Haimson 1955).

The dilemma may be illustrated by the problems faced by Martov and Lenin in their effort to give Social Democratic leadership to the Saint Petersburg labor movement in the 1890s (cf. Pipes 1963; see also Wildman 1967). In this period, the movement consisted of two dissimilar segments. On the one side was the mass of unskilled and semiskilled workers, especially in the textile industry, most of them with yet strong attachments to the peasant milieu from which they had recently come. These laborers distrusted all intellectuals and for long remained immune to their influence. On the other side, a labor aristocracy of skilled workers, mainly from the metal industry, who had been urban dwellers for several generations, displayed considerable social and political awareness. These educated machinists, thirsty for knowledge, furnished the several hundred members of the study circles which Social Democratic as well as Populist revolutionary intellectuals organized in Saint Petersburg in the period from 1885 to 1897.

However, when the first mass strikes occurred in 1896 and 1897, involving as many as 30,000 textile workers, it turned out that the Social

Democratic intellectuals, united by then in the Union of Struggle for the Emancipation of the Working Class, gained only peripheral influence in it. They helped couch demands in precise and literate language, but the demands themselves emerged spontaneously. The whole movement was led and organized by rank-and-file workers who formulated the aims of the strike, among which a reduction in working hours loomed largest. The Social Democratic and the labor movement never merged in Saint Petersburg or elsewhere until 1905, when the two seemed to come together for a brief period. Labor was mainly concerned with economic improvement or, in the case of a section of the labor aristocracy, with intellectual self-improvement. The Social Democratic intelligentsia aimed at the development of revolutionary politics (cf. Pipes 1963, pp. 117ff; and Frankel 1969).

In 1897 Lenin was arrested in Saint Petersburg as a main organizer of the Union of Struggle and spent the next three years in exile in Siberia. When he reached Europe and digested his Russian experiences, he went through a major political and spiritual crisis. He now realized that the aims of labor and of the radical intelligentsia did not necessarily coincide. "On the one hand," he now wrote, "the labor movement separates itself from socialism . . . , on the other, socialism separates itself from the labor movement . . . the labor movement, separated from Social Democracy . . . inevitably become bourgeois" (Pipes 1968, p. 49). Lenin had now come to doubt the revolutionary potential of labor. If labor was not revolutionary, at least potentially, then the whole conception that he had heretofore shared with Plekhanov and all Russian Marxists, namely, that the development of capitalism necessarily entailed the growth of proletarian class consciousness, was put into jeopardy.

Lenin escaped his dilemma by a fundamental revision of previously accepted Marxian doctrine. He now argued that the workers could never spontaneously attain class consciousness, that the working class would become a revolutionary force only if it accepted the leadership of trained professional revolutionists who would inculcate class consciousness, as it were, from the outside. Working-class spontaneity now became the main impediment to political mobilization. "The task of Social Democracy is to combat spontaneity, to divert the labor movement, with its spontaneous trade union strivings, from under the wing of the bourgeoisie, and to bring it under the influence of Social Democracy" (quoted in Haimson 1955, p. 134). Marxists, Lenin now argued, could not afford to follow at the tail of popular movements, for that would be "subservience to spontaneity." Hence, the Marxist party, "the great whole which we are creating for the first time" (Lenin, n.d., p. 464) as the embodiment of disciplined activist drives, became the foremost instrument for achieving revolutionary goals. Consciousness and spontaneity were now definitely severed. Consciousness was embodied in the revolutionary party which imposed its will on the "natural," "spontaneous" course of working-class activity. Revolutionary will became the main drive of history. Optimistic reliance on the idea that the beneficent course of evolution would spontaneously increase working-class consciousness was replaced by a voluntaristic doctrine which proclaimed the need to rape history if it was unwilling to submit.

There is no need here to go into the complicated and intricate political maneuvers, the moves and countermoves, the intrigues and polemics, which led to the split between Bolshevists and Menshevists. At the risk of oversimplification, it can be said that Menshevism, led by such men as Martov, Axelrod, Dan, and, after some initial hesitation, Plekhanov, opted for spontaneity and against Lenin's "consciousness brought from the outside." Only some Marxists adhered to what was called "economism," limiting themselves to support the economic struggles and demands of labor without immediately posing wider political questions. Most Menshevists, in contrast, actively propagandized for their political demands among the workers and attempted to prepare them for the coming democratic revolution against Czardom. But all of them rejected the voluntaristic elitism of Bolshevism. To them, Lenin had abandoned orthodox Marxism for a new version of Jacobinism or Blanquism which subordinated the working class to the heavy hand of the dictatorship of the Bolshevik party.

The voluntaristic Leninist version of Marxism grew in a country and in a social situation in which a young, numerically small, and yet partly peasant-rooted working class did not, or not yet, spontaneously generate the class consciousness on which the politics of all previous Marxist movements had been premised. When Lenin realized that, after all, being does not always determine consciousness, he decided that the radical Marxist intelligentsia would foist it on the working class even against its will. He would force them to become conscious. Consequently, while Menshevism was a version of Western orthodox Marxism, adapted to the conditions of autocratic Russia and hence more revolutionary and activist in orientation than in the West, Leninism was an entirely new variant of Marxism, if it can be called Marxism at all.

We now turn to a brief examination of the Russian Marxist intelligentsia from which Lenin recruited those "professional revolutionaries" in whom he invested all his hopes.

Their social origin is to be found in three strata of Russian society. They were either sons of the gentry and service nobility (like Lenin and Plekhanov), or emancipated Jews (like Trotsky and Martov), or sons of *raznochintsy* (literally, "men of many ranks" or "unrankables"), that is, plebian offspring of priests, servants, shopkeepers, or freed serfs (like Stalin and many secondary leaders of both Menshevism and Bolshevism). It serves no purpose to attempt to distinguish between Leninists and

Menshevists in terms of social origin. All three categories of origin were represented in both organizations, and emancipated Jews took pride of place in the upper echelons of both. Whether a particular individual chose to align himself with one or the other wing depended on specific circumstance and on ideological orientation rather than on origin.

What united the members of the radical intelligentsia was a deep hatred and loathing for Russian backwardness. To Lenin, just as to all other Russian Marxists, the West was "democratic, modern and progressive," and it was sweeping steadily toward social revolution. Russia, by contrast, was "Asiatic, barbarous, and backward" (cf. Wolfe 1955, p. 161). Trotsky expressed this common loathing of the radical intelligentsia most eloquently when he wrote, "The revolution means the final break of the people with Asianism, with the 17th century, with holy Russia, with ikons and cockroaches, not a return to the pre-Petrine period, but on the contrary an assimilation of the people to civilization" (quoted in Carr 1970). Whatever else the radical intellectuals may have been, they were above all men who wished to propel loathsome, sluggish, backward Russia into the 20th century; they were activist modernizers in a hurry.

Russian Marxist intellectuals considered themselves the heirs of the great Populist revolutionary tradition that had preceded their efforts. Even though they differed from populism in both program and orientation, they could not but consider the activist revolutionaries of the previous period as brothers under the skin. By contrast, they sharply attacked those members of the intelligentsia, the great majority, who declined to join the revolutionary struggle. Their emphasis on the supreme importance of *activity* can be interpreted, at least in part, as a reaction against the apathy and intense self-absorption of the nonpolitical intelligentsia. This rejection of the passivity of the intelligentsia was especially pronounced among the Bolsheviks. To Lenin, the heroes of Turgenev and Chekhov, so intensely introspective that they have no capacity to act, seemed the very embodiment of those pernicious tendencies that had to be rooted out if Russia was to be pushed forward. Turgenev's *Rudin*, of whom the author wrote that "nature has . . . denied . . . him the power of action, the ability to carry out his intentions"; the hero of *The Diary of a Superfluous Man*, who "analyzed [himself] to the last shred"; Goncharov's *Oblomov*, that antihero who consumes the first 200 pages of the novel in an effort to get out of bed and the rest with vague dreams of what he will do, dreams he will obviously never realize—these characters were to the Bolshevists and to all Marxists symbols of Russian passivity and sloth. Passivity was the enemy (cf. Coser 1965, pp. 160–61).

When the Marxist radicals turned to the working class, conceiving it to be the privileged instrument for bringing about the revolution that would put an end to Russia's backwardness, they soon faced a dilemma which in another form had faced the Populists when they "went to the people," that is, the peasantry. The Populist Social Revolutionaries found, by and large, that the peasants failed to understand what moved those *intelligentsia* who attempted to propagandize in their villages. Still deeply attached to throne and altar, they often turned the revolutionaries over to the police. The Marxists were not as thoroughly divorced from the workers. As had been seen, small cadres of skilled and self-educated workers served as transmission belts between the Marxists and the emerging labor movement. Yet the working class as a whole still consisted in large part of recent migrants from the villages who had just begun to make the first faltering demands that transcended their immediate economic interests. Hence, the dilemma of choice for the Marxists between "spontaneity"—that is, reliance on the inherent developments within the labor movement coupled with activist efforts to educate workers politically—and "consciousness"— that is, the attempt to force the development through the voluntaristic activism of professional Bolshevist revolutionaries.

The activistic interpretation of Marxism was shared by most Russian Marxists who faced the Czarist autocracy and were forced, for the most part, to operate under conditions of extreme repression and illegality. Extreme voluntaristic activism, on the other hand, was the hallmark of Lenin's doctrine. Both tendencies stemmed from the conditions of a still largely agrarian country in which, in contrast to the West, there existed no strong and self-conscious working-class movement. But the Leninist tendency was rooted in the idea that, when nothing could be expected for the time being from action *by* the workers, then action had to be taken *for* the workers.

Despite superficial similarities, Lenin's and Luxemburg's activism differed fundamentally. Luxemburg based her ideas on her Polish experience, where the working class, although still weak, was considerably more self-conscious and better organized than in the rest of Russia. Disregarding the fundamentally different context in which the German labor movement operated, she then concluded, erroneously, that the German workers, if not held back by bureaucratic fetters, would spontaneously reach for revolutionary goals. Lenin, in contrast, developed his doctrine in the context of a society in which the working class seemed unwilling and unable to act spontaneously in a revolutionary direction. His whole experience having been shaped in this Russian context, Lenin attempted after he had attained power in Russia to transfer his conception of voluntaristic activism by professional revolutionaries to the European scene (cf. Borkenau 1962). He did not trust spontaneity be it in the East or in the West.

In the Leninist as well as the Luxemburgist case, endeavors to transfer the Eastern experience to the West proved a failure. Both foundered on the rock of the fundamentally different class structures of maturing industrial societies. Yet, after the war, voluntaristic interpretations of Marxism found still other defenders in Western Europe. But here again, the theorists expounding such doctrines had their roots in nonindustrial areas and were marginal to the mainstream of the working-class movement in industrial Europe.

GRAMSCI AND LUKACS

It is significant that the only two Marxist theorists of marked originality who emerged after the First World War both came from the agrarian rim of Europe and not from the industrialized heartland. And it is equally significant that these men, just like their Eastern forebears, elaborated a markedly antideterministic and voluntaristic interpretation of Marxism.

Antonio Gramsci came from Sardinia, an utterly backward area, even by southern Italian standards. In Gramsci's time, not even 5 percent of the total population of Sardinia was employed in industry. Its landed aristocracy ran the island in semifeudal fashion and prevented the emergence of a self-conscious middle class. The island was isolated both geographically and culturally. It was one of Europe's most stagnant backwaters.

Gramsci was born in 1891, the son of a petty clerk in the state bureaucracy. When he was six years old, his father was arrested for "administrative irregularity" and sentenced to five years in prison. Two years earlier, young Antonio had fallen down a steep flight of stairs and, as a result, acquired a hunched back. When the father decided that the family could not afford to send Antonio to junior high school, he was sent to work for 10 hours a day in his father's land office for a salary of roughly two dollars a month. Two years later, his mother and sister scraped together enough money from their work as seamstresses to send the boy to *ginnasio*. To say that he had an unhappy childhood risks sounding like an understatement. In later years, he was to reflect that he had "known almost always the most brutal aspects of life" (cf. Cammett 1967, p. 12; and Hughes 1961, pp. 96 ff).

A sense of personal humiliation and alienation merged in Gramsci's mind with his loathing for the backwardness of the island on which he spent the first 20 years of his life. In later years, he referred to the "sewer of my past," and recalled his "continual effort to overcome those backward ways of living and thinking characteristic of Sardinians at the beginning of the century." Imprisoned in a stultifying atmosphere, he spoke of his strong need to break out of the Sardinian swamp to join "national" and "European" life and culture (Cammett 1967, pp. 3–11).

Late in 1911, Gramsci left Sardinia forever and enrolled as a student at the University of Turin. Turin was then the capital of Piedmont and the leader in Italian culture and technology. Gramsci must have felt that he had suddenly moved from the 17th to the 20th century. At the university, he came under the influence of the philosophy of Bennedetto Croce. This neoidealistic historian-philosopher dominated Italian intellectual life and attempted to fuse the heritage of Vico and Hegel into a relativistic historicism somewhat akin to that of Dilthey in Germany. Soon after encountering Crocean ideas, Gramsci joined the socialist movement and familiarized himself with Marxism. Throughout his career, he attempted to infuse a measure of Crocean "idealist" flexibility into the structure of Marxist thought.

The Turin labor movement was the most developed in all Italy. The young rebellious man from the backward provinces was tremendously impressed by it and began soon to see in it the instrumentality that would help bring about revolutionary change in Italy. His diffuse and inchoate hatreds for things as they were became focused and were given coherent shape through his identification with the Turin workers. Working at first as a journalist and pamphleteer at the extreme left wing of the Italian Socialist party, Gramsci came into his own during the large-scale strikes that shook Turin in 1920 and led to the occupation of the major factories by spontaneously emerging factory councils. He saw in these councils the crucible in which the working class could develop those cultural characteristics that would make it fit to impose its "hegemony" on the rest of society. He argued that the working class, before it can seize state power, must establish its claim to power in the political, cultural, and ethical field. It cannot only fight for "crude" economic interests, but as a conscious class must become the carrier of a distinct weltanschauung (Cammett 1967, p. 205).

The factory council movement soon collapsed, and the disunited and rudderless socialist movement proved incapable of stopping Mussolini's march to power. Gramsci became a founding member of the Italian Communist party and worked in its leading cadre. Arrested by Mussolini in 1926, he remained in prison until 1937. He was released three days before his death. His most significant writings are found in his *Letters from Prison*.

Gramsci's unorthodox approach to Marxism had a decidely voluntaristic cast. He argued that traditional Marxism was overly materialistic and deterministic. He opposed to the "economistic superstition" the "philosophy of praxis" (Cammett 1967, p. 191).

Marxism could only become an adequate philosophy, Gramsci argued, by emphasizing the dialectical aspects of the interplay between proletarian action and the ideology developed by intellectuals. His biographer, Cammett (1967, p. 191), puts Gramsci's thought well when he writes: "The Marxist intellectual develops the principles and the problems created by the masses' practical activism, and the conclusions of this theoretical activity are then used to change the practical realm."

Gramsci aspired to a union of "spontaneity" and "conscious leadership" which would eventuate in disciplined praxis of the working class that would establish its hegemony over the rest of society. He rejected the belief that economic conditions determine irrevocably the human condition. Political initiative is always needed to "free the economic thrust from the shackles of traditional politics." In the last analysis, what counts is not the economically and socially given but a determined will to power infused in the working class by its leading intellectual spokesmen.

Despite his admiration for working-class spontaneity, Gramsci's doctrine boiled down to a rejection not only of Marxist determinism but an exaltation of the creative role of intellectuals. Ideas did not spring spontaneously from material conditions; they had an autonomy of their own. Revolutionary advances occurred only when intellectuals, imbued with creative will, fused their energies with a working class ready to conquer the nation. Gramsci did not feel that it was necessary to wait until "all the economic conditions were ripe" to bring about the revolution. Proletarian liberation could be achieved through voluntary praxis in the here and now.

The similarities between Gramsci's and Lenin's view are perhaps more striking than the evident differences in styles of thought and in philosophical sophistication. Gramsci's thought was in tune with contemporary philosophy of history, while Lenin's Marxism was crude indeed. But what is important for my purpose here is not this different level in style or argument but the fact that the son of the school inspector from Simbirsk and the tortured outsider from backward Sardinia both endeavored to impose their vision of a willed transformation of the human condition on a working class that seemed resistant and unwilling to undertake this "historical mission." These rebel "outsiders" could not trust in the comfortable and optimistic evolutionary vision of "insiders" like Kautsky. They bent Marxism in an activistic and voluntaristic direction. In Lenin's Russia, this voluntarism led to a rejection of "spontaneity" and a generalized distrust of the as yet weak and inchoate labor movement. Writing from the vantage point of a more developed labor movement, Gramsci attempted to fuse spontaneity with the consciousness of intellectuals.

It is among the finest ironies of history that the rebellious Sardinian outsider has now become the patron saint of an Italian Communist movement which in its daily practice is almost as respectable and bureaucratic, as complacent and unrevolutionary as the SPD under the Kaiser. There was perhaps more to economic determinism than Gramsci was willing to allow.

At first blush, Georg Lukacs's social origins could hardly be more dissimilar from those of Antonio Gramsci (cf. Lichtheim 1970*b*; and Watnick 1962). His early life was not marked by suffering and poverty; he grew up in a world of abundance. His father was the director of a major bank in Budapest and, despite his Jewishness, had been ennobled by the imperial government. And yet there is much in common between Gramsci's and Lukacs's backgrounds. They both grew up, not in the industrial heartland of Europe, but rather on its agrarian rim. Lukacs's Budapest was a metropolitan center, to be sure, but it was not an industrial center, and, moreover, it was the only major city in Hungary and was all but drowned in the surrounding sea of peasant civilization.

Lukacs spent his formative years in a country in which the major societal forces had reached a kind of stalemate, effectively prohibiting creative innovation in political and social affairs. An essentially traditionalistic peasantry dominated by both Church and landowners seemed impermeable to novel ideas. Labor still had little weight in Hungary's premodern society, and its organizational endeavors in the Social Democratic party and in the unions were more concerned with bread-and-butter issues than with comprehensive reforms. The dominant aristocracy and the impoverished gentry, which did the dirty work for the nobility in the administration of the state, were committed to the maintenance of the existing state of affairs since social changes would undermine the basis of their domination. The oppressed minorities in the countryside, though suffering under the yoke of the Magyars, were isolated from one another and from the urban centers and were therefore unable to make themselves heard in the seats of power. The largely Jewish middle class was conformist to the core and dreaded any transformation that might upset its monopoly on financial and commercial affairs.

Given the stasis of the society, it is understandable that the small layer of alert and activist intellectuals who gathered in Budapest around the turn of the century came to conceive of themselves as the sole voice and conscience of the nation. Even though they were doctrinally committed to the goals of democracy, conditions almost ineluctably drove them to an elitist stance. In their interstitial existence, they came to see themselves as reformers par excellence. Since there was little or no audience for their melioristic ideas, they alone, it seemed to them, could be the source of change, if it were to come at all. In Budapest at that time, as Mannheim used to say later, intellectuals saw themselves as the self-appointed guardians of the well-understood interests of the whole society.

Most of the reform-minded members of the Budapest intelligentsia belonged in the prewar days to the Society for Social Science, a select group of progressive social scientists who saw themselves as the Hungarian counterpart of the Fabian Society. Lukacs, however, was not a member of that group. He had spent a number of years in Germany, where he had made a name for himself as a literary critic and writer on esthetic subjects and where he had gained the friendship of both Georg Simmel and Max Weber. His philosophical orientation at the time was in the tradition of German idealism and historicism, although he had also read widely in mysticism and vitalistic philosophy. Political concerns were then alien to him. When he returned from Heidelberg to Budapest in 1915, he organized a discussion group with like-minded idealist intellectuals which was broadened in 1917 into a Free School for the Humanities, stressing German *Geisteswissenschaft* and idealistic philosophy in contradistinction to the positivism of the Society for Social Sciences. Lukacs's group was beholden to "Soul and Culture," to quote the title of a programmatic lecture given by Mannheim, and scoffed at the primitive "materialism" of Marxist thought.

When the Hungarian revolution broke out in October 1918, the intellectuals of the Society for Social Sciences were in the forefront of the Republican and mildly socialist regime of Count Karolyi. Members of the Lukacs circle seemed unconcerned. But in December 1918, Lukacs suddenly, and to the great surprise of his friends, entered the newly formed Communist party and became a central intellectual figure of the Bela Kun regime during the short-lived Soviet republic (cf. Coser 1971; and Kettler 1967).

All major Hungarian intellectuals had suffered in the prewar years from their impotence and their political as well as social isolation. Many of them had sought for a way out in a sort of a Fabian progressive politics which in fact, though not in theory, would allow them to become a guiding elite. Lukacs, however, had not been part of that movement but had instead been deeply involved in German intellectual circles that had for years stressed the desperate crisis of the European spirit in an age of progressive mechanization and bureaucratization. Hence, the mildly reformist Karolyi regime did not appeal to his romantic yearning for an entirely new beginning, a fundamental recasting of the whole of European culture. The Soviet regime, on the other hand, promised just that. It offered a cure for the torn soul and a road to salvation for the despised *Geist* of European culture. Lukacs became a Marxist out of a deep yearning for cultural renewal. He had never been attracted by humdrum Social Democratic reform activity. Bela Kun's revolution, on the other hand, allowed him to form a vision of the revitalization of European culture on barricades manned by activist workers.

Lukacs himself said almost half a century later that the doctrines he developed in the aftermath of the Hungarian revolution stemmed from certain earlier preoccupations with problems of ethics. He was attracted to syndicalism and the philosophy of Sorel but was "repelled by Social Democratic theory, above all Kautsky." But "ethics exercised pressure in the direction of *praxis*, of action, and hence of politics" (Lukacs 1968, pp. 12–13). With the Russian Revolution, and more directly and immediately with the Hungarian Soviet experience, Lukacs became an activist Marxian. When writing his famous *History and Class Consciousness* in 1922–23, he still believed that "the great revolutionary wave, which would lead the whole world, at least all of Europe, in very short time to socialism . . . had by no means receded." Lukacs later characterized his Marxist orientation of the time as "messianic-utopian" (Lukacs 1968, pp. 16, 27). He says that he passionately hated "mechanical fatalism" and "mechanical materialism" and that his whole thinking was predicated on the notion of revolutionary activity.

Lukacs now idealized the Leninist party as the incarnation of revolutionary voluntarism, as living praxis. The Hegelian *Weltgeist* seemed to him to be embodied in the wisdom of the Communist party. The party could not possibly be wrong. The class consciousness which Lukacs extolled was by no means an empirically ascertainable orientation of concrete workers. It was the "objective consciousness" that was imputed to the proletariat and incarnated in the Communist party. Lukacs argued that it was typical of opportunism to confound "the factual psychological state of consciousness of the proletariat with the class consciousness of the proletariat" (Lukacs 1968, p. 249). The "objective theory of class consciousness," he argued, "is the theory of its objective possibility" (Lukacs 1968, p. 255). And that objective possibility found its adequate embodiment in the omniscient Communist vanguard equipped with a "scientific" understanding of the course of history.

To Lukacs, the proletariat was the potentially revolutionary class par excellence. But potentiality would become reality only if the party would point the correct way through the direction of revolutionary practice. The true subject of history was hence the party, while the masses were only its object as long as they were not energized by the revolutionary will and the scientific praxis of the party. The actual working class, sunk in humdrum existence and nonauthenticity, did not interest Lukacs at all. He was transfixed by what it *could become*. When Caliban absorbed the *Geist* incarnated in the Communist party, he would redeem a fallen world and would make it whole again.

It serves no purpose here to follow Lukacs's later descent into Stalinist conformity and his subsequent recantation of the book on which his reputation as a political thinker inevitably rests. Nor can we deal with his subsequent literary criticism. What concerns us here is exclusively the attempt by a marginal intellectual from the rimland of Europe to develop a voluntaristic Marxism even more extreme than that of Lenin. Lukacs's and Gramsci's attacks against Kautskyan evolutionary orthodoxy were the last major attempts within the period under discussion to develop the voluntaristic and activistic strains that were inherent in the early writings of Marx and Engels.[2]

SUMMARY

This analysis of the major current of Marxist thought in the first quarter of the 20th century focused on the differential interpretation of the teaching of Marx by the main theorists of orthodox Marxism and revisionism in Germany, and by a variety of Marxist revolutionary thinkers from the East, from Italy, and from Hungary. It has been shown that the German Marxists, whether orthodox or revisionist, were "insiders" expressing the desires and hopes of a highly organized working class in a strongly industrialized country. Their evolutionary optimism reflected a movement which saw itself engaged in a confident march toward democratic power and socialist ascendancy. By contrast, the revolutionaries from Russia and Poland who were active in the German movement were "outsiders" who reacted in terms of their different experiences in the East and thought that revolutionary activism would push the spontaneous struggle of the German workers toward an apocalyptic "final struggle" with the forces of capitalist domination. It turned out that they misjudged the character of the work-

---

[2] I originally intended to devote a few pages to the analysis of Georges Sorel's work. His *Reflections on Violence* seem to belong to and indeed anticipate later voluntaristic interpretations of Marxism. I have decided against such discussion, however, since Sorel did not have any impact within the Marxist movement. This was so, not only because a few years after writing his book (1908) he abandoned the Left altogether and endeavored to find a new audience among the conservative Right, but also because his call for energizing myths that would move the working class to action was so far removed from contemporary Marxist thinking of whatever specific coloring that it could not possibly be assimilated by anyone still considering himself a Marxist. Men like Robert Michels or Georg Lukacs might at times read him with a measure of sympathy, but, in the Marxist movement as a whole, the odor of heresy clung to Sorel's name.

It might suffice, hence, to suggest that the extreme voluntarism of this provincial from Cherbourg who had studied at the Ecole polytechnique and for many years pursued a conventional career as an engineer in the road-building services of the government, might best be explained by reference to the specific conditions of France around the turn of the century. France was, of course, one of the leading countries in Europe, but its industry and hence its labor movement was still in many ways more similar to that of Europe in the middle of the century than to conditions in contemporary Germany. Large-scale industry was still rare. Much production was still carried out in enterprises that had not fully shed their artisanal character. The working class was weakened from the bloodletting of the Commune and its trade unions were small, even though militant. Syndicalism, the movement to which Sorel attached himself temporarily, never managed to organize the majority of workers, as the unions of Germany, England, or the Lowlands had managed to do. Given these conditions, it would seem that Sorel's thought, insofar as it expressed real tendencies in the labor movement, if it expressed them at all, was a reflection of its fundamental organizational weakness. In this respect, although obviously not in others, Sorel's voluntarism had much in common with the other varieties that have been discussed here (cf. Ridley 1970).

ing class in a maturing industrial society. They found some acceptance in Germany to the extent that *political* revolution seemed to the orthodox to still be necessary, but they were rejected when they advocated *social* revolution.

In Russia itself, failure of the as yet weak working class to listen to the revolutionary message of the Social Democratic intelligentsia led to the historic split between Bolsheviks and Mensheviks. The former rejected the spontaneous movements of the workers and opted for a voluntaristic activism by professional revolutionaries who were to impose their will on the recalcitrant masses. The latter, though more activistic than their Western counterparts, trusted in the main the evolutionary developments within Russia and hence were fundamentally at one with the evolutionary schemes of orthodox Kautskyan Marxism.

Finally, I analyzed in the case of Gramsci and Lukacs, other types of voluntaristic Marxist thought, nurtured like their Leninist prototype in backward areas by embittered revolutionary intellectuals in a hurry.

In conclusion, it may be stated that the revolutionary and activist Marxism first developed by Marx and Engels in the late 1840s found an echo among 20th century intellectuals in those areas of the rimland of Europe which still resembled in essential respects the conditions prevailing in the heartland of Europe half a century earlier. In the main centers of the European working class, on the other hand, positivistic evolutionary Marxism, adumbrated by Engels in the last period of his life and further developed by Kautsky, carried the day and was later largely replaced by Fabian or Bernsteinian gradualism. Social existence determined social consciousness. The receptivity to variant Marxist doctrine was largely conditioned by the values and attitudes of the men and women whose concrete social and historical existence was mirrored in their world view, whether as producers or as consumers of ideas.

REFERENCES

Baron, Samuel H. 1963. *Plekhanov: The Father of Russian Marxism.* Stanford, Calif.: Stanford University Press.
Bernstein, Eduard. 1961. *Evolutionary Socialism.* New York: Schocken.
Borkenau, Franz. 1962. *World Communism.* Ann Arbor: University of Michigan Press.
Cammett, John M. 1967. *Antonio Gramsci and the Origin of Italian Communism.* Stanford, Calif.: Stanford University Press.
Carr, E. H. 1970. *Socialism in One Country.* Vol. 1. Baltimore: Penguin.
Coser, Lewis A. 1965. *Men of Ideas.* New York: Free Press.
―――. 1971. *Masters of Sociological Thought.* New York: Harcourt Brace Jovanovich.
Coser, Rose Laub. 1951. "An Analysis of the Early German Socialist Movement." M.A. thesis, Columbia University.
Frankel, Jonathan, ed. 1969. *Vladimir Akimov and the Dilemma of Russian Marxism 1895–1903.* Cambridge: Cambridge University Press.

Gay, Peter. 1962. *The Dilemma of Democratic Socialism.* New York: Collier Books.
Haimson, Leopold H. 1955. *The Russian Marxists and the Origin of Bolshevism.* Cambridge, Mass.: Harvard University Press.
Hughes, Stuart H. 1961. *Consciousness and Society.* New York: Vintage.
Kettler, David. 1967. *Marxismus und Kultur.* Neuwied and Berlin: Luchterhand.
Lenin, V. I. n.d. "One Step Forward, Two Steps Backward." In *Selected Works.* Vol. 2. New York: International Publishers.
Lerner, Warren. 1970. *Karl Radek: The Last Internationalist.* Stanford, Calif.: Stanford University Press.
Lichtheim, George. 1961. *Marxism.* New York: Praeger.
———. 1970a. *A Short History of Socialism.* New York: Praeger.
———. 1970b. *Georg Lukacs.* New York: Viking.
Lukacs, Georg. 1968. *Geschichte und Klassenbewusstsein, Werke.* Vol. 2. Neuwied and Berlin: Luchterhand.
Mannheim, Karl. 1936. *Ideology and Utopia.* New York: Harcourt Brace.
Marx, Karl. 1912. *A Contribution to the Critique of Political Economy.* Chicago: Kerr.
Michels, Robert. 1949. *Political Parties.* New York: Free Press.
Nettl, J. P. 1966. *Rosa Luxemburg.* 2 vols. London: Oxford University Press.
Osterroth, F. 1960. *Biographisches Lexicon des Sozialismus.* Hanover: Dietz.
Pipes, Richard. 1963. *Social Democracy and the St. Petersburg Labor Movement, 1885–1897.* Cambridge, Mass.: Harvard University Press.
———. 1968. "The Origin of Bolshevism." In *Revolutionary Russia*, edited by Richard Pipes. Cambridge, Mass.: Harvard University Press.
Ridley, F. F. 1970. *Revolutionary Syndicalism in France.* Cambridge: Cambridge University Press.
Roth, Guenther. 1963. *The Social Democrats in Imperial Germany.* Totowa, N.J.: Bedminster.
Watnick, Morris. 1962. "Relativism and Class Consciousness." In *Revisionism*, edited by Leopold Labedz. London: Allen & Unwin.
Wildman, Allan K. 1967. *The Making of a Workers' Revolution.* Chicago: University of Chicago Press.
Wolfe, Bertram D. 1955. *Three Who Made a Revolution.* Boston: Beacon.
Zeman, Z. B. A., and W. B. Scharlau. 1965. *The Merchant of Revolution: The Life of Alexander Israel Helphand.* London: Oxford University Press.

Review Essay

Science, Technology and Society in Seventeenth-Century England. By Robert K. Merton. New York: Howard Fertig, Inc., 1970. Pp. xxix+279. $11.00 (cloth). New York: Harper & Row, 1970. Pp. xxxii+279. $2.75 (paper).

Benjamin Nelson

New School for Social Research

This precocious masterwork has had to wait 32 years to find its way into separate and full publication in this country. Originally issued in 1938 as a long monograph in *Osiris* magazine (4:360–632), edited by George Sarton under the imprint of the St. Catherine Press in Bruges, the study soon became largely inaccessible, more often cited than read. Now at long last it is available to use in both hardbound and paperback editions, with an intensely revealing new preface in which the author speaks directly to his critics and future readers about his original intentions and his present points of view. Anyone who hopes to follow the developments in Robert Merton's interests and emphases from his days as a graduate student shall henceforth have to study both documents together—the dissertation and the new preface—very closely.

   Although I shall here be limiting myself to only a few aspects of these documents, the reader should not be surprised if certain larger features of Merton's paradigmatic itinerary appear in a new light. Readers of the present essay are offered a continuous center of orientation by one of Merton's most haunting reminiscences now freshly offered us:

> The inquiry began as he [the author] was rummaging about in seventeenth-century England, trying to make some sense of the remarkable efflorescence of science at that time and place, being directed in the search by a general sociological orientation. The orientation was simple enough: various institutions in the society are variously interdependent so that what happens in the economic or religious realm is apt to have some perceptible connections with some of what happens in the realm of science, and conversely. In the course of reading letters, diaries, memoirs and papers of seventeenth-century men of science, the author slowly noted the frequent religious commitments of scientists in this time, and even more, what seemed to be their Puritan orientation. Only then, and almost as though he had not been put through his paces during the course of graduate study, was he belatedly put in mind of that intellectual tradition, established by Max Weber, Troeltsch, Tawney and others, which centered on the interaction between the Protestant Ethic and the emergence of modern capitalism. Swiftly making amends for this temporary amnesia, the author turned to a line-by-line reading of Weber's work to see whether he had anything at all to say about the relation of Puritanism to science and technology. Of course, he had. It turns out that Weber concluded his classic essay by describing one of the "next tasks" as that

of searching out "the significance of ascetic rationalism, which has only been touched in the foregoing sketch, for a variety of cultural and social developments," among them "the development of philosophical and scientific empiricism . . . technical development and . . . spiritual ideals." Once identified, Weber's recommendation became a mandate. [Preface, 1970, p. xvii]

The more carefully we seek to follow the author's entire course against the horizons here adopted as backgrounds, the more surprising the signals suggested by the irregular flickerings of the beacon he has just generously set before us.

I

It seems both prudent and exciting to begin by seeking to retrace the steps Merton took in completing the original dissertation. Already the first lines of the preface and the introductory first chapter of that work reveal the special blend of boldness, caution, rigor and tentativeness which has everywhere become the author's hallmark. The pains he takes to make his purposes and propositions clear are truly extraordinary. It can hardly be his fault that these cautions did not serve to protect him from the stringencies of inclement reviewers and readers.

After a moment's foray—not without its own interest—into the cultural history of Western civilization, Merton proceeds to marshall his evidence in the manner of seasoned professional historians. He sets forth the fruits of in-depth studies of sources, original and secondary alike, illustrating religious and scientific developments among 17th-century British and late 18th early 19th-century German Pietist writers. He strives mightily to master the extensive Continental literature written from varied points of view in the history of science and technology (A. de Candolle, F. Klein, F. M. Feldhaus, Franz Borkenau, and others).

Already in the first two chapters we find Merton doing a great deal more than even the most seasoned historians were attempting in those days: he develops a "data bank" for systematic statistical analysis by intensively collating "some 6000" biographies of 17th-century worthies in all spheres which had appeared in the *Dictionary of National Biography*; he tabulated the record of technological and scientific developments in the work of Darmstädter and in the British materials. On the latter score, to let Merton tell his own story, he goes so far as to codify 2,000 pages published in the *Philosophical Transactions* and hundreds of reports in the minutes of the Royal Society as transcribed in Birch's *History of the Royal Society*. Merton's readiness to bring statistical analysis to bear in his work is further attested by his 13 numbered tables, his many charts, and his use, for comparative purposes, of the findings of M. Offenbach and F. M. Feldhaus.

Beyond all this Merton draws heavily on the frontier researches and developing disciplines of his day: P. A. Sorokin, supervisor of Merton's dissertation and a major influence on Merton's development in sociological theory and research (Sorokin had already begun issuing segments of his work on *Social and Cultural Dynamics*); George Sarton, a mentor in the history of science; several other Harvard luminaries, especially E. F. Gay and A. P. Usher in economic history and history of invention.

It is no wonder that Merton, already a significant contributor to sociological reviews though hardly more than 25 years of age, showed such wide-ranging awareness of the uses and limits of advanced sociological theories. Sorokin and Ogburn were the principal points of reference, but among Americans Merton also drew upon or cited Veblen, Howard Becker, or others. So far as the European writers were concerned, he was already extraordinarily sensitive to the shadings of the work of Max Weber, Alfred Weber, Simmel, Mannheim, Scheler, Pareto, Tarde, Troeltsch, Vierkandt, and others. Even then Merton recognized the importance for his theme of the problematics of Jean Piaget. Nor did he lose any opportunities to draw into his orbit the work going on as he was writing, for example, the lively critique of Hessen by G. N. Clark and the careful discussion of H. M. Robertson by Talcott Parsons, then a junior member of the Harvard staff. Nor is it to be missed that he took a very strong interest in the philosophies and logics of science (Whewell, Rickert, Whitehead, Carnap, and others).

How long did it take Merton to do his dissertation? We have his own word: two years!

II

Merton's work was a unique gem on the day of its first appearance. All his later teaching about the social nature of innovation notwithstanding, his own essay was, without parallel, a "singleton."

Yes, there was the striking 1931 monograph by the Soviet scholar Bernard Hessen, who spoke of the reputed economic and social sources of Newton's *Principia;* yes, there was the scintillating *Ancients and Moderns* (1936) by the American scholar Richard F. Jones, who offered learned discussions of Baconian and other cultural and religious factors in the development *of the scientific movement* in England; indeed, beyond these two works, which were woven into the fabric of Merton's dissertation, were two other wide-ranging studies by men associated with the *Frankfurt Institut für Sozialforschung,* Franz Borkenau and Henryk Grossmann, who offered radically different accounts of the sources of the mechanical world view of the 17th century. (Borkenau claimed that the new world images derived from the rationalization of labor in the era of manufacture in the 16th and 17th centuries. Grossmann sharply challenged Borkenau, insisting Leonardo, Galileo, Descartes, and others were much less inspired by incipient rationalizations of the labor process in manufacture than they were by the observations of—and concerns with—the workings of actual machines and mechanisms.)

But these works and others notwithstanding—of the four mentioned above only Grossmann's is not mentioned by Merton—there was no book which could compare with Merton's unheralded dissertation as a conspectus of the theoretical and empirical problems *at issue from his special perspective;* there was no book which went so far in making explicit the ways in which evidence and proof in need of systematic review might be fruitfully correlated in statistical fashion. (I am not saying that the work was free of flaw!)

Indeed, here the riddles begin. Why has this precocious work had so strange a fate? Why have so few done studies which carefully go over the ground that Merton charts and make advances in the theoretical and empirical mappings of new findings? Why has so much of the discussion of his work come from unfriendly historians of science rather than from sociologists and cultural historians who share his outlooks and methods? Why has Merton himself spoken so little over the years to the issues and sources involved in this area? Why does he now go to such great pains in his important 1970 preface to suggest that very few of his readers and critics have accurately grasped the turns of his argument or, for that matter, have truly appreciated the design and intent of his book?

In the *AJS* (July 1972), reference is made to the fact that this work had to wait 34 years to be reviewed in its pages. This act may be more a symbol of the puzzle than an explanation of the riddles we here hope to explore.

III

To find starting clues to our puzzle we must again and again review the carefully chiseled explanations of Merton's original theses and the—at times caustic and unsparing—assessments of critics he presents in his 1970 preface.

Merton frames his main argument by pointing to the figures which result from applying George Sarton's procedure of quantitative content analysis to Merton's own work: his critics have paid least attention to matters to which he had devoted the greatest number of pages and the highest percentage of content; the "hypotheses about the economic and military influence on the range of scientific inquiry" are given more space in the monograph than "the hypotheses that link up Puritanism with recruitment and commitment to work in science" (p. xix).

Here Merton breaks into open complaint: "The *trio* of chapters on the second subject has received all manner of attention in scholarly print while the *quartet* of chapters on the first subject has received little attention" (p. xii, my italics).

In Merton's reading of his own complex orchestration, the *trio* and *quartet* were harmonically integrated from the beginning. Too few of his readers were able to recognize that the trio and quartet were exploring the same issue in the same manner and in the same key. His 1970 preface is

Benjamin Nelson

a mighty effort to show how the two segments resonate together under his magisterial baton.

It seems strange to me that Merton should now so strongly fault this choice of perspectives. In changing settings different degrees of interest attach to different themes in the orchestration. The latter chapters on economic and military influences probably seemed to his reviewers less problematical, less novel, and composed of quite different thematic elements from the chapters in the trio. Actually, in my own view, these latter chapters do have a wealth of material which carry the reader beyond 17th-century England and come closer than any other parts of the work to having an international flavor. Also, having lately gone over the evidence, I can confirm Merton's recollection on another emphasis of the quartet. In Merton's graduate student days, American sociologists were not nearly so clear about the distinction between "technology" and "science" as they later became, thanks in part to Merton's own efforts.

Moreover, as he now claims, Merton *was* careful "to avoid the mock choice between a vulgar Marxism and an equally vulgar purism"; he did go beyond "arguing that the selection of problems for investigation was either entirely governed by economic and military concerns or was not at all influenced by such concerns"; yes, he did even then establish a distinction "between the *motivational* and *institutional* levels of analysis . . . offering a procedure which, however coarse-grained, may not be inappropriate for analyzing the spectrum of scientific work today."

Despite the strong evidences in support of his current retrospect, I am not surprised that Merton's critics have fastened upon his trio rather than his quartet, nor am I surprised that he himself now strongly calls attention to his quartet rather than his trio. Times change, men change, and the contexts of scientific interests, inquiry, and proof change.

When Merton talked about economic and military influences on the shifts of interests in and estimation of science, he was in many—but not all—respects attempting much more than Hessen or Borkenau or Grossmann. He was, however, not breaking wholly new ground in principle—although careful scholarship and his many subtle distinctions promised a marked improvement in the state of the discussion.

Surely, however, Merton would have to agree that it was the "Puritanism and science hypotheses" which constituted the distinctive feature of his effort in 1938 and which, indeed, constitute it even now. In their original form, the theses about the cultural and social backgrounds of the "institutionalization" of modern science—to adopt Merton's parlance—had the flavor of an adventure into largely unknown but highly contested ground and, in the opinion of many then, and even now, remain an area needing to be carefully studied against wider backgrounds than have so far been brought into focus.

If Merton's 1970 preface does seem to establish that none of his critics has fully perceived his original aims exactly, one finds oneself drawn to retain a lingering doubt despite—perhaps, indeed, because of—the strenuousness of Merton's exertions to set the record straight on page after page of the new statement. Accept these caveats at face value in their full rigor (especially those on pp. x, xvi, xviii), and we are locked into a mystery as to why so few of Merton's most informed readers have known how to read the orchestration of the trio, or why, for that matter, so many echoes of the trio even now seem to sound in the quartet and elsewhere in the work.

There are other too rarely observed indirect corroborations of his present emphasis which Merton might have done more to stress in the new preface. His book did not purport to be a contribution to the history of scientific ideas or of technology. At no point does Merton attempt a detailed or consistent explication of the problems, theories, or presuppositions of 17th-century science and its culture. Nor does he claim to explain "the progressiveness" of science or the replacement of one scientific theory by another, a fact which is currently being forgotten in the writings of those who are trying to wed Merton to Thomas Kuhn by vastly expanding the scope of Merton's work on reference groups and role sets.

The 1970 preface leaves readers little recourse but to agree that the overriding aim of the dissertation was to explicate the processes of sociocultural *legitimation* of an "emerging social institution" and outlook—an *institution* and *outlook*—which required strong support from society on a sustaining basis in order to thrive. At one point Merton puts the matter in a rather general way: "The substantial and persistent development of science occurs only in societies of a certain kind, which provide both cultural and material conditions for that development. This becomes particularly evident in the early days of modern science before it was established as a major institution with its own presumably manifest value" (p. xix). Elsewhere the stresses are stronger and elaborated in greater detail; in other places they are weaker. Soon these variations may be expected to become the theme of many special monographs by a new generation of readers.

It will be for them to decide how truly the 1970 preface registers the latent content—and intent—of the original dissertation. Will they agree that the issues are now resolved by Merton's latest statements? I can hardly close this section without citing one such statement:

> In the case in hand, it is certainly not the case that Puritanism was indispensable in the sense that if it had not found historical expression at that time, modern science would not then have emerged. The historically concrete movement of Puritanism is not being put forward as a prerequisite to the substantial thrust of English science in that time; other functionally equivalent ideological movements could have served to provide the emerging science with widely acknowledged claims to legitimacy. The interpretation in this study assumes the functional requirement of providing socially and culturally patterned support for a not yet institutionalized science; it does not presuppose that only Puritanism could have served that function. [P. xviii]

It is hard at this point to refrain from turning to an implicit wider horizon of these remarks—the work of Max Weber.

IV

A second piece in the puzzle is brought into focus by exploring the contrast between the fortunes of Merton's dissertation and Weber's essays on "The Protestant Ethic and the Spirit of Capitalism." The latter papers were no sooner published in the *Archiv für Sozialwissenschaft und Sozialpolitik* for 1904–5 than they were under discussion by political and economic historians who felt that Weber had failed to prove and had overstated his case. The discussions continued extensively until 1910 when Weber himself decided to call a halt and served notice, in an essay entitled "Anti-Critical Last Word," that he preferred to leave this phase of the issue without further polemic. There were other questions crying out to be answered.

In the case of Merton's dissertation, most of the controversy is of relatively recent vintage. Efforts to relate to the pages to which, by Merton's own account, he was most partial—namely, those dealing with the economic and military spectrum of scientific work—have been extremely rare. Nor have many cared to review the details he offers as evidence of the fluctuations in the cultural profiles and trends he has particularly studied. There is something in the contrast which asks for clarification.

A more impressive aspect of the puzzle is the difference in the way Weber and Merton moved from these first statements. For Weber, the *Protestant Ethic* was a prelude to a larger effort that was begun with the publication in 1916 of the first of his sequence of masterly essays on the "Economic Ethic of the World Religions," which is now known as "The Social Psychology of the World Religions." He had now embarked upon a series of extraordinary special studies in which he sought to explain by a special comparative method how rationalism and rationalization had fared in the Orient—in Far East and Near East alike, in China, ancient India, ancient Judea. He was determined to develop a wider understanding of the particular influences which may have worked to promote or to inhibit the full functionalization and rationalization of all elements of the cultural, political, economic life of the different areas which had been the settings of the development of world religions.

There have been some moves of a comparable sort in the work of Merton, but these have been only hints. His thrust has been different; instead of moving out toward the comparative historical sociology of sociocultural process, he has tended to develop an ever more keen concentration on the areas or the boundaries of the sociological psychology of social and cultural process.

Actually, an impressive fact about his dissertation which might easily escape notice is that Merton was already launched on the sorts of studies which were to highlight his later career down to the present day. Thus we must be attentive here to the footnotes or we shall miss this fact. Already he is pointing to the critical importance of struggles over priorities and competitive advantage—shades of the Matthew Effect; he is promising to do later studies on science in its social ambience; he is striving to establish the relation of rates of change to the levels of frequencies of social interaction among fellow professionals; he is striving to document the fact that extra-logical factors of allocations operate to create settings for scientific research which produce outstanding innovations.

An interim summary may help us here:

A) Merton's doctoral dissertation was the work of a young pioneering scholar with an extraordinary range of skills, interests, and sympathies—a range rarely matched in the history of sociology. Few aspects of human activity, experience, and expression failed to interest him deeply. He had read widely and had come to have insights which allowed him to innovate on almost every page.

B) To the great loss of instruction and research in our country—in my view—the several strains of his orientation tended to draw apart during the years after his dissertation. In place of the model of analysis he exhibited in what he calls the trio, we witness a thrust toward frames which come to serve as the formats of highly institutionalized theoretical and empirical work mainly in the sphere of a sophisticated sociological social psychology oriented to narrower temporal horizons.

Here we are on the verge of solving a critical part of the puzzle. For Merton this dissertation may be said to represent the high point of his efforts in historical sociology rather than a point of departure for new work along these lines. Even before his dissertation appeared, Merton had already published several essays dealing with fluctuations in the development of rates of industrial invention and in the course of Arabian intellectual development (the latter was done in collaboration with Sorokin). Merton's own "Puritanism, Pietism, and Science" appeared in 1936. Sorokin's *Social and Cultural Dynamics* was already in progress and was, indeed, to be published in the following year (1937), a year before the appearance of Merton's dissertation in *Osiris*.

As I read the evidence, it was Merton's seminal paper, "Social Structure and Anomie," published in the same year as his dissertation, which was to set the pattern for the "normal science" in departments of sociology at American universities, to become the "launching pad" for a great number of American doctoral dissertations and research monographs. This was the study which was to become the model of the so-called structural-functional analysis in the manner now regularly ascribed to Durkheim.

I am saddened to report that much of the research which developed out of his interest in the sociology of science served to elaborate neither his trio nor his quartet, nor, for that matter, his duo (the two first chapters), but came to be concentrated on the documentation of the more miniscule theoretical elements at the level of social interaction. Nowadays work done in his fashion, except when it is done by him, is likely to seem a far cry from his original intentions. Elsewhere in this issue we will be reminded of how Merton sounds when he recovers his full range. I refer to his exceptional article on "Insiders and Outsiders."

Benjamin Nelson

A LAST WORD

Nothing I have here written is to be construed as arguing that Merton has ever abandoned the immensely deep interest he showed from the beginning in historical sociology of culture. Any review of the essays he has written since 1938 would prove that this field has remained near and dear to him across the years. It is simply being suggested that a shift in focus reduced the importance of the wider perspectives which manifested themselves with great penetration in his paper on "Puritanism, Pietism, and Science" and throughout the course of his dissertation.

One is reminded of Robert Frost's poem that recalls how two roads diverged in the wood and he (the poet) "took the one less travelled by."

The suggestion of the present review is that the road Merton was to take was to become the high road of American sociology and the one he was to visit only occasionally was to undergo very great neglect. The fact is that the issues, as they come to be circumscribed within sociology largely developed in the shadows of his work, forfeit much substance and scope and too often seem to lose rather than benefit from the immense attention accorded to them. On the other hand, the areas too soon abandoned because of apparent difficulties in introducing system and rigor continue to call for the kinds of insight and skill which are only rarely wedded in extremely well-trained men like Merton.

The "road less travelled by" was the road which led toward the comparative historical sociology of sociocultural process in the spirit of Max Weber, Alfred Weber, Durkheim, Mauss, the Durkheimians, Joseph Needham, and a number of contemporary historians and philosophers of science. Merton's dissertation is clearly a pioneering first step on that road. May one not hope that he and some of his future readers will recover the wider purposes which first drew him forth on this quest?

I have my own reasons for being persuaded that this must happen before too long.

Epilogue: To Be a Phoenix—Reflections on Two Noisy Ages of Prose

E. Digby Baltzell
University of Pennsylvania

I

Heroic ages of poetry are often followed by hesitant ages of prose, literary creativity by literary criticism, and the doing of sociology by the sociology of sociology. At least as I see it, the central thrust of this volume of the *American Journal of Sociology*, largely concerned as it is with the sociology of sociology, nicely reflects our hesitant age of prose. The poetic core of sociology, I like to think on the other hand, lies in the doing tradition of the great problematic monographs like *Le suicide, L'ancien régime, The Protestant Ethic, The Polish Peasant, The Gang, Yankee City, Deep South,* and *Middletown, White Collar, The Lonely Crowd, Black Bourgeoisie, Union Democracy, Asylums,* and so forth. Merton's *Science, Technology and Society in Seventeenth-Century England* is very much a part of this poetic tradition. Its review by Benjamin Nelson, more than three decades after its original publication, may well be the most symbolically important thing about this volume.

All civilizations, at one unfortunate time or another, have been pushed to the polar, *lawless* extremes of autocracy or anarchy. If autocracy is the anarchy of lawless, lonely tyrants, anarchy is the tyranny of lawless, lonely crowds. It is interesting that such a timeless and poetic work as Solzhenitsyn's *First Circle* was produced in autocratic Moscow, while the timely prose of Mailer's *Advertisements for Myself* seems such a telling symptom of anarchic New York. Perhaps the silence of autocracy is less of an obstacle to real poetic genius than the infernal noise of anarchy. In our own discipline, for example, the major monographs of Erving Goffman, poetic doer par excellence, were all done before the noise began. On the other hand, it is probably inevitable that sociologists, at the end of the noisiest decade in modern history, should be preoccupied with the sociology of sociology (see the recent books by Friedrichs (1970), Gouldner (1970), and Tiryakian (1971)). Thus the relevant problem today, so they say, is *not* the doing of sociology but rather *how* it should be done, for *whom* (adults or children, boozers, or potheads!), and by persons of *what* theoretical, political, sexual, racial, class, or sartorial persuasions. But surely, as even Becker and Horowitz admit, it is "good sociology" which will last, regardless of what contemporaries think of the theoretical, political, or social positions of the doers. When the doing of political sociology, as for example Lipset's *Political Man*, gives way to the concentration on the politics of sociological theorists (as shown in Lipset and Ladd), the discipline is betraying its best and most fruitful traditions. When my own graduate students, so often the less secure and talented among them, are noisily engaged in arguing the pros and cons of the Tumin criticisms of the "iniquitous" Davis and Moore thesis, I urge them instead to take some problem, preferably dear to their own hearts or personal experiences, and to go to work in the hopes of adding something, however great or small, to the great doing tradition, from Durkheim to Goffman.

When asked by the editor for my "reactions" to these articles, I hesitated to interrupt my own work on the problem of the rise of Quakerism in Puritan England. I accepted the invitation, however, because I was convinced that an understanding of this crucial period in English history had something to tell us about our own age.[1] During the anarchical and violent years of the Puritan Revolution, for example, John Milton shelved his poetic genius and produced a series of polemical and relevant pamphlets, including his famous defense of freedom of the press and a less famous justification of regicide; he survived the Restoration of 1660, though he was arrested as an Enemy of the State and two of his pamphlets were burned by the public hangman, only because of his friends at court; and he did not publish *Paradise Lost* until 1667, a year before his sixtieth birthday. Milton witnessed the rise and agonizing death of Puritanism which a modern historian, Alan Simpson, has briefly outlined as follows: "The origins of English Puritanism are to be found among the Protestant reformers of the mid-sixteenth century; it takes shape in the reign of Elizabeth; produces thrust after thrust of energy in the seventeenth century, until the final thrust throws up the Quakers; and then ebbs away."

Alvin Gouldner's brilliant book, which is the subject of two of the essays in this collection, as well as the articles by Janowitz, Merton, and Becker and Horowitz, are all very much a product of our anarchic age and the consequent "balcanization of social science," as Merton puts it. In other words, as I see it, they are a reflection of sociology's attempt to cope with and understand the agonizing death of liberalism, about which some future, intellectual historian may write as follows: "The origins of Western Liberalism are to be found among the Utilitarian reformers of the mid-19th century; it takes shape in the Victorian age; produces thrust after thrust in America during the Progressive, New Freedom, New Deal, and New

---

[1] According to the Oxford dictionary, the term "anarchism" came into the English language in 1642, the year the English Revolution broke out ("antinomianism," the theological counterpart of our own sociological jargon-term, "anomie," was introduced in 1645).

Frontier years of the 20th century, until the final thrust throws up the New Left and a host of other secular-sectarian movements; and then, like the Puritans of another day, ebbs away."

Now the content and the ideas of 17th-century Puritanism were hardly similar to those of 20th-century liberalism; for one thing the rhetoric of one was religious, the other secular. But 17th-century Puritans and modern liberals, on the other hand, played functionally equivalent roles, as reformers and advocates of change, in their respective societies. As Weber, Tawney, Merton, and others have shown, Puritans took the lead in science, law, medicine, manufacturing, and in military tactics. Their political leaders were largely members of the country gentry whose power lay in the House of Commons. These gentlemen reformers, allied with city merchants and lawyers, were seeking to enlarge their power and authority as against the establishment of Church, Lords, and Monarchy. Oliver Cromwell, for example, was a prominent member of this gentry class. He was born in the last years of Elizabeth's reign, in 1599, to the poorer branch of a wealthy and prominent family in the county of Huntington, near the Puritan stronghold of Cambridge. Before going to Parliament in 1628, he had spent a year at Sidney Sussex, a Puritan college at Cambridge, and then settled down as a gentleman farmer and leader in local county affairs. In social background and in politics, then, he was not unlike the gentlemen reformers who followed the leadership of Theodore and Franklin Roosevelt, both of whom challenged the established power and authority of big business in 20th-century America. And this 17th-century English gentleman would have been quite at home among the Roosevelts at Oyster Bay or Hyde Park. Just as the two Roosevelts were essentially Victorians in education, background, and temperament, so the leading men of the great Puritan generation were essentially Elizabethans and men of order, who nevertheless believed in change, the continual reform of the inevitable abuses of authority, and the steady equalizing of opportunity. They *never*, however, advocated the abolition of authority or the possibility, or desirability, of complete equality of conditions; they were reformers but not radicals, equalizers but certainly not egalitarians.

For approximately a century, Puritan and liberal reformers were successful in backing more or less orderly and evolutionary change in their respective eras. Then suddenly and in times of seeming victory, reform turned upon itself and died in a period of radicalism and anarchy. Among other things, there was a generation problem. Thus John Winthrop, who brought Puritanism to New England, was born in the Armada year of 1588, while William Penn, founder of Quaker Pennsylvania, was born the year of the great parliamentary victory at Marston Moor (1644). Winthrop was born the same year as Hobbes, while Penn was a friend of Locke. To put it another way, Winthrop and Penn were born as far apart in time and societal values as Franklin Roosevelt was from the younger generation of the sixties.

At any rate, in England both the reformers and the radicals eventually lost out at the Restoration of 1660. What will happen here nobody knows. Marx, following Hegel, saw historical patterns repeating themselves at least twice, first as tragedy and second as farce. There is a haunting similarity between the pattern of anarchy which followed the execution of England's king, in January 1649, and the years in America since the assassination of our president in November 1963.[2] In the interest of avoiding farce, I should like to take a look at the first tragedy. Though I must be brief, I shall try to include enough concrete detail to make the historical parallels meaningful and more than mere abstractions.

II

The 1630s in England were much like the Eisenhower years in America. Society went through a period of confident calm under the benevolent authority of Charles I. As a contemporary poet wrote, with smugness and pride:

> Tourneys, masques, theatres better become
> Our Halcyon days; what though German drums
> Bellow for freedom and revenge, the noise
> Concerns us not, nor should divert our joys.

But the placid thirties were followed by the revolutionary forties and anarchical fifties, when Englishmen, for the first and last time in their history, fought each other to the bloody and bitter end, abolishing bishops and lords, beheading their king, and eventually setting up a kind of military dictatorship in the face of increasing anarchy.

This is no place to go into the causes of the Civil War. But it is safe to say, I think, that war broke out in 1642, not because the leaders on either side wanted it, but rather because, as with our own involvement in Vietnam today, they failed to see the collective and cumulative consequences of their individual actions.

[2] There are, according to Webster, at least two meanings of the term anarchy: (1) a state of political disorder, and (2) a state of confusion or disorder. In the British, French, and Russian revolutions, the states were overthrown, creating political as well as societal disorder (1 and 2). The 20th-century welfare state, on the other hand, is highly centralized and strong: thus the anarchy of our sixties in America was largely societal confusion and normlessness (2) rather than political anarchy (1). Anarchy, chaos, and lawlessness, according to Webster, are synonyms: anarchy implies absence or suspension of government; chaos, the utter negation of law and order; lawlessness, a prevalent or habitual disregard for law and order. I use the term "anarchy" here more in the sense of chaos or lawlessness than in simple political anarchy. In many ways, the theological term "antinomian" and the sociological term "anomie" might better serve my purpose than "anarchy."

The vast majority of leaders of both parties, for instance, believed in a monarchical form of government and an established church. When the members of the Long Parliament passed the Grand Remonstrance, a mild-mannered listing of the abuses of monarchical and Episcopal authority, they included the following statement of their belief in religious uniformity and authority: "We do here declare that it is far from our purpose or desire to let loose the golden reigns of discipline and government in the Church, to leave private persons of particular congregations to take up what form of divine service they please, for we hold it requisite that there should be through-out the whole realm a conformity to that order which the laws enjoin according to the word of God." The parliamentary army, moreover, was raised "for the safety of the King's person, defence of both Houses of Parliament, the preservation of the true religion, the laws, liberty and peace of the kingdom." The commissions of its officers, moreover, ran "in the name of King and Parliament."

The Long Parliament was certainly no revolutionary body. Its members were essentially a conservative cousinhood of knights, squires, and gentlemen from the counties, along with some city lawyers and wealthy merchants. When young Cromwell first went to Parliament in 1628, for instance, he found nine cousins there; at the opening of the Long Parliament, he sat with 11 cousins, including John Hampden, then the richest man in England; six more cousins and three other relatives joined him there later on. In addition to the gentry-merchant cousinage, no less than 48 members were sons of peers. That the extremely mild Grand Remonstrance was passed by a slim majority of only 11 votes out of 307 members present attested to the conservative and conciliatory mood as of December 1641. Unfortunately, Charles rejected the mild criticism and impeached six members for treason (including Hampden, one of the most widely respected men of his day). It was the slender straw that broke the camel's back, and war broke out at the Battle of Edgehill. The Parliamentary party eventually won a military victory due, among other things, to the efficiency and leadership of the New Model Army.

The New Model was something new in English history. In the Puritan tradition of the calling, Cromwell had a great sense of professional pride. In striking contrast to the aristocratic ideal, he organized the New Model on the basis of merit rather than status: "The officers," wrote his more conservative contemporary, Clarendon, "are of no better family than the common soldiers." The New Model not only provided for careers open to talents; it was also an ideological army made up of voluntary, true believers in the righteousness of the Holy Crusade. Unfortunately it was this Cromwellian tradition, transplanted to America, which has produced such moral disillusionment after each of our own military crusades in the 20th century, from the days of Wilson and Roosevelt through Kennedy and Johnson. All this was, of course, quite in contrast to the aristocratic ideal of warfare as a sport, with rules protecting priests, women, and children, and fought for limited interests rather than ideological abstractions.

As was to be expected with this new ideological army, there soon developed, from colonel to common soldier, a belief in the right of self-expression, or a kind of participatory democracy. We often forget the revolutionary potential of all standing armies, of which the New Model was the first in English history. Down to 1640, for example, most Englishmen were extremely provincial. Even after years of Tudor and Stuart attempts at centralization, there was little sense of nationhood; one's *country* meant one's *county*, where everyone was bound together by local loyalties of family, lord and manor, vicar and village, all reinforcing the established customs of degree, priority, and place. Now, for the first time, large numbers of Englishmen were away from home and easily influenced by the sway of opinion so characteristic of the all-male and atomized life in the ranks.

And the men of the New Model were exposed to all kinds of new enthusiasms. According to George Sabine, the great political scientist and biographer of the "Digger" leader, Gerrard Winstanley, the debates and heated discussions which took place around the army campfires marked the first appearance of public opinion as a factor in British politics. These debates, mirroring and reinforcing those of revolutionary society as a whole, were part of the greatest outpouring of pamphleteering in British history (a fine collection of the pamphlets in the British Museum includes some 20,000 titles, obviously only part of the whole). In order to organize and regulate the expression of opinion, there was set up a Council of the Army, representing the officers, and a Council of Agitators, representing the ranks. As Clarendon, the first great historian of the Rebellion and a contemporary witness, wrote, the army had "set itself up as a rival parliament with the agitators as the house of commons and the officers as peers."

The most famous of the army debates took place in the little village church at Putney, in the autumn of 1647, after military victory in the Civil War had been won. Although the Leveller leader, John Lilburne, was imprisoned in the Tower at the time, the debates centered around his draft constitution, called *Agreement of the People*, which was concerned mainly with the franchise. This was the first time in English history that the possibility of manhood suffrage was taken seriously: in the now-famous words of Colonel Rainsborough (kin by marriage to John Winthrop of New England), "The poorest he that is in England has a life to live as the greatest he, and therefore . . . every man that is to live under a government ought first by his own consent to put himself under that government." The Putney debates dragged on through October, many of the generals and colonels being horrified at the extreme views of the agitators with all their leveling ideas. Finally in November, Cromwell terminated the debates and ordered the men back to their regiments, shooting one agitator on the spot for insubordination.

Events now moved steadily to the left, toward the logical conclusion of the revolution: execution of the king. During the course of the next year (1648) the generals revived their alliance with the Levellers and proceeded to occupy London. In December, Colonel Pride forcefully expelled 96 conservative Presbyterians from Parliament. This left only some 60 more radical members, called the Rump, who abolished the House of Lords and brought Charles before the High Court of Justice, which sent him to the scaffold on January 30, 1649. "All is quiet," wrote John Winthrop's son, Stephen, from London, in the hush which followed the execution of the king: "All is quiet, but I know not how long it will last. . . . New England seems the only safe place."

Stephen Winthrop's premonitions of strife were justified. With the final abolition of all traditional authorities, only anarchy or the sword remained. Even the perpetual opponent of authority, John Lilburne, was horrified. He denied the lawfulness of both Pride's purge and the king's trial: "To have the name of Commonwealth imposed upon us by the Sword," he told Cromwell at the time, "wherein we are and shall be more slaves than ever we were under kingship. . . . and therefore I had rather be under a King reasonable bound than under you, and your new Sword Tyranny called Common-wealth."

As long as history had recorded, authority in England had been symbolized in the now-abolished orders of kings, lords, and bishops. The regicide had so uniquely shocked the people that, according to a contemporary witness, "Women miscarried, men fell into melancholy, some with consternation expired." The great physician, William Harvey, told a bishop at the time that he met with "more diseases generated by the mind than from any other cause." All indeed was now in doubt, all coherence gone, and a host of "seekers" began to populate the melancholy land of England, very much in the style of the lonely and lost souls of our own day who once gathered at Woodstock and are now joining the Jesus cults. Clarendon was horrified at the decline in traditional authority: "All relations," he wrote, "were confounded by the several Sects in Religion, which discountenanced all Forms of Reverence and Respect. . . . Parents had no Manner of Authority over their Children, nor Children any Obedience or Submission to their Parents; but everyone did that which was good in their own Eyes." Quite naturally Clarendon saw the extreme egalitarianism abroad in the land as a reversion to primitivism: "In all well instituted governments," he wrote, "the heirs and descendants from worthy and eminent parents, if they do not degenerate from their virtue, have always been allowed a preference and kind of title to employments and offices of honour and trust. . . . Whatever is of Civility and good Manners, all that is Art and

Beauty, or of real and solid Wealth in the World, is the . . . child of be-loved Propriety; and they who would strangle this Issue, desire to de-molish all Buildings, eradicate all Plantations, to make the Earth barren, and Mankind to live again in Tents, and nourish his Cattle where the grass grows. Nothing but the joy in Propriety reduc'd us from barbarity; and nothing but security in the same, can preserve us from returning into it again." Clarendon's view of the barbaric consequences of the proposed "greening" of his England would also apply to the proposals of our academic seekers for the "Greening of America."

All revolts against the inevitable hypocricies of established authority have called for the return to the simplicities of naked and nonliterate primitivisms. Thus many of the early founders of Quakerism went naked through marketplaces, and even into churches, as a witness of their mar-tyrdom to the "naked truth." Even as late as 1672, the one and only great Quaker theologian, Robert Barkley, went "naked as a sign through the chilly streets of Aberdeen." George Fox and other leaders of the Quaker movement preached the futility of "mere book knowledge" which only tended to pervert the purity of the untainted prompting of the "inner light." Gerrard Winstanley, in his relevant pamphlet *The New Law of Righteous-ness* (1649), wrote that "the Universities are the standing ponds of stink-ing waters." Even Emanuel College, at Cambridge, once the seat of Puritan intellectualism and the founding seed of Harvard College, went through a period of extreme mysticism during this period. It is no wonder that at both Oxford and Cambridge there was the smashing of stained-glass windows and the decimation of altar decorations, all in the name of Puritan and sectarian relevance.

Among a host of other parallels of our own noisy years, there was, finally, the digging up and replanting of the Common land on St. George's Hill, in Surrey, by the followers of Winstanley, a once-religious mystic turned utopian "communist." The Diggers, in appealing their arrest to the House of Commons, demanded, much in the manner of their modern imitators, "whether the common people shall have the quiet enjoyment of the Com-mons, or Waste Land, or whether they shall be under the will of the Lords of the Manor." In that anarchical regicide year, similar diggings took place in Buckinghamshire, Middlesex, Hertfordshire, and Berkshire, altogether in some 34 towns. The following lines, attributed to Winstanley, would have appealed to the modern "Diggers" of the People's Park at Berkeley:

> The gentrye are all round, on each side they are found,
> Theire wisdom's so profound, to cheat us of our ground. . .
> The clergy they come in, and say it is a sin
> That we should now begin, our freedom for to win.
>
> Stand up now, Diggers all.
> To conquer them by love . . .

To conquer them by love, as it does you behove,
For he is King above; no power is like to love:
Glory here, Diggers all.

Viable civilizations, are, almost literally, *clothed* in authority; and when the emperor's clothes are removed his only recourse is the exercise of *naked* power. The Diggers dug up St. George's Hill in April, and in May mutinies broke out in the army which soon turned into a full-scale Leveller revolt. Parliament immediately declared mutiny in the army to be treason, and Cromwell led a lightning night attack on the rebels at Buford; three leaders were shot on the spot and a fourth was caught and shot three days later. Cromwell and Fairfax now returned to Oxford, Royalist stronghold in Charles's last days, where they were feasted by the conservative city fathers. After Buford, the Revolution turned conservative.

As part of the reactionary trend, John Lilburne was brought to trial for sedition in October. If Cromwell was respected, admired, and feared, Lilburne was undoubtedly the most popular man in England at this time. When he was finally acquitted by a jury of his peers, the people shouted with joy. A cheering mob followed him all the way from the Guild Hall to the Tower, where, in spite of his recent acquittal, and another in 1652, he was to remain until the end of his life. In the meantime, Lilburne lost all hope of secular solutions and became a Quaker, "renouncing all weapons except the Sword of the Spirit." When he died in 1657, his funeral was held at the Bull and Mouth Meeting House, in London; some 4,000 Quakers accompanied his body to the burial grounds.

Lilburne, who had spent almost two-thirds of his life in jail and was in perpetual revolt against authority, whether monarchical, Episcopal, Presbyterian, or Cromwellian, was an ideal spiritual ancestor of a sect of martyrs. The great Quaker preacher and historian, Rufus Jones, considered him, along with Winstanley, a noble ancestor of both modern democracy and Quakerism. Thus it was that "the Quakers passed on the Leveller torch to the New World."

When formalism declines fanaticism comes to the fore, and the church is replaced by a host of sects. Just as we are witnessing the spread of fanatical sectarianism in America today, so the Puritan Interregnum was faced with the rise of the Ethringtonians, Grindlestonians, Mugglestonians, Fifth Monarchy Men, Family of Love, Ranters, and a veritable swarm of other seeking sectarians. It is always the ex-radicals who hate and hunt the newer radicals. Thus the Reverend Thomas Edwards, who back in 1628 had been dismissed from his post as University Preacher at Cambridge for his violent attacks on the establishment of bishops, now turned around and attacked, in even more fanatical terms, the fanaticisms and heresies of the 199 sects which he now found abroad in the land. Many of the new sectarians and seekers joined the Quaker movement, which was unquestionably the most interesting and important of them all.

In striking contrast to the university educated, and theologically sophisticated, builders of Puritanism, the founder of Quakerism, George Fox, was not unlike that "rough beast slouching towards Bethlehem" which Yeats saw as the only possible savior of our own seeking and anarchic generation. Born the son of a humble weaver in a small village in the North Country—the most backward, feudal, royalist, and Catholic part of England—Fox was almost entirely self-educated and a charismatic mystic whom many have called the only religious genius of the English Reformation. A year after the outbreak of the Civil War, young Fox, at the age of 19, left home like so many of today's soul-hungry seekers of the counterculture, and wandered through the countryside, dressed in leather breeches, sleeping in haystacks, under hedges, and even, as legend has it, in the trunks of hollow trees. He was desperately seeking for some new vision of life outside the establishment of hated "steeplehouses" and their hypocritical "professors." After four years of lonely seeking, five years of preaching to other seekers (and two periods in prison), he came to Pendle Hill, famous in local folklore as the haunt of witches and warlocks, where he had a vision of "a great people to be gathered." Modern Quakers have always dated the founding of their sect with this vision on Pendle Hill, in the spring of 1652.

Just as the hated Anabaptists rose to haunt the reformers and Lutherans during the 15th-century Reformation on the Continent, so the Quakers marked the extreme left wing of the English Reformation. "The Society of Friends," wrote Ernst Troeltsch, "represents the final expression in its purest form of the Anabaptist Movement." After a century of reform, religious authority in England—once lodged in the pope and the priestly control of the seven sacraments, then in the Anglican bishops and the priestly control of two sacraments, and finally in local preachers interpreting the Bible—was suddenly transformed by the radically individualistic and subjective doctrine of the "inner-light." The hierarchical yet reforming ethic of the Puritans now gave way to the radical egalitarianism of the Quakers: "When the Lord sent me into the world," so Fox says in one of the key passages of his *Journal*, "He forbade me to put off my hat to any, high or low: and I was required to 'thee' and 'thou' all men and women, without any respect to rich or poor, great or small." While the Puritans were closer to Hobbes, the Quakers anticipated the tradition of Rousseau.

This is no time to go into a detailed discussion of the differences between the Puritan and Quaker ethics. The following skeleton list of the differences (in emphasis, of course) should, however, show how similar they were to our present conflicts between culture and counterculture.

Puritan Ethic	Quaker Ethic
God transcendent (man anxious to prove himself)	God imminent (peace of mind)
Old Testament (Decalogue)	New Testament (Sermon on Mount)
Head (learning)	Heart (feeling)
Law	Love
Danger: legalism and rationalism	Danger: anarchy and mysticism
Elitism (elect of Saints)	Egalitarianism (that of God in every man)
Institution building	Anti-institutional (spontaneity)
Aristocratic (antimonarchical)	Democratic (anti–all hierarchy)
Representative democracy (majority 51% rule)	Direct democracy (sense of meeting, like "general will" of Rousseau)
Calling (great professional pride in ministry and magistry)	Calling (more like Thomism: to God rather than profession; exaltation of laymen and amateurs)
Ideal man: magistrate	Ideal person: martyr
Evil: in sinful man	Evil: in corrupt institutions
Major vice: arrogance	Major vice: self-righteousness

"Anyone who knows anything about history," Marx once wrote to a friend, "knows that great social changes are impossible without the feminine ferment." It is happening today as it did in the 17th century, as a voguish ditty of that day put it:

> We will not be wives
> And tie up our lives
> To villainous slavery.

As might be expected, women played a major role in the Quaker movement. In fact, Clarendon thought the Quakers were a female sect, as well he might have: Fox's first convert was Elizabeth Hooton, of whom more later; his most important early convert, later his wife and mother of the movement, was Margeret Fell, mistress of Swarthmoor Hall which became the movement's headquarters; the first Quaker "publishers of truth" in London, in the universities, and in Dublin, were women; Mary Fisher, a young Yorkshire house servant, was the first Quaker in America; even in England today more women than men are registered as ministers.

The Quakers of the first generation were a hardy, fanatical, and apocalyptical band of martyrs who were hated, hunted down, and hung, imprisoned, and tortured for their convictions. Puritan England was no permissive age. That the female "Friends of Truth" had a particular affinity for fanaticism and martyrdom was illustrated in the career of Fox's first convert. Elizabeth Hooton. A woman of good position, 47 years old and the mother of seven children when she first met Fox in 1646, Elizabeth took up the active ministry in 1650 and almost immediately went to prison, first at Derby then at York Castle (16 months). After continuing her ministry in England, where she was imprisoned six months in 1654 and three months in 1655, she set sail for America in 1657, but was soon shipped back by the Boston authorities (after they had nearly starved her in the wilderness). At the age of 65 she went back to New England where, according to her *Journal*, she suffered fantastic hardships including four days in prison without bread or water and being whipped "for a wandering vagabond Quaker at three towns, ten stripes at whipping post in Cambridge, and ten at Watertown and ten stripes at Dedham at the cart's tail with a three cord whip three knots at the end, and a handful of willow rods at Watertown on a cold frosty morning. Then they put me on a horse and carried me into the wilderness many miles, where was many wild beasts both bears and wolves . . . but the Lord delivered me." Before leaving New England, she was sent to prison for attending, and probably preaching at, the funeral of Governor Endicott, the great opponent of the Quakers who had previously ordered the hanging of Mary Dyer on Boston Commons, where her statue now stands. Elizabeth Hooton's last service to the cause was when she went with George Fox, as one of his "twelve" companions, on her third trip to America, where she died in Jamaica at the age of 73.

Like Elizabeth Hooton, hundreds of Quakers in the first generation were martyrs for their cause. In England, some 3,000 were sent to prison under Cromwell (20 died there) and over 15,000 during the Restoration (300 deaths). Almost every leader, from George Fox and Margeret Fell to Robert Barclay and William Penn, went to prison, usually more than once. But of course the martyr thrives on, and often seeks out punishment and persecution, and the movement spread rapidly throughout England, Ireland, and Wales, and thence to the New World. By 1700 there were over 40,000 Quakers in the American and Caribbean colonies and 50,000 at home in Britain. The evangelical zeal of the first generation eventually spent itself and the movement became a very solid, bourgeois sect which reached its numerical peak in the middle of the 18th century. The miracle of the Quakers is that they have survived both persecution and prosperity.

III

C. Wright Mills once wrote that we sociologists must "try to understand men and women as historical and social actors." My reaction to this volume of the *AJS* is to place it within some historical context. The two excellent articles by Coser and Dibble, for instance, might have appeared in this *Journal* a decade or two ago. On the other hand, as I have said above, the Gouldner book and the comments on it here, as well as Merton's concept of the "Insider," are all infinitely relevant to the Oz-like world which Becker and Horowitz describe in the following lines at the beginning of their article:

> Greater sensitivity to the undemocratic character of ordinary institutions and relationships (ironically fostered by social scientists themselves) has revealed how research frequently represents the interests of adults and teachers instead of those of children and students; of men instead of women; of the white middle class instead of the lower class, blacks, chicanos, and other minorities; of the conventional straight world instead of freaks; of boozers instead of potheads. . . . Younger men have debated whether it was moral to be affiliated with the sociological enterprise. Older sociologists have searched their work and their consciences to see if, far from being the political liberals they imagined themselves, they were in fact lackeys of capitalist repression.
>
> In the midst of these reconsiderations, positions hardened. The language of scholarly journals became increasingly polemical. Meetings thought to be scientific were disrupted by political protest and discussion. Presidential addresses at national and regional meetings were interrupted. . . . Some teachers found themselves unable to bear the discourtesies of their radical students. Some professors saw attempts to change the hierarchical relations of a department as an attack on the very idea of scholarship. They assumed that a student who called their ideas "bullshit" was attacking rational thought.

Once again the "Church" has disintegrated and a host of self-righteous sectarians are loosed upon the world. In this climate of opinion, it is understandable that the anti-institutional, egalitarian, perfectionist, and mystical ideals of the Quakers are now more popular in America, especially among intellectuals and academics, than at any other time in our history. Since the close of the Second World War, for example, there has been both a reversal of the downward trend in numbers and a very real renaissance within the Society, such as the winning of the Nobel Peace Prize by the American Friends Service Committee.

The Quaker ranks have been swelled by all sorts of refugees from the institutional "Church" of their ancestors. In a recent, excellent study of the American Friends Service Committee by a *New Yorker* writer, for instance, it was interesting to observe that a majority of the leaders of various projects he mentioned were "convinced" rather than "birthright" Friends. As the rabbi put it: "some of my best Jews are Friends."

Most of the new Quaker meetings which have sprung up around the country since the war have been formed, often by academics, in and around college or university communities. Today, for instance, the largest meeting in Massachusetts is located in Cambridge, right off fashionable Brattle Street. Only a few years ago, moreover, several departments in the humanities and the social sciences (including Parsons's own department) had chairmen who were "convinced" Friends and members of the Cambridge Meeting. As the Cambridge meetings are unstructured, permissive, and antiauthoritarian in the extreme, the sober and square families, in recent years, apparently avoid the freaks from the Yard by attending the earlier of the First Day meetings.

It is indeed part of the irony of this age of the absurd that the quiet Quakers have really come into their own once again in America during the 1960s, the decade of noise. But when martyrs of all kinds are abroad in the land, it is quite appropriate that the Quakers, by now having institutionalized their perfectionist and pacifist ideals, should be drawn into the very heart of the various protests and antiwar movements.[3] Three centuries after George Fox personally appealed to Cromwell to lay down his "carnal weapons," his spiritual descendants were "visiting" with leaders in Hanoi and Washington, "treating" with them to do the same.

It was indeed a fitting forecast of the shape of things to come that, when he died in March 1962, the great disestablishmentarian guru, C. Wright Mills, the John Lilburne of modern social science, was buried after a Quaker memorial service. He, unlike Lilburne, died "unconvinced" and an atheist, or as Mills himself would have more dramatically put it, a Pagan. It is fitting, too, that virtually before the ink was dry on Mills's death certificate, to put it figuratively, Professor Horowitz should have published a collection of Mills's essays, in the introduction to which he called Mills the "singular intellectual 'hero' of our age." And Horowitz went on to say that Mills, in the good tradition of George Fox, "was singularly unimpressed with titles, honors, degrees, positions and the entire world of inherited feudal values [?] that have been mysteriously grafted on to present-day status-conscious America." Now I should have thought that men and women have been "status conscious" ever since they put on clothes after their emergence forever (except in the minds of perfectionist sectarians) from the Garden of Eden. In point of historical fact, men in feudal times were far more interested in the state of their souls than in their secular status, which, being fixed by fate, produced little of the status anxiety which so marks our own age. But it must be said that in my day at Columbia, when ambitious graduate students still looked to Brooks Brothers rather than the local Army and Navy Store for their sartorial standards, Professor Mills was a prophet in life-styles, as well as in sociology, as he roared up to

---

[3] Even Quaker ideals do not operate in a vacuum. Thus during the First World War, Haverford College let one of its spirited young faculty members go when he allowed as how perhaps the German people were not all representatives of Satan He went on to Harvard, where he eventually became Hollis Professor of Divinity and a great New Testament scholar. Hollis was a wealthy English Baptist, which did not prevent Cotton Mather from putting his loyalty to Harvard above ideology in influencing Hollis to endow this oldest chair in America

Fayerweather Hall on a motorcycle, clothed more often than not in the style now cultivated, as a badge of baptism, by the followers of Professor Gouldner.

Gouldner, like Mills, is very much in the anti-institutional and egalitarian tradition of the 17th-century sectarians. Thus a great deal of space in his prophetic book is devoted to denouncing the sociological establishment, now dominated, so he says, by a priestly caste of Parsonian functionalists. Its prophetic tone can be summed up, I think, in his antinomian concept of "authenticity" which he wants to substitute for the priestly concept of "legitimacy." In the 17th century, John Donne, great metaphysical poet and famous preacher at St. Paul's Cathedral, put it this way:

> The new philosophy calls all in doubt;
> 'Tis all in pieces, all coherence gone;
> All just supply and all relation.
> Prince, subject, father, son, are things forgot,
> For every man alone thinks he has got
> To be a Phoenix, and that he can be
> None of that kind of which he is but he.

A society of Phoenixes would surely be a sociological monstrosity, though a few "authentic" geniuses are always needed, in every generation, to change the meaning of "legitimacy." What the egalitarian perfectionists will not face is the moral ambiguity of all institutional life; "authenticities" in one generation forever become legitimacies in the next. As the late Reinhold Niebuhr once wrote: "But the fact is that not only property, but the two institutions of property and social stratification are in the same position of moral ambiguity. Both are necessary instruments of justice and order, and yet both are fruitful of injustice. Both have, no less than government, grown up organically in traditional civilizations in the sense that they are unconscious adaptations to the needs of justice and order. The revolts against both of them by both the radical Christians and the radical secular idealists of the seventeenth and eighteenth centuries tended to be indiscriminate."

This is what I think Gouldner means in his description of the functionalists: "Functionalism postulates that, even if a society might be reformed in some ways, there are other profound ways in which it cannot be reformed and which men must accept." In spite of the poetic license taken by Edward Hicks in *The Peaceable Kingdom*, the most famous and popular painting ever done by a Quaker, the lion will probably never lie down with the lamb.

Ages are known by the questions they raise; not by the answers they may seem to give. By definition, important questions are never answered. Thus the debate between Gouldner and the Parsonian functionalists is, in many fundamental ways, a continuation of the Quaker-Puritan debate of the

E. Digby Baltzell

1650s, which Hugh Barbour, in his book on *The Quakers in Puritan England*, summarizes as follows: "The Quaker preacher and the Puritan pastor worked in opposite directions and never understood each other. . . . The Puritan leaders were men who had known life in all its complexity. They knew the ambiguous mixture of sin and grace in their own best actions and in the motives they least admired. They had discovered new levels of sin and evil in the moment of seeming victory, when Cromwell and the forces of Parliament broke apart in the struggle to remake England. Inevitably they regarded the Quakers as self-righteous and unrealistic. . . . While Baxter was daily praying to receive God's Spirit, Friends insisted that they had it."

IV

Noisy and ideological ages raise questions which sober ages somehow have to solve, preferably in compromise. Who knows what solutions lie ahead for tragically troubled America? Here again, I think, we have something to learn from 17th-century England. For there is something in the English character which tells them that, in the long run, order and civility are only possible in sober societies where left and right extremists, though always necessary as critics of the status quo and stimulants to change, are *never* allowed to *win*. In both the French and Russian Revolutions, for example, the revolutionaries *won out*, but, at the same time, the French and Russian people *lost out* to the one-party and autocratic regimes of Napoleon and Stalin. In the English Revolution, on the other hand, both the revolutionary puritans and the radical sectarians *lost out* when the traditional authorities of throne and altar were finally restored.

Though cruel and vindictive at first, the Restoration Settlement eventually produced a vigorous two-party system which lasted down through the Victorian age; Cavalier squires, supporters of throne and altar, became Tories; and Roundhead, gentry-merchants, supporters of parliamentary authority, became dissenters and Whigs. After a period of bitter party battles, including a series of plots and counterplots, the more moderate leaders of both parties were finally united, as G. M. Trevelyan once put it, by "the wit and wisdom of George Savile, Marquis of Halifax, 'the Trimmer,' the Philosopher Statesman, whose dislike of extremes always caused him to 'trim' away from whichever party was at the moment enjoying and abusing power." Trimmer politics of Halifax, which incidentally became a Whig tradition in England, led the way to the bloodless, Glorious Revolution of 1688 and the Toleration Act of 1689, thereby securing parliamentary authority and religious toleration. This final settlement of the Reformation in England was, as usual, quite in contrast to the extreme positions taken on the Continent. While the reactionary princes of Germany, for instance, abolished all sectarian dissent after the bloody Peasant Wars and settled for Caesaropapism (the religion of the prince is the religion of all his subjects), and Louis XIV, in 1685, exiled the valuable and prosperous Huguenots from France, the English Toleration Act allowed dissenters or nonconformists to act as a continuing and liberating balance to the conserving, Anglican Establishment. Power warmly clothed in authority can always afford to be tolerant, naked power never. Thus it was the tolerating of this dissenting-nonconformist tradition which produced the reforming approach to social change, so often led by the Quakers, which characterized 19th-century England; the lack of a dissenting religious tradition in France and Germany, on the other hand, allowed for the growth of a stronger socialist-Marxist approach to social change, with its endless cycles of revolution and reaction. If history and sociology are any guide, we in America are surely in for a conservative reaction of one sort or another. Let us hope that it is not too late to follow in the English, rather than the Continental, tradition.

V

Finally, does the spirit of the Restoration compromise and the Trimmer-inspired Glorious Revolution have anything to tell us about the possible future course of sociology? In the first place, I should like to argue that we are *all* functionalists. If sociology is a cumulative science rather than a mildly disguised ideology, a moot assumption at best, then social theory is primarily a *point of departure*, a conceptual guide in the endless adventure of doing research, and never an end in itself or a final answer. To be brief, and unavoidably to simplify, there are two functionalist points of departure: (1) the *order-hierarchical* and (2) the *conflict-egalitarian*. Take, for instance, the following statement by Karl Marx: "The more a ruling class is able to assimilate the most prominent men of the dominated classes, the more stable and *dangerous* its rule." This is a functionalist generalization, and a valid one of course, from the *conflict-egalitarian* point of departure. Change the word "dangerous" to "desirable," on the other hand, and one has an equally valid generalization from the *order-hierarchical* point of view. To say, however, that the use of the word "dangerous" derives from a more or less valid social theory than the use of the word "desirable" is, or so it seems to me, to confuse ideology with social theory. Or take another generalization about human behavior which I find this morning, as I write these lines, in the *Wall Street Journal*. Thus the *Journal*'s diplomatic correspondent, in sociological rather than ideological style, contrasts the *order* with the *conflict* theories of international relations: "The U.S. contends that tensions in international relations are abnormal: smoothing things over is the prime reason for having diplomats. The Soviets, on the other

227

hand, find such tensions an inevitable result of conflicting social systems; their diplomats strive for competitive advantage while hoping to stave off disasters. Compromise and self-restraint for their own sake have little appeal; they are often considered weaknesses."

The quotation above, as it stands, is a perfectly valid outline of two approaches to international tension. And the *Journal*'s correspondent does not, like all too many sociologists today, go on to say that one is more valid than the other.

In the Trimmer spirit of the last lines of Merton's article, then, I would urge that Order and Conflict functionalists unite: "We have nothing to loose but our claims. We have a world of understanding to win" (p. 44). Let us all, above all, get away from the ideological, from the sociology of sociology, and get down to the doing of it, as best we can, in the grand tradition of Durkheim and Weber. And if we have some sort of restoration of authority in this country, instead of a blind reaction into some kind of violent anti-intellectualism, we may yet experience a flowering of social science much like that which England experienced in their 17th century of genius in the natural and biological sciences. One more backward glance should serve as a guide to hope.

The foundations of science in England were laid in the great Elizabethan age of poetry. It first flourished, as might have been expected, outside the conservative and church-controlled universities. Many of the early followers of the New Philosophy, as the scientific attitude was then called, congregated at Gresham College, a kind of adult-education center in the heart of London, founded in 1575 by one of Elizabeth's first councillors and son of the Lord Mayor of London, Thomas Gresham. Despite pleas from Cambridge, his alma mater, that he leave his money to them, Gresham amply endowed his college and made sure that it would remain in control of merchants like himself rather than the clerical guardians of the old tradition. The theoretician of the New Philosophy was Francis Bacon, twice related to Gresham, and attorney general under James I. His famous *Novum Organum* was published in 1620. The popularity of the New Philosophy may be measured by the fact that Bacon's *Essays* went through 17 editions in the years before the outbreak of the Revolution. Another pioneer, William Harvey, discovered the circulation of the blood in 1617 and published his findings in 1628. Harvey was appointed physician extraordinary by James I and was on the Royalist side during the Revolution. The two ideological decades of anarchy witnessed a definite decline in the doing of science, which finally flowered after the Restoration. In the single year of 1662, for instance, the Royal Society was founded (four of the 12 founding members had been teachers at Gresham College), Robert Boyle published his famous law on the behavior of gases, and William Petty, in his *Treatises of Taxes and Contributions*, founded the science of vital statistics. Three years later, Thomas Sydenham, often called the "English Hippocrates," published his first book, which brought him fame throughout Europe. In the doing tradition, Sydenham insisted on the importance of clinical observation rather than theory. Finally, the *summa* of mechanistic science was given to the world in the year preceding the Glorious Revolution, in 1687, when Edmond Halley, discoverer of the comet named in his honor, brought out Newton's classic, *Principia*. Halley not only constantly encouraged Newton to finish and publish his *Principia*; he also published his good friend's work at his own expense. I have, of course, only mentioned the few outstanding leaders of this great age of English science. For more quantitative evidence of how the doing of science declined during the two ideological decades and then flowered under the Restoration compromise, I should like to refer to a table in Merton's early book on England:

TABLE 3

NUMBER OF IMPORTANT DISCOVERIES AND INVENTIONS (5)
ENGLAND, 1601–1700

Years	Number	Years	Number
1601–1610	10	1651–1660	13
1611–1620	13	1661–1670	44
1621–1630	7	1671–1680	29
1631–1640	12	1681–1690	32
1641–1650	3	1691–1700	17

SOURCE.—Robert K. Merton, *Science, Technology and Society in Seventeenth-Century England* (New York: Harper Torchbooks, 1970), p. 40. Originally published in *Osiris: Studies on the History and Philosophy of Science, and on the History of Learning and Culture* (Bruges: St. Catherine Press, 1938).

CONTRIBUTORS

TOM BOTTOMORE is professor of sociology at the University of Sussex. He was president of the British Sociological Association from 1969 to 1971 and is the author of *Sociology* (rev. ed., 1971) and *Elites and Society* (1964). He is currently finishing a book on the various sociological schools of Marxism.

ROBERT K. MERTON, the Giddings Professor of Sociology at Columbia University, works mainly in the sociology of science and the theory of social structure.

HOWARD S. BECKER is professor of sociology and urban affairs at Northwestern University. He is currently working in the sociology of the arts.

IRVING LOUIS HOROWITZ is professor of sociology at Livingston College, Rutgers University, and editor-in-chief of *Society*. His most recent book is *Foundations of Political Sociology*.

SEYMOUR MARTIN LIPSET is professor of government and sociology at Harvard University. He is the author of *Rebellion in the University* (1972); with Earl Raab, *Politics of Unreason: Right Wing Extremism in the U.S.* (1970); and *Revolution and Counterrevolution* (rev. ed., 1970). He was the recipient of the Gunnar Myrdal Award in 1970. He is currently holding a Guggenheim Fellowship for the study of intellectuals.

EVERETT CARLL LADD, JR., is professor of political science at the University of Connecticut. He is the author of *Negro Political Leadership in America* (1966), *Ideology in America* (1969), and *American Political Parties* (1970). He also holds a Guggenheim Fellowship this year, for a study of American academics.

MORRIS JANOWITZ is professor of sociology at the University of Chicago. He is currently engaged in a study of theories of social control and macrosociology. He will spend the academic year 1972–73 as Pitt Professor at the University of Cambridge.

JOHN K. RHOADS is associate professor of sociology at Northern Illinois University. He is presently attempting to construct a synthesis of social systems theory. He is also interested in the history of social thought.

VERNON K. DIBBLE is associate professor of sociology at Wesleyan University and an intermittent political activist. His papers on the young Max Weber, in the *European Journal of Sociology* (1968), and on the connection between sociology and ethics in the social thought of Albion W. Small, to be presented at the 1972 meetings of the American Sociological Association, are closely related to his article in this issue.

LEWIS A. COSER is Distinguished Professor of Sociology at the State University of New York at Stony Brook. Among his recent books are *Masters of Sociological Thought* and *Men of Ideas*. He is currently at work on a series of papers in historical sociology dealing with different types of servants of power in patrimonial regimes and bureaucratic systems.

BENJAMIN NELSON is professor of sociology and history in the Graduate Faculty of the New School for Social Research. Within the last several years he has written papers and given addresses on the comparative historical sociology of science against the background of changing structures of consciousness in East and West. The Winter 1971–72 number of *Social Research* carries his translation of Durkheim and Mauss's "Note on the Notion of Civilization." In 1969 the University of Chicago and Phoenix Books issued a second enlarged edition of his book *The Idea of Usury: From Tribal Brotherhood to Universal Otherhood.*

E. DIGBY BALTZELL is professor of sociology at the University of Pennsylvania. He is the author of *Philadelphia Gentlemen: The Making of a National Upper Class* (1958) and the *Protestant Establishment* (1966) among other works.